SOME PRINCIPLES OF MARITIME STRATEGY

BY THE SAME AUTHOR

DRAKE AND THE TUDOR NAVY: with a History of the Rise of England as a Maritime Power. With Portraits, Illustrations and Maps. 2 vols. Crown. 8vo. *Out of print*

THE SUCCESSORS OF DRAKE. With 4 Portraits (2 Photogravures) and 12 Maps and Plans. 8vo. *Out of print*

ENGLAND IN THE MEDITERRANEAN: A Study of the Rise and Influence of British Power within the Straits, 1603-1713. 2 vols. 8vo. *Out of print*

ENGLAND IN THE SEVEN YEARS' WAR. A Study in Combined Strategy. With 14 Maps and Plans. 2 vols. 8vo. *Out of print*

THE CAMPAIGN OF TRAFALGAR. With 13 Charts and Diagrams. 8vo. *Out of print*

FIGHTING INSTRUCTIONS, 1530-1816. The art of naval tactics and its history. Roy. 8vo. £4.75

SIGNALS AND INSTRUCTIONS 1776-1794 Sailing Tactics based upon the Bridport Papers, the Rodney Papers, and the Collection of Admiral Sir Thomas Graves, K.B. Roy. 8vo. £4.75

SOME PRINCIPLES OF

MARITIME STRATEGY

BY

JULIAN S. CORBETT, LL.M.

NAVAL INSTITUTE PRESS

1972

© Conway Maritime Press Ltd.,
7 Nelson Road, Greenwich, London, S.E.10

First Edition 1911
New Impression 1972

Published and distributed in the United States of America by the
NAVAL INSTITUTE PRESS
ISBN 087021 880 8

Library of Congress Catalog Card No. 72-184622

Printed in Great Britain by
Unwin Brothers Limited
The Gresham Press
Old Woking, Surrey

CONTENTS

CONTENTS

FOREWORD

It is generally accepted that Sir Julian Corbett's *Some Principles of Maritime Strategy,* first published in 1911, was based on his lectures at the Royal Naval War College, although the exact relationship between text of the book and the lectures as delivered has not been established. When the War College was founded at Greenwich in 1900 it was the only forum in which the senior officers of the Royal Navy could study the principles of maritime war and strategy. Corbett was also a close associate of Admiral Sir John Fisher at the peak of his reforming career. He was not an uncritical admirer of that erratic genius but approved of his general policies, especially his changes in the pattern of officers' entry and education at the new Colleges at Osborne and Dartmouth. Quite apart from its intrinsic merit therefore as an analysis of the theory and principles of maritime war, the book is significant as the work of a man who had the ear of the architect of the Royal Navy which fought the war against Germany and who had expounded his doctrines to many of the officers destined to responsible positions in the conduct of that war.

Corbett's intentions in his lectures are clear. He knew his audience and realised that they were professionally obsessed by the revolutionary changes in naval material which dominated their lives at sea. He also knew that, except for rare individuals, they had not felt the need for any systematic study of how technological change had affected traditional patterns of strategy and warfare. This lack of reflection did not prevent many of them having dogmatic opinions on every aspect of their profession. It was these opinions which he tried to persuade them to reconsider or establish on firmer ground. His first aim was to convince an audience, which for the most part believed that technical change had made the study of all past naval warfare irrelevant, that there were principles of maritime strategy which could be deduced from a study of history and which could help them to carry out their future tasks. By the time he began to lecture at Greenwich Corbett had published three of his major historical works and the other two were to appear before his lectures were put into book form.[1] His research had brought him to firm conclusions about the permanent features of maritime war. He never claimed that historical study could produce detailed rules for the future conduct of battles and campaigns. The practical experience and personal qualities of commanders and the unique circumstances of every war and battle were of primary significance, but systematic study could help. It could give an understanding of the particular character-istics of maritime war and naval forces which could help in assessing individual situations. If study could produce some rational principles of maritime war it would enable naval commanders to communicate more clearly with their colleagues and to argue more cogently with their military and political counterparts. Thus a fuller appreciation of the role of maritime power in the country's policy would be gained.

In more directly naval matters Corbett sought to

[1] For an illuminating account of Corbett's life and work, see:—
D. M. Schurman; *The Education of a Navy;* Cassell, London, 1965.

convince his audience that there was far more to naval warfare than the seeking out and destroying the enemy's main fleet, which was likely to be the beginning and end of their strategic doctrine. He emphasised that the Navy could never by itself gain total victory and must learn to work in close harmony with the Army for the political objectives of war established by government. In this context, Corbett urged the importance of Combined Operations, which he regarded as the highest product of Britain's maritime genius and the necessity of the Navy having the proper organisation and techniques for them.

It is impossible to judge the impact of Corbett's teaching on individual officers but the naval policies of the 1914-1918 war show little of his influence. The desire to bring the German fleet to action dominated the naval command. Combined Operations were regarded as a dangerous diversion of resources from this essential task. Only on the subject of Protection of Trade were Corbett's ideas followed, probably because they fitted in with general naval opinion. The irony is, that it is here that Corbett's thought is most open to criticism. During the War some critics tried to make his teaching responsible for the lack of decisive naval actions and the Admiralty dealt him a last bitter blow when the Board insisted on inserting the following disclaimer at the beginning of Volume III of his *Naval Operations* in the Official History of the Great War, when it appeared in 1923,

> "Their Lordships find that some of the principles advocated in this book, especially the tendency to minimise the importance of seeking battle and of forcing it to a conclusion, are directly in conflict with their views."

However little Corbett was appreciated by those whom

he sought directly to influence, students of a later day when the whole concept of war has been revolutionised by the advent of nuclear weapons and when the continued usefulness of conventional naval forces is seriously questioned, will find much of value in his pages. For maritime historians, his work is still essential reading, and the quality of his analysis of the principles of maritime war which had emerged from his historical study and is embodied in this book, puts him alongside Clausevitz in the ranks of the great theorists of war. A modern student seeking a balanced exposition of the classical theory of maritime war as a basis for considering its future, can find no better starting point.

The book's structure is that of a well-designed lecture course. The Introduction seeks to establish the validity of its main theme, the existence of permanent principles of maritime strategy and their value to naval commanders. Part I is an analysis of the general theory of war as it had been developed by Jomini and Clausevitz and continues with Corbett's own development of that thought taking into account Britain's experience in maritime war which the continental writers had largely ignored. Parts II and III must have taken the lecture audience into more familiar waters with their interpretation of such well known but perhaps imperfectly understood terms such as 'Command of the Sea,' and 'Concentration of Force,' before concluding with a systematic analysis of the various forms of naval operations. Each stage of the argument is buttressed by well chosen illustrations from Corbett's wide and precise historical knowledge. There is no trace of shallow propaganda and the overall impression is that of a measured exposition by a confident expert.

Corbett's balanced view of the relationship between land and sea power emerges clearly in his definition of maritime strategy; "The principles which govern a war in which the sea is a substantial factor," and in his insistence that such a maritime strategy must be seen as part of a larger national strategy and directed towards those objectives which are the aims of national policy. As men live on land not in the sea, it is on land that the final decision must be found. In a successful maritime strategy the relationship between land and sea forces are of paramount importance. This insistence that the nature of maritime war must take into account national policy is a clear derivation from Clausevitz as is Corbett's examination of the Offensive and Defensive in warfare. It is only when he deals with the concept of Limited War that this originality emerges. Both Jomini and Clausevitz had distinguished wars fought for a limited objective from the "Absolute War" aimed at the complete destruction of an enemy's will to resist. The latter could only be won by the destruction of the enemy's main fighting strength, the former by the seizure of a designated limited objective and the deterrence of the enemy from launching major operations to regain it. Corbett pointed out that in the Continental warfare with which Clausevitz was concerned, Limited Wars had never been of very great significance because of the impossibility of isolating a limited objective. In maritime war they were of supreme importance because a nation exercising command of the seas could seize important territory geographically distant from a metropolitan country and be confident of retaining it whatever the military strength of its opponent. Obvious examples of this were the British taking of Havana and Canada in the Seven Years War, but for extra measure Corbett added the illustration of the capture of Sevastapol in the Crimean War. It was to success in this type of Limited War that Corbett ascribed Britain's rise to imperial greatness despite the opposition of stronger nations. Like other exponents of maritime strategy he tended to minimise the contribution of Continental allies whose land campaigns prevented France from concentrating her entire strength against Britain. In this context Corbett makes large claims for what he terms "Limited Intervention in Unlimited Wars," in the form of assaults on a Continental enemy from the sea designed to make him weaken his strength on the central front. He asserts that even the apparently disastrous Walcheren expedition was a success of this kind because it forced Napoleon to reconsider his whole defensive strategy. In a telling aphorism, Corbett states that the Emperor reacted thus because he realised, "That in war to ignore a threat is often to create an opportunity."

Corbett's main doctrine of naval warfare is concerned with command of the sea and the particular nature of concentration of force in sea as distinct from land warfare. "Command of the sea therefore means nothing but the control of maritime communications, whether for commercial or military purposes. The object of naval warfare therefore is the control of communications, and not, as in land warfare, the conquest of territory." To achieve this control, either offensively, by depriving the enemy of use of the seas, or defensively, by protecting one's own shipping, a different form of concentration is required compared with the physical massing of troops at a vital point in land warfare. The mobility and flexibility of naval forces makes it possible to disperse them widely to attack or defend sea communications as long as the organisation and the means exist to concentrate them rapidly when and where a major threat appears. This was the basis of Corbett's attempt in his lectures to wean his audience away from their preconception that the only task of the Navy was to fight fleet actions and that it must be kept physically concentrated until the enemy fleet had been destroyed.

His further treatment of this emotive subject was academic and calm. He strongly restated the validity of the traditional British doctrine that the primary task was to gain command of the seas by seeking out and destroying the enemy's battle fleet and admitted it to be an un-challengeable maxim. He then slyly inserted the academic goad, "Yet nothing is so dangerous in the study of war as to permit maxims to become a substitute for judgement." From there he continued with a magnificent set of historical illustrations, ranging from the Armada to the Spanish-American war of 1898, to demonstrate the folly of believing that decisive battles could be brought about simply by chasing and hunting out the enemy. The enemy may be impossible to find or he may very sensibly decline major action and keep his fleet in being to hamper your use of the seas. He may even raid your coasts and harass your shipping because you have withdrawn all protection, to concentrate against his main force. Battles have to be planned and worked for and naval forces must be used in such a way and positioned in such places that the enemy will be compelled to accept battle if he designs to make any effective use of his own naval forces. Such operations as attacking enemy trade, placing strong naval contingents around your own or threatening his coast with attack must be given as much thought as are preparations for decisive fleet action; otherwise that action may never happen.

Not only his own insistence on the close inter-relation of naval and military affairs but also the violent controversy of the day on the prospects of a successful invasion of Britain, made it inevitable that Corbett should devote considerable attention to this topic. His conclusions are clear and confident. As long as the Navy adhered to its traditional policy of concentrating against the troop transports rather than the naval escort and support of an invading force, the attempt would fail. He was sure that all the technical developments of the previous century, by increasing the speed, freedom of movement and fire-power of the flotilla vessels, the main force for repelling invasion attempts, had resulted in a strengthening of the defence.

He was equally confident, perhaps on less firm grounds, of the converse type of operation, the escort, landing and support of British military expeditions overseas, being successful under modern conditions. As long as there was a joint planning staff and close co-operation between naval and military commanders, (he opposed unified command on the grounds that no one man could understand both the military and the naval art), and as long as general command of the seas prevented the expedition being threatened by the enemy's navy, all would be well. As in an earlier section of the book on the influence of the torpedo on naval operations, Corbett here seems to find difficulty in assessing the impact of new weapons. The existence of mines, long range coastal artillery and mobile defensive artillery, as used in the Dardanelles, was to make landings from the sea much more hazardous than they had been in the French wars.

It was however in his teaching on the attack and defence of sea-borne trade that Corbett most signally failed to anticipate correctly the impact of technical change.

From his first major historical work, *Drake and the Tudor Navy* (1898), Corbett had followed Mahan in asserting that commerce destruction was an indecisive form of naval warfare which could never prevail against a nation with a strong navy, a large mercantile marine and efficient shipbuilding resources. Thus though attacks on her trade could be a serious irritant to Britain, her losses would never be such as to defeat her. On the other hand Britain, with her naval superiority, could impose an effective commercial blockade severe enough to cripple an enemy's will and ability to resist. This view is still maintained in this book although with some caution. "Modern developments and changes in shipping and naval material have indeed so profoundly modified the whole conditions of commerce protection, that there is no part of strategy where historical deduction is more difficult or more liable to error." His own conclusions were, that all recent developments had made the threat to Britain less than it had been in the past. The abolition of privateering by the Declaration of Paris in 1854 had removed what had been the greatest menace in home waters in earlier wars. All that would have to be guarded against was a small number of regular and auxiliary cruisers which would be limited in their range of action by coal supplies and the problems of providing prize crews and accommodation for prisoners taken from captured vessels. He admitted the possibility, but not the probability of raiders sinking their prizes and making no provision for survivors. "But this course has objections scarcely less weighty than the other. No Power will incur the odium of sinking a prize with all hands."

On the methods of protection against enemy cruisers Corbett made little detailed comment. He did consider that technical change in the nature of merchant ships, especially the freedom of movement and additional speed given by steam, had made them less vulnerable and that therefore the continued need for a convoy system needed reconsideration. "It now becomes doubtful whether the additional security which convoys afforded, is sufficient to outweigh their economic drawbacks and their liability to cause strategic disturbance." These last two words are the clue to Corbett's treatment of the protection of trade. He was convinced that there was no truth in the widely held opinion, strongly publicised by Sir John Colomb, that the vast increase in Britain's mercantile marine since the Napoleonic wars, had made her more vulnerable. He believed the contrary to be true. Britain had adequate enough margins to be able to accept the scale of losses to be expected, and it was most undesirable that public panic and outcry over the few losses which would inevitably occur, should force the Admiralty to divert large forces to trade protection from more important strategic tasks.

In the light of what happened between 1915 and 1917 when Britain was brought to the verge of defeat by losses of merchant shipping, it is natural to attack Corbett for lack of foresight and to forget that Germany's cruiser campaign against trade very closely bore out his predictions. His failure to anticipate the nature of the submarine's use against merchant shipping was shared by virtually all authoritative naval opinion, except for Fisher. Two valid charges can be brought against him. By playing down the threat of commerce war he encouraged an already dangerous tendency in the Navy not to give its problems adequate consideration. By not following Mahan's example in emphasising the permanent tactical advantages of the convoy system, he made himself a party to the most costly mistake in British naval thinking ever made. It was an ironic failure in the work of a man who had devoted a great deal of his life to the encouragement of the kind of thought among naval officers which would have avoided a gross error of this kind.

14th August 1971   B. McL. Ranft.
Professor of History, the Royal Naval College, Greenwich, Visiting Professor in War Studies, King's College, University of London

SOME PRINCIPLES OF MARITIME STRATEGY

INTRODUCTION

THE THEORETICAL STUDY OF WAR

ITS USE AND LIMITATIONS

At first sight nothing can appear more unpractical, less promising of useful result, than to approach the study of war with a theory. There seems indeed to be something essentially antagonistic between the habit of mind that seeks theoretical guidance and that which makes for the successful conduct of war. The conduct of war is so much a question of personality, of character, of common-sense, of rapid decision upon complex and ever-shifting factors, and those factors themselves are so varied, so intangible, so dependent upon unstable moral and physical conditions, that it seems incapable of being reduced to anything like true scientific analysis. At the bare idea of a theory or "science" of war the mind recurs uneasily to well-known cases where highly "scientific" officers failed as leaders. Yet, on the other hand, no one will deny that since the great theorists of the early nineteenth century attempted to produce a reasoned theory of war, its planning and conduct have acquired a method, a precision, and a certainty of grasp which were unknown before. Still less will any one deny the value which the shrewdest and most successful leaders in war have placed upon the work of the classical strategical writers.

The truth is that the mistrust of theory arises from a misconception of what it is that theory claims to do. It does not pretend to give the power of conduct in the field; it claims no more than to increase the effective power of conduct. Its main practical value is that it can assist a capable man to acquire a broad outlook whereby he may be the surer his plan shall cover all the ground, and whereby he may with greater rapidity and certainty seize all the factors of a sudden situation. The greatest of the theorists himself puts the matter quite frankly. Of theoretical study he says, " It should educate the mind of the man who is to lead in war, or rather guide him to self-education, but it should not accompany him on the field of battle."

Its practical utility, however, is not by any means confined to its effects upon the powers of a leader. It is not enough that a leader should have the ability to decide rightly; his subordinates must seize at once the full meaning of his decision and be able to express it with certainty in well-adjusted action. For this every man concerned must have been trained to think in the same plane; the chief's order must awake in every brain the same process of thought; his words must have the same meaning for all. If a theory of tactics had existed in 1780, and if Captain Carkett had had a sound training in such a theory, he could not possibly have misunderstood Rodney's signal. As it was, the real intention of the signal was obscure, and Rodney's neglect to explain the tactical device it indicated robbed his country of a victory at an hour of the direst need. There had been no previous theoretical training to supply the omission, and Rodney's fine conception was unintelligible to anybody but himself.

Nor is it only for the sake of mental solidarity between a chief and his subordinates that theory is indispensable. It is of still higher value for producing a similar solidarity between him and his superiors at the Council table at home. How often have officers dumbly acquiesced in ill-advised operations simply for lack of the mental power and verbal apparatus to convince an impatient Minister where the errors of his plan lay? How often, moreover, have statesmen and officers, even in the most harmonious conference, been unable to decide on a coherent plan of war from inability to analyse scientifically the situation they had to face, and to recognise the general character of the struggle in which they were about to engage. That the true nature of a war should be realised by contemporaries as clearly as it comes to be seen afterwards in the fuller light of history is seldom to be expected. At close range accidental factors will force themselves into undue prominence and tend to obscure the true horizon. Such error can scarcely ever be eliminated, but by theoretical study we can reduce it, nor by any other means can we hope to approach the clearness of vision with which posterity will read our mistakes. Theory is, in fact, a question of education and deliberation, and not of execution at all. That depends on the combination of intangible human qualities which we call executive ability.

This, then, is all the great authorities ever claimed for theory, but to this claim the chief of them at least, after years of active service on the Staff, attached the highest importance. " In actual operations," he wrote in one of his latest memoranda, " men are guided solely by their judgment, and it will hit the mark more or less accurately according as they possess more or less genius. This is the way all great generals have acted. . . . Thus it will always be in action, and so far judgment will suffice. But when it is a question not of taking action yourself, but of convincing others at the Council table, then everything depends on clear conceptions and the exposition of the inherent relations of things. So little progress has been made in this respect that most deliberations are merely verbal contentions which rest on no firm foundation, and end either in every one retaining his own opinion, or in a compromise from considerations of mutual respect—a middle course of no actual value." [1]

The writer's experience of such discussions was rich and at first hand. Clear conceptions of the ideas and factors involved in a war problem, and a definite exposition of the relations between them, were in his eyes the remedy for loose and purposeless discussion ; and such conceptions and expositions are all we mean by the theory or the science of war. It is a process by which we co-ordinate our ideas, define the meaning of the words we use, grasp the difference between essential and unessential factors, and fix and expose the fundamental data on which every one is agreed. In this way we prepare the apparatus of practical discussion ; we secure the means of

---

[1] Clausewitz *On War*, p. ix. The references are to Colonel Graham's translation of the third German edition, but his wording is not always followed exactly.

arranging the factors in manageable shape, and of deducing from them with precision and rapidity a practical course of action. Without such an apparatus no two men can even think on the same line ; much less can they ever hope to detach the real point of difference that divides them and isolate it for quiet solution.

In our own case this view of the value of strategical theory has a special significance, and one far wider than its continental enunciators contemplated. For a world-wide maritime Empire the successful conduct of war will often turn not only on the decisions of the Council chamber at home, but on the outcome of conferences in all parts of the world between squadronal commanders and the local authorities, both civil and military, and even between commanders-in-chief of adjacent stations. In time of war or of preparation for war, in which the Empire is concerned, arrangements must always be based to an exceptional degree on the mutual relation of naval, military, and political considerations. The line of mean efficiency, though indicated from home, must be worked out locally, and worked out on factors of which no one service is master. Conference is always necessary, and for conference to succeed there must be a common vehicle of expression and a common plane of thought. It is for this essential preparation that theoretical study alone can provide ; and herein lies its practical value for all who aspire to the higher responsibilities of the Imperial service.

So great indeed is the value of abstract strategical study from this point of view, that it is necessary to guard ourselves against over-valuation. So far from claiming for their so-called science more than the possibilities we have indicated, the classical strategists insist again and again on the danger of seeking from it what it cannot give. They even repudiate the very name of " Science." They prefer the older term " Art." They will permit no laws or rules. Such laws, they say, can only mislead in practice, for the friction to which they are subject from the incalculable human factors alone is such that the friction is stronger than the law. It is an old adage of lawyers that nothing is so misleading as a legal maxim, but a strategical maxim is undoubtedly and in every way less to be trusted in action.

What then, it will be asked, are the tangible results which we can hope to attain from theory ? If all on which we have to build is so indeterminate, how are any practical conclusions to be reached ? That the factors are infinitely varied and difficult to determine is true, but that, it must be remembered, is just what emphasises the necessity of reaching such firm standpoints as are attainable. The vaguer the problem to be solved, the more resolute must we be in seeking points of departure from which we can begin to lay a course, keeping always an eye open for the accidents that will beset us, and being always alive to their deflecting influences. And this is just what the theoretical study of strategy can do. It can at least determine the normal. By careful colla- tion of past events it becomes clear that certain lines of conduct tend normally to produce certain effects ; that wars tend to take certain forms each with a marked idiosyncrasy ; that these forms are normally related to the object of the war and to its value to one or both belligerents ; that a system of operations which suits one form may not be that best suited

to another. We can even go further. By pursuing
an historical and comparative method we can detect
that even the human factor is not quite indetermin-
able. We can assert that certain situations will
normally produce, whether in ourselves or in our
adversaries, certain moral states on which we may
calculate.

Having determined the normal, we are at once in
a stronger position. Any proposal can be compared
with it, and we can proceed to discuss clearly the
weight of the factors which prompt us to depart from
the normal. Every case must be judged on its merits,
but without a normal to work from we cannot form
any real judgment at all; we can only guess. Every
case will assuredly depart from the normal to a
greater or less extent, and it is equally certain that
the greatest successes in war have been the boldest
departures from the normal. But for the most part
they have been departures made with open eyes by
geniuses who could perceive in the accidents of the
case a just reason for the departure.

Take an analogous example, and the province of
strategical theory becomes clear at once. Navigation
and the parts of seamanship that belong to it have
to deal with phenomena as varied and unreliable as
those of the conduct of war. Together they form
an art which depends quite as much as generalship
on the judgment of individuals. The law of storms
and tides, of winds and currents, and the whole of
meteorology are subject to infinite and incalculable
deflections, and yet who will deny nowadays that
by the theoretical study of such things the seaman's art has gained in coherence and strength?
Such study will not by itself make a seaman or

a navigator, but without it no seaman or navigator can nowadays pretend to the name. Because storms do not always behave in the same way, because currents are erratic, will the most practical seaman deny that the study of the normal conditions are useless to him in his practical decisions?

If, then, the theoretical study of strategy be approached in this way—if, that is, it be regarded not as a substitute for judgment and experience, but as a means of fertilising both, it can do no man harm. Individual thought and common-sense will remain the masters and remain the guides to point the general direction when the mass of facts begins to grow bewildering. Theory will warn us the moment we begin to leave the beaten track, and enable us to decide with open eyes whether the divergence is necessary or justifiable. Above all, when men assemble in Council it will hold discussion to the essential lines, and help to keep side issues in their place.

But beyond all this there lies in the theory of war yet another element of peculiar value to a maritime Empire. We are accustomed, partly for convenience and partly from lack of a scientific habit of thought, to speak of naval strategy and military strategy as though they were distinct branches of knowledge which had no common ground. It is the theory of war which brings out their intimate relation. It reveals that embracing them both is a larger strategy which regards the fleet and army as one weapon, which co-ordinates their action, and indicates the lines on which each must move to realise the full power of both. It will direct us to assign to each its proper function in a plan of war; it will enable each service to realise the better the limitations and the possibilities of the function with which it is charged, and how and when its own necessities must give way to a higher or more pressing need of the other. It discloses, in short, that naval strategy is not a thing by itself, that its problems can seldom or never be solved on naval considerations alone, but that it is only a part of maritime strategy—the higher learning which teaches us that for a maritime State to make successful war and to realise her special strength, army and navy must be used and thought of as instruments no less intimately connected than are the three arms ashore.

It is for these reasons that it is of little use to approach naval strategy except through the theory of war. Without such theory we can never really understand its scope or meaning, nor can we hope to grasp the forces which most profoundly affect its conclusions.

PART I

THEORY OF WAR

CHAPTER I

THE THEORY OF WAR

THE last thing that an explorer arrives at is a complete map that will cover the whole ground he has travelled, but for those who come after him and would profit by and extend his knowledge his map is the first thing with which they will begin. So it is with strategy. Before we start upon its study we seek a chart which will show us at a glance what exactly is the ground we have to cover and what are the leading features which determine its form and general characteristics. Such a chart a "theory of war" alone can provide. It is for this reason that in the study of war we must get our theory clear before we can venture in search of practical conclusions. So great is the complexity of war that without such a guide we are sure to go astray amidst the bewildering multiplicity of tracks and obstacles that meet us at every step. If for continental strategy its value has been proved abundantly, then for maritime strategy, where the conditions are far more complex, the need of it is even greater.

By maritime strategy we mean the principles which govern a war in which the sea is a substantial factor. Naval strategy is but that part of it which determines the movements of the fleet when maritime strategy has determined what part the fleet must play in relation to the action of the land forces ; for it scarcely needs saying that it is almost impossible that a war can be decided by naval action alone. Unaided, naval pressure can only work by a process of exhaustion. Its effects must always be slow, and so galling both to our own commercial community and to neutrals, that the tendency is always to accept terms of peace that are far from conclusive. For a firm decision a quicker and more drastic form of pressure is required. Since men live upon the land and not upon the sea, great issues between nations at war have always been decided— except in the rarest cases—either by what your army can do against your enemy's territory and national life, or else by the fear of what the fleet makes it possible for your army to do.

The paramount concern, then, of maritime strategy is to determine the mutual relations of your army and navy in a plan of war. When this is done, and not till then, naval strategy can begin to work out the manner in which the fleet can best discharge the function assigned to it.

The problem of such co-ordination is one that is susceptible of widely varying solutions. It may be that the command of the sea is of so urgent an importance that the army will have to devote itself to assisting the fleet in its special task before it can act directly against the enemy's territory and land forces; on the other hand, it may be that the immediate duty of the fleet will be to forward military action ashore before it is free to devote itself whole-heartedly to the destruction of the enemy's fleets. The crude maxims as to primary objects which seem to have served well enough in continental warfare have never worked so clearly where the sea enters seriously into a war. In such cases it will not suffice to say the primary object of the army is to destroy the enemy's army, or that of the fleet to destroy the enemy's fleet. The delicate interactions of the land and sea factors produce conditions too intricate for such blunt solutions. Even the initial equations they present are too complex to be reduced by the simple application of rough-and-ready maxims. Their right handling depends upon the broadest and most fundamental principles of war, and it is as a standpoint from which to get a clear and unobstructed view of the factors in their true relations that a theory of war has perhaps its highest value.

The theory which now holds the field is that war in a fundamental sense is a continuation of policy by other means. The process by which the continental strategists arrived at it involved some hard philosophical reasoning. Practical and experienced veterans as they were, their method is not one that works easily with our own habit of thought. It will be well, therefore, to endeavour first to present their conclusions in a concrete form, which will make the pith of the matter intelligible at once. Take, now, the ordinary case of a naval or military Staff being asked to prepare a war plan against a certain State and to advise what means it will require. To any one who has considered such matters it is obvious the reply must be another question — What will the war be about? Without a definite answer or alternative answers to that question a Staff can scarcely do more than engage in making such forces as the country can afford as efficient as possible. Before they take any sure step further they must know many things. They must know whether they are expected to take something from the enemy, or to prevent his taking something either from us or from some other State. If from some other State, the measures to be taken will depend on its geographical situation and on its relative

strength by land and sea. Even when the object is
clear it will be necessary to know how much value
the enemy attaches to it. Is it one for which he will
be likely to fight to the death, or one which he will
abandon in the face of comparatively slight resistance?
If the former, we cannot hope to succeed without entirely
overthrowing his powers of resistance. If the latter,
it will suffice, as it often has sufficed, to aim at something less costly and hazardous and better within
our means. All these are questions which lie in the
lap of Ministers charged with the foreign policy of
the country, and before the Staff can proceed with a
war plan they must be answered by Ministers.

In short, the Staff must ask of them what is the
policy which your diplomacy is pursuing, and where,
and why, do you expect it to break down and force
you to take up arms? The Staff has to carry on in
fact when diplomacy has failed to achieve the object in
view, and the method they will use will depend on the
nature of that object. So we arrive crudely at our
theory that war is a continuation of policy, a form of
political intercourse in which we fight battles instead
of writing notes.

It was this theory, simple and even meaningless
as it appears at first sight, that gave the key to the
practical work of framing a modern war plan and
revolutionised the study of strategy. It was not till
the beginning of the nineteenth century that such
a theory was arrived at. For centuries men had
written on the "Art of War," but for want of a
working theory their labours as a whole had been
unscientific, concerned for the most part with the
discussion of passing fashions and the elaboration of
platitudes. Much good work it is true was done on

details, but no broad outlook had been obtained to enable us to determine their relation to the funda-mental constants of the subject. No standpoint had been found from which we could readily detach such constants from what was merely accidental. The result was a tendency to argue too exclusively from the latest examples and to become entangled in erroneous thought by trying to apply the methods which had attained the last success to war as a whole. There was no means of determining how far the particular success was due to special conditions and how far it was due to factors common to all wars.

It was the Revolutionary and Napoleonic wars, coinciding as they did with a period of philosophic activity, that revealed the shallowness and empirical nature of all that had been done up to that time. Napoleon's methods appeared to his contemporaries to have produced so strenuous a revolution in the conduct of land warfare that it assumed a wholly new aspect, and it was obvious that those conceptions which had sufficed previously had become inadequate as a basis of sound study. War on land seemed to have changed from a calculated affair of thrust and parry between standing armies to a headlong rush of one nation in arms upon another, each thirsting for the other's life, and resolved to have it or perish in the attempt. Men felt themselves faced with a mani-festation of human energy which had had no counter-part, at least in civilised times.

The assumption was not entirely true. For al-though the Continent had never before adopted the methods in question, our own country was no stranger to them either on sea or land. As we shall see, our own Revolution in the seventeenth century had pro-

duced strenuous methods of making war which were
closely related to those which Napoleon took over from
the French Revolutionary leaders. A more philosophic
outlook might have suggested that the phenomenon
was not really exceptional, but rather the natural outcome of popular energy inspired by a stirring political
ideal. But the British precedent was forgotten, and
so profound was the disturbance caused by the new
French methods that its effects are with us still. We
are in fact still dominated by the idea that since the
Napoleonic era war has been essentially a different
thing. Our teachers incline to insist that there is now
only one way of making war, and that is Napoleon's
way. Ignoring the fact that he failed in the end, they
brand as heresy the bare suggestion that there may
be other ways, and not content with assuming that
his system will fit all land wars, however much their
natures and objects may differ, they would force naval
warfare into the same uniform under the impression
apparently that they are thereby making it presentable
and giving it some new force.

Seeing how cramping the Napoleonic idea has
become, it will be convenient before going further to
determine its special characteristics exactly, but that is
no easy matter. The moment we approach it in a critical
spirit, it begins to grow nebulous and very difficult)
to define. We can dimly make out four distinct ideas
mingled in the current notion. First, there is the
idea of making war not merely with a professional
standing army, but with the whole armed nation—a
conception which of course was not really Napoleon's.
It was inherited by him from the Revolution, but was
in fact far older. It was but a revival of the universal
practice which obtained in the barbaric stages of social

development, and which every civilisation in turn had abandoned as economically unsound and subversive of specialisation in citizenship. The results of the abandonment were sometimes good and sometimes bad, but the determining conditions have been studied as yet too imperfectly to justify any broad generalisation. Secondly, there is the idea of strenuous and persistent effort—not resting to secure each minor advantage, but pressing the enemy without pause or rest till he is utterly overthrown—an idea in which Cromwell had anticipated Napoleon by a century and a half. Scarcely distinguishable from this is a third idea—that of taking the offensive, in which there was really nothing new at all, since its advantages had always been understood, and Frederick the Great had pressed it to extremity with little less daring than Napoleon himself—nay even to culpable rashness, as the highest exponents of the Napoleonic idea admit. Finally, there is the notion of making the armed forces of the enemy and not his territory or any part of it your main objective. This perhaps is regarded as the strongest characteristic of Napoleon's methods, and yet even here we are confused by the fact that undoubtedly on some very important occasions — the Austerlitz campaign, for example—Napoleon made the hostile capital his objective as though he believed its occupation was the most effective step towards the overthrow of the enemy's power and will to resist. He certainly did not make the enemy's main army his primary objective—for their main army was not Mack's but that of the Archduke Charles.

On the whole then, when men speak of the Napoleonic system they seem to include two groups of ideas—one which comprises the conception of war made with the whole force of the nation; the other, a group which includes the Cromwellian idea of persistent effort, Frederick's preference for the offensive at almost any risk, and finally the idea of the enemy's armed forces as the main objective, which was also Cromwell's.

It is the combination of these by no means original or very distinct ideas that we are told has brought about so entire a change in the conduct of war that it has become altogether a different thing. It is unnecessary for our purpose to consider how far the facts seem to support such a conclusion, for in the inherent nature of things it must be radically unsound. Neither war nor anything else can change in its essentials. If it appears to do so, it is because we are still mistaking accidents for essentials, and this is exactly how it struck the acutest thinkers of Napoleonic times.

For a while it is true they were bewildered, but so soon as they had had time to clear their heads from the din of the struggle in which they had taken part, they began to see that the new phenomena were but accidents after all. They perceived that Napoleon's methods, which had taken the world by storm, had met with success in wars of a certain nature only, and that when he tried to extend those methods to other natures of war he had met with failure and even disaster. How was this to be explained? What theory, for instance, would cover Napoleon's successes in Germany and Italy, as well as his failures in Spain and Russia? If the whole conception of war had changed, how could you account for the success of England, who had not changed her methods? To us the answer to these questions is of living and infinite importance. Our standpoint remains still un-changed. Is there anything inherent in the conception of war that justifies that attitude in our case? Are we entitled to expect from it again the same success it met with in the past?

The first man to enunciate a theory which would explain the phenomena of the Napoleonic era and co-ordinate them with previous history was General Carl von Clausewitz, a man whose arduous service on the Staff and the actual work of higher instruction had taught the necessity of systematising the study of his profession. He was no mere professor, but a soldier bred in the severest school of war. The pupil and friend of Sharnhorst and Gneisenau, he had served on the Staff of Blücher in 1813, he had been Chief of the Staff to Wallmoden in his campaign against Davoust on the Lower Elbe, and also to the Third Prussian Army Corps in the campaign of 1815. Thereafter for more than ten years he was Director of the General Academy of War at Berlin, and died in 1831 as Chief of the Staff to Marshal Gneisenau. For the fifty years that followed his death his theories and system were, as he expected they would be, attacked from all sides. Yet to-day his work is more firmly established than ever as the necessary basis of all strategical thought, and above all in the " blood and iron " school of Germany.

The process by which he reached his famous theory can be followed in his classical work *On War* and the *Notes* regarding it which he left behind him. In accordance with the philosophic fashion of his time he began by trying to formulate an abstract idea of war. The definition he started with was that " War is an act of violence to compel our opponent to do our will."

But that act of violence was not merely " the shock of armies," as Montecuculi had defined it a century and a half before. If the abstract idea of war be followed to its logical conclusion, the act of violence must be performed with the whole of the means at our disposal and with the utmost exertion of our will. Consequently we get the conception of two armed nations flinging themselves one upon the other, and continuing the struggle with the utmost strength and energy they can command till one or other is no longer capable of resistance. This Clausewitz called " Absolute War." But his practical experience and ripe study of history told him at once that " Real War " was something radically different. It was true, as he said, that Napoleon's methods had approximated to the absolute and had given some colour to the use of the absolute idea as a working theory. " But shall we," he acutely asks, " rest satisfied with this idea and judge all wars by it however much they may differ from it—shall we deduce from it all the requirements of theory? We must decide the point, for we can say nothing trustworthy about a war plan until we have made up our minds whether war should only be of this kind or whether it may be of another kind." He saw at once that a theory formed upon the abstract or absolute idea of war would not cover the ground, and therefore failed to give what was required for practical purposes. It would exclude almost the whole of war from Alexander's time to Napoleon's. And what guarantee was there that the next war would conform to the Napoleonic type and accommodate itself to the abstract theory ? " This theory," he says, " is still quite powerless against the force of circumstances." And so it proved, for the wars of the middle nineteenth century did in fact revert to the pre-Napoleonic type.

In short, Clausewitz's difficulty in adopting his abstract theory as a working rule was that his practical mind could not forget that war had not begun with the Revolutionary era, nor was it likely to end with it. If that era had changed the conduct of war, it must be presumed that war would change again with other times and other conditions. A theory of war which did not allow for this and did not cover all that had gone before was no theory at all. If a theory of war was to be of any use as a practical guide it must cover and explain not only the extreme manifestation of hostility which he himself had witnessed, but every manifestation that had occurred in the past or was likely to recur in the future.

It was in casting about for the underlying causes of the oscillations manifested in the energy and intensity of hostile relations that he found his solution. His experience on the Staff, and his study of the inner springs of war, told him it was never in fact a question of purely military endeavour aiming always at the extreme of what was possible or expedient from a purely military point of view. The energy exhibited would always be modified by political considerations and by the depth of the national interest in the object of the war. He saw that real war was in fact an international relation which differed from other international relations only in the method we adopted to achieve the object of our policy. So it was he arrived at his famous theory—"that war is a mere continuation of policy by other means."

At first sight there seems little enough in it. It may seem perhaps that we have been watching a mountain in labour and nothing but a mouse has been produced. But it is only upon some such simple, even obvious, formula that any scientific system can be constructed with safety. We have only to develop the meaning of this one to see how important and practical are the guiding lines which flow from it.

With the conception of war as a continuation of political intercourse before us, it is clear that everything which lies outside the political conception, everything, that is, which is strictly peculiar to military and naval operations, relates merely to the means which we use to achieve our policy. Conseqently, the first desideratum of a war plan is that the means adopted must conflict as little as possible with the political conditions from which the war springs. In practice, of course, as in all human relations, there will be a compromise between the means and the end, between the political and the military exigencies. But Clausewitz held that policy must always be the master. The officer charged with the conduct of the war may of course demand that the tendencies and views of policy shall not be incompatible with the military means which are placed at his disposal; but however strongly this demand may react on policy in particular cases, military action must still be regarded only as a manifestation of policy. It must never supersede policy. The policy is always the object; war is only the means by which we obtain the object, and the means must always keep the end in view.

The practical importance of this conception will now become clear. It will be seen to afford the logical or theoretical exposition of what we began by stating in its purely concrete form. When a Chief

of Staff is asked for a war plan he must not say we
will make war in such and such a way because it
was Napoleon's or Moltke's way. He will ask what
is the political object of the war, what are the political
conditions, and how much does the question at issue
mean respectively to us and to our adversary. It is
these considerations which determine the nature of
the war. This primordial question settled, he will be
in a position to say whether the war is of the same
nature as those in which Napoleon's and Moltke's
methods were successful, or whether it is of another
nature in which those methods failed. He will then
design and offer a war plan, not because it has the
hall-mark of this or that great master of war, but
because it is one that has been proved to fit the
kind of war in hand. To assume that one method
of conducting war will suit all kinds of war is to
fall a victim to abstract theory, and not to be a
prophet of reality, as the narrowest disciples of the
Napoleonic school are inclined to see themselves.

Hence, says Clausewitz, the first, the greatest and
most critical decision upon which the Statesman and
the General have to exercise their judgment is to
determine the nature of the war, to be sure they do not
mistake it for something nor seek to make of it something which from its inherent conditions it can never
be. "This," he declares, "is the first and the most
far-reaching of all strategical questions."

The first value, then, of his theory of war is that it
gives a clear line on which we may proceed to determine the nature of a war in which we are about to
engage, and to ensure that we do not try to apply to
one nature of war any particular course of operations
simply because they have proved successful in another

nature of war. It is only, he insists, by regarding war
not as an independent thing but as a political instrument that we can read aright the lessons of history and
understand for our practical guidance how wars must
differ in character according to the nature of the
motives and circumstances from which they proceed.
This conception, he claims, is the first ray of light to
guide us to a true theory of war and thereby enable us
to classify wars and distinguish them one from another.

Jomini, his great contemporary and rival, though
proceeding by a less philosophical but no less lucid
method, entirely endorses this view. A Swiss soldier
of fortune, his experience was much the same as that
of Clausewitz. It was obtained mainly on the Staff of
Marshal Ney and subsequently on the Russian head-
quarter Staff. He reached no definite theory of war,
but his fundamental conclusions were the same. The
first chapter of his final work, *Précis de l'art de la
Guerre*, is devoted to " La Politique de la Guerre." In
it he classifies wars into nine categories according to
their political object, and he lays it down as a base
proposition "That these different kinds of war will
have more or less influence on the nature of the operations which will be demanded to attain the end in view,
on the amount of energy that must be put forth, and
on the extent of the undertakings in which we must
engage." "There will," he adds, " be a great difference
in the operations according to the risks we have to
run."

Both men, therefore, though on details of means
they were often widely opposed, are agreed that the
fundamental conception of war is political. Both of
course agree that if we isolate in our mind the forces
engaged in any theatre of war the abstract conception

reappears. So far as those forces are concerned, war is a question of fighting in which each belligerent should endeavour by all the means at his command and with all his energy to destroy the other. But even so they may find that certain means are barred to them for political reasons, and at any moment the fortune of war or a development of the political conditions with which it is entangled may throw them back upon the fundamental political theory.

That theory it will be unprofitable to labour further at this point. Let it suffice for the present to mark that it gives us a conception of war as an exertion of violence to secure a political end which we desire to attain, and that from this broad and simple formula we are able to deduce at once that wars will vary according to the nature of the end and the intensity of our desire to attain it. Here we may leave it to gather force and coherence as we examine the practical considerations which are its immediate outcome.

CHAPTER II

HAVING determined that wars must vary in character according to the nature and importance of their object, we are faced with the difficulty that the variations will be of infinite number and of all degrees of distinction. So complex indeed is the graduation presented that at first sight it appears scarcely possible to make it the basis of practical study. But on further examination it will be seen that by applying the usual analytical method the whole subject is susceptible of much simplification. We must in short attempt to reach some system of classification; that is, we must see if it is not possible to group the variations into some well-founded categories. With a subject so complex and intangible the grouping must of course be to some extent arbitrary, and in some places the lines of demarcation will be shadowy; but if classification has been found possible and helpful in Zoology or Botany, with the infinite and minute individual variations with which they have to deal, it should be no less possible and helpful in the study of war.

The political theory of war will at any rate give us two broad and well-marked classifications. The first is simple and well known, depending on whether the political object of the war is positive or negative. If it be positive—that is, if our aim is to wrest something from the enemy—then our war in its main lines will be offensive. If, on the other hand, our aim be negative, and we simply seek to prevent the enemy wresting some advantage to our detriment, then the war in its general direction will be defensive.

It is only as a broad conception that this classification has value. Though it fixes the general trend of our operations, it will not in itself affect their character. For a maritime Power at least it is obvious that this must be so. For in any circumstances it is impossible for such a Power either to establish its defence or develop fully its offence without securing a working control of the sea by aggressive action against the enemy's fleets. Furthermore, we have always found that however strictly our aim may be defensive, the most effective means of securing it has been by counter-attack over-sea, either to support an ally directly or to deprive our enemy of his colonial possessions. Neither category, then, excludes the use of offensive operations nor the idea of overthrowing our enemy so far as is necessary to gain our end. In neither case does the conception lead us eventually to any other objective than the enemy's armed forces, and particularly his naval forces. The only real difference is this—that if our object be positive our general plan must be offensive, and we should at least open with a true offensive movement; whereas if our object be negative our general plan will be preventive, and we may bide our time for our counter-attack. To this extent our action must always tend to the offensive. For counter-attack is the soul of defence. Defence is not a passive attitude, for that is the negation of war. Rightly conceived, it is an attitude of alert expectation. We wait for the moment when the enemy shall expose himself to a counter-stroke, the success of which will so far cripple him as to render us relatively strong enough to pass to the offensive ourselves.

From these considerations it will appear that, real and logical as the classification is, to give it the designation " offensive and defensive " is objectionable from every point of view. To begin with, it does not emphasise what the real and logical distinction is. It suggests that the basis of the classification is not so much a difference of object as a difference in the means employed to achieve the object. Consequently we find ourselves continually struggling with the false assumption that positive war means using attack, and negative war being content with defence.

That is confusing enough, but a second objection to the designation is far more serious and more fertile of error. For the classification " offensive and defensive " implies that offensive and defensive are mutually exclusive ideas, whereas the truth is, and it is a fundamental truth of war, that they are mutually complementary. All war and every form of it must be both offensive and defensive. No matter how clear our positive aim nor how high our offensive spirit, we cannot develop an aggressive line of strategy to the full without the support of the defensive on all but the main lines of operation. In tactics it is the same. The most convinced devotee of attack admits the spade as well as the rifle. And even when it comes to men and material, we know that without a certain amount of protection neither ships, guns, nor men can develop their utmost energy and endurance in striking power. There is never, in fact, a clean choice between attack and defence. In aggressive operations the question always is, how far must defence enter into the methods we employ in order to enable us to do the utmost within our resources to break or paralyse the strength of the enemy. So also with defence. Even in its most legitimate use, it must always be supplemented by attack. Even behind the walls of a fortress men know that sooner or later the place must fall unless by counter-attack on the enemy's siege works or communications they can cripple his power of attack.

It would seem, therefore, that it were better to lay aside the designation " offensive and defensive " altogether and substitute the terms " positive and negative." But here again we are confronted with a difficulty. There have been many wars in which positive methods have been used all through to secure a negative end, and such wars will not sit easily in either class. For instance, in the War of Spanish Succession our object was mainly to prevent the Mediterranean becoming a French lake by the union of the French and Spanish crowns, but the method by which we succeeded in achieving our end was to seize the naval positions of Gibraltar and Minorca, and so in practice our method was positive. Again, in the late Russo-Japanese War the main object of Japan was to prevent Korea being absorbed by Russia. That aim was preventive and negative. But the only effective way of securing her aim was to take Korea herself, and so for her the war was in practice positive.

On the other hand, we cannot shut our eyes to the fact that in the majority of wars the side with the positive object has acted generally on the offensive and the other generally on the defensive. Unpractical therefore as the distinction seems to be, it is impossible to dismiss it without inquiring why this was so, and it is in this inquiry that the practical results of the classification will be found to lie—that is, it forces us to analyse the comparative advantages of offence and defence. A clear apprehension of their relative possibilities is the corner stone of strategical study.

Now the advantages of the offensive are patent and admitted. It is only the offensive that can produce positive results, while the strength and energy which are born of the moral stimulation of attack are of a practical value that outweighs almost every other consideration. Every man of spirit would desire to use the offensive whether his object were positive or negative, and yet there are a number of cases in which some of the most energetic masters of war have chosen the defensive, and chosen with success. They have chosen it when they have found themselves inferior in physical force to their enemy, and when they believed that no amount of aggressive spirit could redress that inferiority.

Obviously, then, for all the inferiority of the defensive as a drastic form of war it must have some inherent advantage which the offensive does not enjoy. In war we adopt every method for which we have sufficient strength. If, then, we adopt the less desirable method of defence, it must be either that we have not sufficient strength for offence, or that the defence gives us some special strength for the attainment of our object.

What, then, are these elements of strength? It is very necessary to inquire, not only that we may know that if for a time we are forced back upon the defensive all is not lost, but also that we may judge with how much daring we should push our offensive to prevent the enemy securing the advantages of defence.

As a general principle we all know that possession is nine points of the law. It is easier to keep money in our pocket than to take it from another man's. If one man would rob another he must be the stronger or better armed unless he can do it by dexterity or stealth, and there lies one of the advantages of offence. The side which takes the initiative has usually the better chance of securing advantage by dexterity or stealth. But it is not always so. If either by land or sea we can take a defensive position so good that it cannot be turned and must be broken down before our enemy can reach his objective, then the advantage of dexterity and stealth passes to us. We choose our own ground for the trial of strength. We are hidden on familiar ground; he is exposed on ground that is less familiar. We can lay traps and prepare surprises by counter-attack, when he is most dangerously exposed. Hence the paradoxical doctrine that where defence is sound and well designed the advantage of surprise is against the attack.

It will be seen therefore that whatever advantages lie in defence they depend on the preservation of the offensive spirit. Its essence is the counter-attack —waiting deliberately for a chance to strike—not cowering in inactivity. Defence is a condition of restrained activity—not a mere condition of rest. Its real weakness is that if unduly prolonged it tends to deaden the spirit of offence. This is a truth so vital that some authorities in their eagerness to enforce it have travestied it into the misleading maxim, "That attack is the best defence." Hence again an amateurish notion that defence is always stupid or pusillanimous, leading always to defeat, and that what is called "the military spirit" means nothing but taking the offensive. Nothing is further from the teaching or the practice of the best masters. Like Wellington at Torres Vedras, they all at times used the defensive till the elements of strength inherent in that form of war, as opposed to the exhausting strain inherent in the form that they had fixed upon their opponents, lifted them to a position where they in their turn were relatively strong enough to use the more exhausting form.

The confusion of thought which has led to the misconceptions about defence as a method of war is due to several obvious causes. Counter-attacks from a general defensive attitude have been regarded as a true offensive, as, for instance, in Frederick the Great's best-known operations, or in Admiral Tegethoff's brilliant counterstroke at Lissa, or our own operations against the Spanish Armada. Again, the defensive has acquired an ill name by its being confused with a wrongly arrested offensive, where the superior Power with the positive object lacked the spirit to use his material superiority with sufficient activity and perseverance. Against such a Power an inferior enemy can always redress his inferiority by passing to a bold and quick offensive, thus acquiring a momentum both moral and physical which more than compensates his lack of weight. The defensive has also failed by the choice of a bad position which the enemy was able to turn or avoid. A defensive attitude is nothing at all, its elements of strength entirely disappear, unless it is such that the enemy must break it down by force before he can reach his ultimate objective. Even more often has it failed when the belligerent adopting it, finding he has no available defensive position which will bar the enemy's progress, attempts to guard every possible line of attack. The result is of course that by attenuating his force he only accentuates his inferiority.

Clear and well proven as these considerations are for land warfare, their application to the sea is not so obvious. It will be objected that at sea there is no defensive. This is generally true for tactics, but even so not universally true. Defensive tactical positions are possible at sea, as in defended anchorages. These were always a reality, and the mine has increased their possibilities. In the latest developments of naval warfare we have seen the Japanese at the Elliot Islands preparing a real defensive position to cover the landing of their Second Army in the Liaotung Peninsula. Strategically the proposition is not true at all. A strategical defensive has been quite as common at sea as on land, and our own gravest problems have often been how to break down such an attitude when our enemy assumed it. It usually meant that the enemy remained in his own waters and near his own bases, where it was almost impossible for us to attack him with decisive result, and whence he always threatened us with counter-attack at moments of exhaustion, as the Dutch did at Sole Bay and in the Medway. The difficulty of dealing decisively with an enemy who adopted this course was realised by our service very early, and from first to last one of our chief preoccupations was to prevent the enemy availing himself of this device and to force him to fight in the open, or at least to get between him and his base and force an action there.

Probably the most remarkable manifestation of the advantages that may be derived in suitable conditions from a strategical defensive is also to be found in the late Russo-Japanese War. In the final crisis of the naval struggle the Japanese fleet was able to take advantage of a defensive attitude in its own waters which the Russian Baltic fleet would have to break down to attain its end, and the result was the most decisive naval victory ever recorded.

The deterrent power of active and dexterous operations from such a position was well known to our old tradition. The device was used several times, particularly in our home waters, to prevent a fleet, which for the time we were locally too weak to destroy, from carrying out the work assigned to it. A typical position of the kind was off Scilly, and it was proved again and again that even a superior fleet could not hope to effect anything in the Channel till the fleet off Scilly had been brought to decisive action. But the essence of the device was the preservation of the aggressive spirit in its most daring form. For success it depended on at least the will to seize every occasion for bold and harassing counter-attacks such as Drake and his colleagues struck at the Armada.

To submit to blockade in order to engage the attention of a superior enemy's fleet is another form of defensive, but one that is almost wholly evil. For a short time it may do good by permitting offensive operations elsewhere which otherwise would be impossible. But if prolonged, it will sooner or later destroy the spirit of your force and render it incapable of effective aggression.

The conclusion then is that although for the practical purpose of framing or appreciating plans of war the classification of wars into offensive and defensive is of little use, a clear apprehension of the inherent relative advantages of offence and defence is essential. We must realise that in certain cases, provided always we preserve the aggressive spirit, the defensive will enable an inferior force to achieve points when the offensive would probably lead to its destruction. But the elements of strength depend entirely on the will and insight to deal rapid blows in the enemy's unguarded moments. So soon as the defensive ceases to be regarded as a means of fostering power to strike and of reducing the enemy's power of attack it loses all its strength. It ceases to be even a suspended activity, and anything that is not activity is not war.

With these general indications of the relative advantages of offence and defence we may leave the subject for the present. It is possible of course to catalogue the advantages and disadvantages of each form, but any such bald statement—without concrete examples to explain the meaning—must always appear controversial and is apt to mislead. It is better to reserve their fuller consideration till we come to deal with strategical operations and are able to note their actual effect upon the conduct of war in its various forms. Leaving therefore our first classification of wars into offensive and defensive we will pass on to the second, which is the only one of real practical importance.

CHAPTER III

NATURES OF WARS—LIMITED AND UNLIMITED

THE second classification to which we are led by the political theory of war, is one which Clausewitz was the first to formulate and one to which he came to attach the highest importance. It becomes necessary therefore to examine his views in some detail—not because there is any need to regard a continental soldier, however distinguished, as an indispensable authority for a maritime nation. The reason is quite the reverse. It is because a careful examination of his doctrine on this point will lay open what are the radical and essential differences between the German or Continental School of Strategy and the British or Maritime School—that is, our own traditional School, which too many writers both at home and abroad quietly assume to have no existence. The evil tendency of that assumption cannot be too strongly emphasised, and the main purpose of this and the following chapters will be to show how and why even the greatest of the continental strategists fell short of realising fully the characteristic conception of the British tradition.

By the classification in question Clausewitz distinguished wars into those with a "Limited" object and those whose object was "Unlimited." Such a classification was entirely characteristic of him, for it rested not alone upon the material nature of the object, but on certain moral considerations to which he was the first to attach their real value in war. Other writers such as Jomini had attempted to classify wars by the special purpose for which they were fought, but Clausewitz's long course of study convinced him that such a distinction was unphilosophical and bore no just relation to any tenable theory of war. Whether, that is, a war was positive or negative mattered much, but its special purpose, whether, for instance, according to Jomini's system, it was a war " to assert rights " or " to assist an ally " or " to acquire territory," mattered not at all.

Whatever the object, the vital and paramount question was the intensity with which the spirit of the nation was absorbed in its attainment. The real point to determine in approaching any war plan was what did the object mean to the two belligerents, what sacrifices would they make for it, what risks were they prepared to run? It was thus he stated his view. "The smaller the sacrifice we demand from our opponent, the smaller presumably will be the means of resistance he will employ, and the smaller his means, the smaller will ours be required to be. Similarly the smaller our political object, the less value shall we set upon it and the more easily we shall be induced to abandon it." Thus the political object of the war, its original motive, will not only determine for both belligerents reciprocally the aim of the force they use, but it will also be the standard of the intensity of the efforts they will make. So he concludes there may be wars of all degrees of importance and energy from a war of extermination down to the use of an army of observation. So also in the naval sphere there may be a life and death struggle for maritime supremacy or hostilities which never rise beyond a blockade.

Such a view of the subject was of course a wide

departure from the theory of "Absolute War" on
which Clausewitz had started working. Under that
theory "Absolute War" was the ideal form to which
all war ought to attain, and those which fell short
of it were imperfect wars cramped by a lack of true
military spirit. But so soon as he had seized the
fact that in actual life the moral factor always must
override the purely military factor, he saw that he
had been working on too narrow a basis—a basis
that was purely theoretical in that it ignored the
human factor. He began to perceive that it was
logically unsound to assume as the foundation of
a strategical system that there was one pattern to
which all wars ought to conform. In the light of
his full and final apprehension of the value of the
human factor he saw wars falling into two well-
marked categories, each of which would legitimately
be approached in a radically different manner, and
not necessarily on the lines of "Absolute War."

He saw that there was one class of war where
the political object was of so vital an importance
to both belligerents that they would tend to fight
to the utmost limit of their endurance to secure it.
But there was another class where the object was
of less importance, that is to say, where its value
to one or both the belligerents was not so great
as to be worth unlimited sacrifices of blood and
treasure. It was these two kinds of war he designated
provisionally "Unlimited" and "Limited," by which
he meant not that you were not to exert the force
employed with all the vigour you could develop,
but that there might be a limit beyond which it
would be bad policy to spend that vigour, a point
at which, long before your force was exhausted or

even fully developed, it would be wiser to abandon your object rather than to spend more upon it.

This distinction it is very necessary to grasp quite clearly, for it is often superficially confused with the distinction already referred to, which Clausewitz drew in the earlier part of his work—that is, the distinction between what he called the character of modern war and the character of the wars which preceded the Napoleonic era. It will be remembered he insisted that the wars of his own time had been wars between armed nations with a tendency to throw the whole weight of the nation into the fighting line, whereas in the seventeenth and eighteenth centuries wars were waged by standing armies and not by the whole nation in arms. The distinction of course is real and of far-reaching consequences, but it has no relation to the distinction between " Limited " and " Unlimited " war. War may be waged on the Napoleonic system either for a limited or an unlimited object.

A modern instance will serve to clear the field. The recent Russo-Japanese War was fought for a limited object—the assertion of certain claims over territory which formed no part of the possessions of either belligerent. Hostilities were conducted on entirely modern lines by two armed nations and not by standing armies alone. But in the case of one belligerent her interest in the object was so limited as to cause her to abandon it long before her whole force as an armed nation was exhausted or even put forth. The expense of life and treasure which the struggle was involving was beyond what the object was worth.

This second distinction—that is, between Limited and Unlimited wars—Clausewitz regarded as of greater importance than his previous one founded on the negative or positive nature of the object. He was long in reaching it. His great work *On War* as he left it proceeds almost entirely on the conception of offensive or defensive as applied to the Napoleonic ideal of absolute war. The new idea came to him towards the end in the full maturity of his prolonged study, and it came to him in endeavouring to apply his strategical speculations to the practical process of framing a war plan in anticipation of a threatened breach with France. It was only in his final section *On War Plans* that he began to deal with it. By that time he had grasped the first practical result to which his theory led. He saw that the distinction between Limited and Unlimited war connoted a cardinal distinction in the methods of waging it. When the object was unlimited, and would consequently call forth your enemy's whole war power, it was evident that no firm decision of the struggle could be reached till his war power was entirely crushed. Unless you had a reasonable hope of being able to do this it was bad policy to seek your end by force—that is, you ought not to go to war. In the case of a limited object, however, the complete destruction of the enemy's armed force was beyond what was necessary. Clearly you could achieve your end if you could seize the object, and by availing yourself of the elements of strength inherent in the defensive could set up such a situation that it would cost the enemy more to turn you out than the object was worth to him.

Here then was a wide difference in the fundamental postulate of your war plan. In the case of an unlimited war your main strategical offensive must be directed against the armed forces of the enemy; in the case

of a limited war, even where its object was positive,
it need not be. If conditions were favourable, it
would suffice to make the object itself the objective
of your main strategical offensive. Clearly, then, he
had reached a theoretical distinction which modified
his whole conception of strategy. No longer is there
logically but one kind of war, the Absolute, and no
longer is there but one legitimate objective, the enemy's
armed forces. Being sound theory, it of course had an
immediate practical value, for obviously it was a distinction from which the actual work of framing a war
plan must take its departure.

A curious corroboration of the soundness of these
views is that Jomini reached an almost identical standpoint independently and by an entirely different road.
His method was severely concrete, based on the comparison of observed facts, but it brought him as surely
as the abstract method of his rival to the conclusion
that there were two distinct classes of object. "They
are of two different kinds," he says, " one which may be
called territorial or geographical . . . the other on the
contrary consists exclusively in the destruction or dis-
organisation of the enemy's forces without concerning
yourself with geographical points of any kind." It is
under the first category of his first main classification
" Of offensive wars to assert rights," that he deals with
what Clausewitz would call " Limited Wars." Citing
as an example Frederick the Great's war for the conquest
of Silesia, he says, " In such a war . . . the offensive
operations ought to be proportional to the end in view.
The first move is naturally to occupy the provinces
claimed " (not, be it noted, to direct your blow at
the enemy's main force). " Afterwards," he proceeds,
" you can push the offensive according to circumstances

and your relative strength in order to obtain the desired cession by menacing the enemy at home." Here we have Clausewitz's whole doctrine of "Limited War"; firstly, the primary or territorial stage, in which you endeavour to occupy the geographical object, and then the secondary or coercive stage, in which you seek by exerting general pressure upon your enemy to force him to accept the adverse situation you have set up.

Such a method of making war obviously differs in a fundamental manner from that which Napoleon habitually adopted, and yet we have it presented by Jomini and Clausewitz, the two apostles of the Napoleonic method. The explanation is, of course, that both of them had seen too much not to know that Napoleon's method was only applicable when you could command a real physical or moral preponderance. Given such a preponderance, both were staunch for the use of extreme means in Napoleon's manner. It is not as something better than the higher road that they commend the lower one, but being veteran staff-officers and not mere theorists, they knew well that a belligerent must sometimes find the higher road beyond his strength, or beyond the effort which the spirit of the nation is prepared to make for the end in view, and like the practical men they were, they set themselves to study the potentialities of the lower road should hard necessity force them to travel it. They found that these potentialities in certain circumstances were great. As an example of a case where the lower form was more appropriate Jomini cites Napoleon's campaign against Russia in 1812. In his opinion it would have been better if Napoleon had been satisfied to begin on the lower method with a limited territorial object, and he attributes his failure

to the abuse of a method which, however well suited to
his wars in Germany, was incapable of achieving success
in the conditions presented by a war with Russia.

Seeing how high was Napoleon's opinion of Jomini
as a master of the science of war, it is curious how
his views on the two natures of wars have been
ignored in the present day. It is even more curious
in the case of Clausewitz, since we know that in the
plenitude of his powers he came to regard this classification as the master-key of the subject. The explanation is that the distinction is not very clearly formulated
is his first seven books, which alone he left in anything
like a finished condition. It was not till he came to
write his eighth book *On War Plans* that he saw the
vital importance of the distinction round which he had
been hovering. In that book the distinction is clearly
laid down, but the book unhappily was never completed. With his manuscript, however, he left a
"Note" warning us against regarding his earlier books
as a full presentation of his developed ideas. From
the note it is also evident that he thought the classification on which he had lighted was of the utmost
importance, that he believed it would clear up all the
difficulties which he had encountered in his earlier
books—difficulties which he had come to see arose
from a too exclusive consideration of the Napoleonic
method of conducting war. "I look upon the first
six books," he wrote in 1827, "as only a mass of
material which is still in a manner without form and
which has still to be revised again. In this revision
the two kinds of wars will be kept more distinctly
in view all through, and thereby all ideas will gain in
clearness, in precision, and in exactness of application."
Evidently he had grown dissatisfied with the theory

of Absolute War on which he had started. His new
discovery had convinced him that that theory would
not serve as a standard for all natures of wars. " Shall
we," he asks in his final book, " shall we now rest
satisfied with this idea and by it judge of all wars,
however much they may differ ? " [1] He answers his
question in the negative. " You cannot determine the
requirements of all wars from the Napoleonic type.
Keep that type and its absolute method before you
to use *when you can* or *when you must*, but keep
equally before you that there are two main natures
of war."

In his note written at this time, when the distinction
first came to him, he defines these two natures of war
as follows : " First, those in which the object is the
overthrow of the enemy, whether it be we aim at his
political destruction or merely at disarming him and
forcing him to conclude peace on our terms ; and
secondly, those in which our object is *merely to make
some conquests on the frontiers of his country*, either
for the purpose of retaining them permanently or of
turning them to account as a matter of exchange in
settling terms of peace." [2] It was in his eighth book
that he intended, had he lived, to have worked out
the comprehensive idea he had conceived. Of that
book he says, " The chief object will be to make good
the two points of view above mentioned, by which
everything will be simplified and at the same time be
given the breath of life. I hope in this book to iron
out many creases in the heads of strategists and statesmen, and at least to show the object of action and the
real point to be considered in war." [3]

---

[1] *On War*, Book viii. chap. ii.   [2] *Ibid.*, Prefatory Notice, p. vii.
[3] *Ibid.*, p. viii.

That hope was never realised, and that perhaps is why his penetrating analysis has been so much ignored. The eighth book as we have it is only a fragment. In the spring of 1830—an anxious moment, when it seemed that Prussia would require all her best for another struggle single-handed with France—he was called away to an active command. What he left of the book on "War Plans" he describes as "merely a track roughly cleared, as it were, through the mass, in order to ascertain the points of greatest moment." It was his intention, he says, to "carry the spirit of these ideas into his first six books"—to put the crown on his work, in fact, by elaborating and insisting upon his two great propositions, viz. that war was a form of policy, and that being so it might be Limited or Unlimited.

The extent to which he would have infused his new idea into the whole every one is at liberty to judge for himself; but this indisputable fact remains. In the winter in view of the threatening attitude of France in regard to Belgium he drew up a war plan, and it was designed not on the Napoleonic method of making the enemy's armed force the main strategical objective, but on seizing a limited territorial object and forcing a disadvantageous counter-offensive upon the French. The revolutionary movement throughout Europe had broken the Holy Alliance to pieces. Not only did Prussia find herself almost single-handed against France, but she herself was sapped by revolution. To adopt the higher form of war and seek to destroy the armed force of the enemy was beyond her power. But she could still use the lower form, and by seizing Belgium she could herself force so exhausting a task on France that success was well within her strength.

It was exactly so we endeavoured to begin the Seven Years' War; and it was exactly so the Japanese successfully conducted their war with Russia; and what is more striking, it was on similar lines that in 1859 Moltke in similar circumstances drew up his first war plan against France. His idea at that time was on the lines which Jomini held should have been Napoleon's in 1812. It was not to strike directly at Paris or the French main army, but to occupy Alsace-Lorraine and hold that territory till altered conditions should give him the necessary preponderance for proceeding to the higher form or forcing a favourable peace.

In conclusion, then, we have to note that the matured fruit of the Napoleonic period was a theory of war based not on the single absolute idea, but on the dual distinction of Limited and Unlimited. Whatever practical importance we may attach to the distinction, so much must be admitted on the clear and emphatic pronouncements of Clausewitz and Jomini. The practical importance is another matter. It may fairly be argued that in continental warfare—in spite of the instances quoted by both the classical writers —it is not very great, for reasons that will appear directly. But it must be remembered that continental warfare is not the only form in which great international issues are decided. Standing at the final point which Clausewitz and Jomini reached, we are indeed only on the threshold of the subject. We have to begin where they left off and inquire what their ideas have to tell for the modern conditions of world-wide imperial States, where the sea becomes a direct and vital factor.

CHAPTER IV

LIMITED WAR AND MARITIME EMPIRES—DEVELOPMENT
OF CLAUSEWITZ'S AND JOMINI'S THEORY OF A
LIMITED TERRITORIAL OBJECT, AND ITS APPLICA-
TION TO MODERN IMPERIAL CONDITIONS

THE German war plans already cited, which were
based respectively on the occupation of Belgium and
Alsace-Lorraine, and Jomini's remarks on Napoleon's
disastrous Russian campaign serve well to show the
point to which continental strategists have advanced
along the road which Clausewitz was the first to indicate
clearly. We have now to consider its application to
modern imperial conditions, and above all where the
maritime element forcibly asserts itself. We shall
then see how small that advance has been compared
with its far-reaching effects for a maritime and above
all an insular Power.

It is clear that Clausewitz himself never apprehended the full significance of his brilliant theory.
His outlook was still purely continental, and the
limitations of continental warfare tend to veil the
fuller meaning of the principle he had framed. Had
he lived, there is little doubt he would have worked
it out to its logical conclusion, but his death condemned
his theory of limited war to remain in the inchoate
condition in which he had left it.

It will be observed, as was natural enough, that
all through his work Clausewitz had in his mind war
between two contiguous or at least adjacent continental

States, and a moment's consideration will show that in
that type of war the principle of the limited object can
rarely if ever assert itself in perfect precision.   Clausewitz himself put it quite clearly.   Assuming a case
where " the overthrow of the enemy "—that is, unlimited
war—is beyond our strength, he points out that we
need not therefore necessarily act on the defensive.
Our action may still be positive and offensive, but
the object can be nothing more than " the conquest
of part of the enemy's country."   Such a conquest he
knew might so far weaken your enemy or strengthen
your own position as to enable you to secure a satisfactory peace.   The path of history is indeed strewn
with such cases.   But he was careful to point out that
such a form of war was open to the gravest objections.
Once you had occupied the territory you aimed at, your
offensive action was, as a rule, arrested.   A defensive
attitude had to be assumed, and such an arrest of
offensive action he had previously shown was inherently
vicious, if only for moral reasons.   Added to this you
might find that in your effort to occupy the territorial
object you had so irretrievably separated your striking
force from your home-defence force as to be in no
position to meet your enemy if he was able to retort by
acting on unlimited lines with a stroke at your heart.
A case in point was the Austerlitz campaign, where
Austria's object was   to   wrest   North   Italy   from
Napoleon's empire.   She sent her main army under
the Archduke Charles to seize the territory she desired.
Napoleon immediately struck at Vienna, destroyed her
home army, and occupied the capital before the Archduke could turn to bar his way.

The argument is this : that, as all strategic attack
tends to leave points of your own uncovered, it always

involves greater or less provision for their defence.   It
is obvious, therefore, that if we are aiming at a limited
territorial object the proportion of defence required
will tend to be much greater than if we are directing
our attack on the main forces of the enemy.   In unlimited war our attack will itself tend to defend everything elsewhere, by forcing the enemy to concentrate
against our attack.   Whether the limited form is
justifiable or not therefore depends, as Clausewitz points
out, on the geographical position of the object.

So far British experience is with him, but he then
goes on to say the more closely the territory in question
is an annex of our own the safer is this form of war,
because then our offensive action will the more surely
cover our home country.   As a case in point he cites
Frederick the Great's opening of the Seven Years' War
with the occupation of Saxony—a piece of work which
materially strengthened Prussian defence.   Of the
British opening in Canada he says nothing.   His
outlook was too exclusively continental for it to
occur to him to test his doctrine with a conspicuously
successful case in which the territory aimed at was
distant from the home territory and in no way covered
it.   Had he done so he must have seen how much
stronger an example of the strength of limited war
was the case of Canada than the case of Saxony.
Moreover, he would have seen that the difficulties,
which in spite of his faith in his discovery accompanied
his attempt to apply it, arose from the fact that the
examples he selected were not really examples at all.

When he conceived the idea, the only kind of
limited object he had in his mind was, to use his own
words, " some conquests on the frontiers of the enemy's
country," such as Silesia and Saxony for Frederick the

Great, Belgium in his own war plan, and Alsace-Lorraine in that of Moltke. Now it is obvious that such objects are not truly limited, for two reasons. In the first place, such territory is usually an organic part of your enemy's country, or otherwise of so much importance to him that he will be willing to use unlimited effort to retain it. In the second place, there will be no strategical obstacle to his being able to use his whole force to that end. To satisfy the full conception of a limited object, one of two conditions is essential. Firstly, it must be not merely limited in area, but of really limited political importance; and secondly, it must be so situated as to be strategically isolated or to be capable of being reduced to practical isolation by strategical operations. Unless this condition exists, it is in the power of either belligerent, as Clausewitz himself saw, to pass to unlimited war if he so desires, and, ignoring the territorial objective, to strike at the heart of his enemy and force him to desist.

If, then, we only regard war between contiguous continental States, in which the object is the conquest of territory on either of their frontiers, we get no real generic difference between limited and unlimited war. The line between them is in any case too shadowy or unstable to give a classification of any solidity. It is a difference of degree rather than of kind. If, on the other hand, we extend our view to wars between world-wide empires, the distinction at once becomes organic. Possessions which lie oversea or at the extremities of vast areas of imperfectly settled territory are in an entirely different category from those limited objects which Clausewitz contemplated. History shows that they can never have the political importance of objects which are organically part of the European system, and it shows further that they can be isolated by naval action sufficiently to set up the conditions of true limited war.

Jomini approaches the point, but without clearly detaching it. In his chapter " On Great Invasions and Distant Expeditions," he points out how unsafe it is to take the conditions of war between contiguous States and apply them crudely to cases where the belligerents are separated by large areas of land or sea. He hovers round the sea factor, feeling how great a difference it makes, but without getting close to the real distinction. His conception of the inter-action of fleets and armies never rises above their actual co-operation in touch one with the other in a distant theatre. He has in mind the assistance which the British fleet afforded Wellington in the Peninsula, and Napoleon's dreams of Asiatic conquest, pronouncing such distant invasions as impossible in modern times except perhaps in combination with a powerful fleet that could provide the army of invasion with successive advanced bases. Of the paramount value of the fleet's isolating and preventive functions he gives no hint.

Even when he deals with oversea expeditions, as he does at some length, his grip of the point is no closer. It is indeed significant of how entirely continental thought had failed to penetrate the subject that in devoting over thirty pages to an enumeration of the principles of oversea expeditions, he, like Clausewitz, does not so much as mention the conquest of Canada; and yet it is the leading case of a weak military Power succeeding by the use of the limited form of war in forcing its will upon a strong one, and succeeding because it was able by naval action to secure its home defence and isolate the territorial object.

For our ideas of true limited objects, therefore, we must leave the continental theatres and turn to mixed or maritime wars. We have to look to such cases as Canada and Havana in the Seven Years' War, and Cuba in the Spanish-American War, cases in which complete isolation of the object by naval action was possible, or to such examples as the Crimea and Korea, where sufficient isolation was attainable by naval action owing to the length and difficulty of the enemy's land communications and to the strategical situation of the territory at stake.

These examples will also serve to illustrate and enforce the second essential of this kind of war. As has been already said, for a true limited object we must have not only the power of isolation, but also the power by a secure home defence of barring an unlimited counterstroke. In all the above cases this condition existed. In all of them the belligerents had no contiguous frontiers, and this point is vital. For it is obvious that if two belligerents have a common frontier, it is open to the superior of them, no matter how distant or how easy to isolate the limited object may be, to pass at will to unlimited war by invasion. This process is even possible when the belligerents are separated by a neutral State, since the territory of a weak neutral will be violated if the object be of sufficient importance, or if the neutral be too strong to coerce, there still remains the possibility that his alliance may be secured.

We come, then, to this final proposition—that limited war is only permanently possible to island Powers or between Powers which are separated by sea, and then only when the Power desiring limited war is able to command the sea to such a degree as to be able not only to isolate the distant object, but also to render impossible the invasion of his home territory.

Here, then, we reach the true meaning and highest military value of what we call the command of the sea, and here we touch the secret of England's success against Powers so greatly superior to herself in military strength. It is only fitting that such a secret should have been first penetrated by an Englishman. For so it was, though it must be said that except in the light of Clausewitz's doctrine the full meaning of Bacon's famous aphorism is not revealed. "This much is certain," said the great Elizabethan on the experience of our first imperial war; "he that commands the sea is at great liberty and may take as much or as little of the war as he will, whereas those that be strongest by land are many times nevertheless in great straits." It would be difficult to state more pithily the ultimate significance of Clausewitz's doctrine. Its cardinal truth is clearly indicated—that limited wars do not turn upon the armed strength of the belligerents, but upon the amount of that strength which they are able or willing to bring to bear at the decisive point.

It is much to be regretted that Clausewitz did not live to see with Bacon's eyes and to work out the full comprehensiveness of his doctrine. His ambition was to formulate a theory which would explain all wars. He believed he had done so, and yet it is clear he never knew how complete was his success, nor how wide was the field he had covered. To the end it would seem he was unaware that he had found an explanation of one of the most inscrutable problems in history—the expansion of England—at least so far as it has been due to successful war. That a small country with a weak army should have been able to gather to herself the most desirable regions of the earth, and to gather them at the expense of the greatest military Powers, is a paradox to which such Powers find it hard to be reconciled. The phenomenon seemed always a matter of chance—an accident without any foundation in the essential constants of war. It remained for Clausewitz, unknown to himself, to discover that explanation, and he reveals it to us in the inherent strength of limited war when means and conditions are favourable for its use.

We find, then, if we take a wider view than was open to Clausewitz and submit his latest ideas to the test of present imperial conditions, so far from failing to cover the ground they gain a fuller meaning and a firmer basis. Apply them to maritime warfare and it becomes clear that his distinction between limited and unlimited war does not rest alone on the moral factor. A war may be limited not only because the importance of the object is too limited to call forth the whole national force, but also because the sea may be made to present an insuperable physical obstacle to the whole national force being brought to bear. That is to say, a war may be limited physically by the strategical isolation of the object, as well as morally by its comparative unimportance.

CHAPTER V

WARS OF INTERVENTION—LIMITED INTERFERENCE IN UNLIMITED WAR

BEFORE leaving the general consideration of limited war, we have still to deal with a form of it that has not yet been mentioned. Clausewitz gave it provisionally the name of " War limited by contingent," and could find no place for it in his system. It appeared to him to differ essentially from war limited by its political object, or as Jomini put it, war with a territorial object. Yet it had to be taken into account and explained, if only for the part it had played in European history.

For us it calls for the most careful examination, not only because it baffled the great German strategist to reconcile it with his theory of war, but also because it is the form in which Great Britain most successfully demonstrated the potentiality for direct continental interference of a small army acting in conjunction with a dominant fleet.

The combined operations which were the normal expression of the British method of making war on the limited basis were of two main classes. Firstly, there were those designed purely for the conquest of the objects for which we went to war, which were usually colonial or distant oversea territory; and secondly, operations more or less upon the European seaboard designed not for permanent conquest, but as a method of disturbing our enemy's plans and strengthening the hands of our allies and our own position. Such operations might take the form of insignificant coastal diversions, or they might rise through all degrees of importance till, as in Wellington's operations in the Peninsula, they became indistinguishable in form from regular continental warfare.

It would seem, therefore, that these operations were distinguished not so much by the nature of the object as by the fact that we devoted to them, not the whole of our military strength, but only a certain part of it which was known as our "disposal force." Consequently, they appear to call for some such special classification, and to fall naturally into the category which Clausewitz called "War limited by contingent."

It was a nature of war well enough known in another form on the Continent. During the eighteenth century there had been a large number of cases of war actually limited by contingent—that is, cases where a country not having a vital interest in the object made war by furnishing the chief belligerent with an auxiliary force of a stipulated strength.

It was in the sixth chapter of his last book that Clausewitz intended to deal with this anomalous form of hostility. His untimely death, however, has left us with no more than a fragment, in which he confesses that such cases are "embarrassing to his theory." If, he adds, the auxiliary force were placed unreservedly at the disposal of the chief belligerent, the problem would be simple enough. It would then, in effect, be the same thing as unlimited war with the aid of a subsidised force. But in fact, as he observes, this seldom happened, for the contingent was always more or less controlled in accordance with the special political aims of the Government which furnished it. Consequently, the only conclusion he succeeded in reaching was that it was a form of war that had to be taken into account, and that it was a form of limited war that appeared to differ essentially from war limited by object. We are left, in fact, with an impression that there must be two kinds of limited war.

But if we pursue his historical method and examine the cases in which this nature of war was successful, and those in which it was unsuccessful, we shall find that wherever success is taken as an index of its legitimate employment, the practical distinction between the two kinds of limited war tends to disappear. The indications are that where the essential factors which justify the use of war limited by object are present in war limited by contingent, then that form of war tends to succeed, but not otherwise. We are brought, in fact, to this proposition, that the distinction " Limited by contingent " is not one that is inherent in war, and is quite out of line with the theory in hand—that, in reality, it is not a *form* of war, but a *method* which may be employed either for limited or unlimited war. In other words, war limited by contingent, if it is to be regarded as a legitimate form of war at all, must take frankly the one shape or the other. Either the contingent must act as an organic unit of the force making unlimited war without any reservations whatever, or else it should be given a definite territorial object, with an independent organisation and an independent limited function.

Our own experience seems to indicate that war by contingent or war with " a disposal force " attains the highest success when it approaches most closely to true limited war—that is, as in the case of the Peninsula and the Crimea, where its object is to wrest or secure from the enemy a definite piece of territory that to a greater or less extent can be isolated by naval action. Its operative power, in fact, appears to bear some direct relation to the intimacy with which naval and military action can be combined to give the contingent a weight and mobility that are beyond its intrinsic power.

If, then, we would unravel the difficulties of war limited by contingent, it seems necessary to distinguish between the continental and the British form of it. The continental form, as we have seen, differs but little in conception from unlimited war. The contingent is furnished at least ostensibly with the idea that it is to be used by the chief belligerent to assist him in overthrowing the common enemy, and that its objective will be the enemy's organised forces or his capital. Or it may be that the contingent is to be used as an army of observation to prevent a counterstroke, so as to facilitate and secure the main offensive movement of the chief belligerent. In either case, however small may be our contribution to the allied force, we are using the unlimited form and aiming at an unlimited and not a mere territorial object.

If now we turn to British experience of war limited by contingent, we find that the continental form has frequently been used, but we also find it almost invariably accompanied by a popular repugnance, as though there were something in it antagonistic to the national instinct. A leading case is the assistance we sent to Frederick the Great in the Seven Years' War. At the opening of the war, so great was the popular repugnance that the measure was found impossible, and it was not till Frederick's dazzling resistance to the Catholic powers had clothed him with the glory of a Protestant hero, that Pitt could do what he wanted. The old religious fire was stirred. The most potent of all national instincts kindled the people to a generous warmth which overcame their inborn antipathy to continental operations, and it was possible to send a substantial contingent to Frederick's assistance. In the end the support fully achieved its purpose, but it must be noted that even in this case the operations were limited not only by contingent but also by object. It is true that Frederick was engaged in an unlimited war in which the continued existence of Prussia was at stake, and that the British force was an organic element in his war plan. Nevertheless, it formed part of a British subsidised army under Prince Ferdinand of Brunswick, who though nominated by Frederick was a British commander-in-chief. His army was in organisation entirely distinct from that of Frederick, and it was assigned the very definite and limited function of preventing the French occupying Hanover and so turning the Prussian right flank. Finally it must be noted that its ability to perform this function was due to the fact that the theatre of operations assigned to it was such that in no probable event could it lose touch with the sea, nor could the enemy cut its lines of supply and retreat.

These features of the enterprise should be noted. They differentiate it from our earlier use of war limited by contingent in the continental manner, of which Marlborough's campaigns were typical, and they exhibit the special form which Marlborough would have chosen had political exigencies permitted and which was to become characteristic of British effort from Pitt's time onward. In the method of our greatest War Minister we have not only the limit by contingent but also the limit of a definite and independent function, and finally we have touch with the sea. This is the really vital factor, and upon it, as will presently appear, depends the strength of the method.

In the earlier part of the Great War we employed the same form in our operations in North-Western Europe. There we had also the limited function of securing Holland, and also complete touch with the sea, but our theatre of operations was not independent. Intimate concerted action with other forces was involved, and the result in every case was failure. Later on in Sicily, where absolute isolation was attainable, the strength of the method enabled us to achieve a lasting result with very slender means. But the result was purely defensive. It was not till the Peninsular War developed that we found a theatre for war limited by contingent in which all the conditions that make for success were present. Even there so long as our army was regarded as a contingent auxiliary to the Spanish army the usual failure ensued. Only in Portugal, the defence of which was a true limited object, and where we had a sea-girt theatre independent of extraneous allies, was success achieved from the first. So strong was the method here, and so exhausting the method which it forced on the enemy, that the local balance of force was eventually reversed and we were able to pass to a drastic offensive.

The real secret of Wellington's success—apart from his own genius—was that in perfect conditions he was applying the limited form to an unlimited war. Our object was unlimited. It was nothing less than the overthrow of Napoleon. Complete success at sea had failed to do it, but that success had given us the power of applying the limited form, which was the most decisive form of offence within our means.

Its substantial contribution to the final achievement of the object is now universally recognised.

The general result, then, of these considerations is that war by contingent in the continental form seldom or never differs generically from unlimited war, for the conditions required by limited war are seldom or never present. But what may be called the British or maritime form is in fact the application of the limited method to the unlimited form, as ancillary to the larger operations of our allies—a method which has usually been open to us because the control of the sea has enabled us to select a theatre in effect truly limited.[1]

But what if the conditions of the struggle in which we wish to intervene are such that no truly limited theatre is available? In that case we have to choose between placing a contingent frankly at the disposal of our ally, or confining ourselves to coastal diversion, as we did at Frederick the Great's request in the early campaigns of the Seven Years' War. Such operations can seldom be satisfactory to either party. The small positive results of our efforts to intervene in this way have indeed done more than anything to discredit this form of war, and to brand it as unworthy of a first-class Power. Yet the fact remains that all the great continental masters of war have feared or valued British intervention of this character even in the most unfavourable

---

[1] Wellington's view of the essential factor was expressed to Rear-Admiral Markham, who was sent to Spain by the Admiralty to confer with him in September 1813. "If any one," he said, "wishes to know the history of this war, I will tell them it is our maritime superiority gives me the power of maintaining my army while the enemy are unable to do so." (*Letters of Sir T. Byam Martin* (Navy Record Society), ii. p. 499.)

conditions. It was because they looked for its effects rather in the threat than in the performance. They did not reckon for positive results at all. So long as such intervention took an amphibious form they knew its disturbing effect upon a European situation was always out of all proportion to the intrinsic strength employed or the positive results it could give. Its operative action was that it threatened positive results unless it were strongly met. Its effect, in short, was negative. Its value lay in its power of containing force greater than its own. That is all that can be claimed for it, but it may be all that is required. It is not the most drastic method of intervention, but it has proved itself the most drastic for a Power whose forces are not adapted for the higher method. Frederick the Great was the first great soldier to recognise it, and Napoleon was the last. For years he shut his eyes to it, laughed at it, covered it with a contempt that grew ever more irritable. In 1805 he called Craig's expedition a "pygmy combination," yet the preparation of another combined force for an entirely different destination caused him to see the first as an advance guard of a movement he could not ignore, and he sacrificed his fleet in an impotent effort to deal with it.

It was not, however, till four years later that he was forced to place on record his recognition of the principle. Then, curiously enough, he was convinced by an expedition which we have come to regard as above all others condemnatory of amphibious operations against the Continent. The Walcheren expedition is now usually held as the leading case of fatuous war administration. Historians can find no words too bad for it. They ignore the fact that it was a step—the final and most difficult step—in our post-Trafalgar policy of using the army to perfect our command of the sea against a fleet acting stubbornly on the defensive. It began with Copenhagen in 1807. It failed at the Dardanelles because fleet and army were separated; it succeeded at Lisbon and at Cadiz by demonstration alone. Walcheren, long contemplated, had been put off till the last as the most formidable and the least pressing. Napoleon had been looking for the attempt ever since the idea was first broached in this country, but as time passed and the blow did not fall, the danger came to be more and more ignored. Finally, the moment came when he was heavily engaged in Austria and forced to call up the bulk of his strength to deal with the Archduke Charles. The risks were still great, but the British Government faced them boldly with open eyes. It was now or never. They were bent on developing their utmost military strength in the Peninsula, and so long as a potent and growing fleet remained in the North Sea it would always act as an increasing drag on such development. The prospective gain of success was in the eyes of the Government out of all proportion to the probable loss by failure. So when Napoleon least expected it they determined to act, and caught him napping. The defences of Antwerp had been left incomplete. There was no army to meet the blow— nothing but a polyglot rabble without staff or even officers. For a week at least success was in our hands. Napoleon's fleet only escaped by twenty-four hours, and yet the failure was not only complete but disastrous. Still so entirely were the causes of failure accidental, and so near had it come to success, that Napoleon received a thorough shock and looked for a quick repetition of the attempt. So seriously indeed did he regard his narrow escape that he found himself driven to reconsider his whole system of home defence. Not only did he deem it necessary to spend large sums in increasing the fixed defences of Antwerp and Toulon, but his Director of Conscription was called upon to work out a scheme for providing a permanent force of no less than 300,000 men from the National Guard to defend the French coasts. "With 30,000 men in transports at the Downs," the Emperor wrote, "the English can paralyse 300,000 of my army, and that will reduce us to the rank of a second-class Power."[1] The concentration of the British efforts in the Peninsula apparently rendered the realisation of this project unnecessary—that is, our line of operation was declared and the threat ceased. But none the less Napoleon's recognition of the principle remains on record—not in one of his speeches made for some ulterior purpose, but in a staff order to the principal officer concerned.

It is generally held that modern developments in military organisation and transport will enable a great continental Power to ignore such threats. Napoleon ignored them in the past, but only to verify the truth that in war to ignore a threat is too often to create an opportunity. Such opportunities may occur late or early. As both Lord Ligonier and Wolfe laid it down for such operations, surprise is not necessarily to be looked for at the beginning. We have usually had to create or wait for our opportunity—too often because we were either not ready or not bold enough to seize the first that occurred.

The cases in which such intervention has been most potent have been of two classes. Firstly, there is the intrusion into a war plan which our enemy has

---

[1] *Correspondance de Napoleon,* xix. 421, September 4,

designed without allowing for our intervention, and
to which he is irrevocably committed by his opening
movements. Secondly, there is intervention to deprive
the enemy of the fruits of victory. This form finds its
efficacy in the principle that unlimited wars are not
always decided by the destruction of armies. There
usually remains the difficult work of conquering the
people afterwards with an exhausted army. The intrusion of a small fresh force from the sea in such
cases may suffice to turn the scale, as it did in the
Peninsula, and as, in the opinion of some high
authorities, it might have done in France in 1871.

Such a suggestion will appear to be almost heretical
as sinning against the principle which condemns a
strategical reserve. We say that the whole available
force should be developed for the vital period of the
struggle. No one can be found to dispute it nowadays. It is too obviously true when it is a question of
a conflict between organised forces, but in the absence
of all proof we are entitled to doubt whether it is true
for that exhausting and demoralising period which lies
beyond the shock of armies.

CHAPTER VI

CONDITIONS OF STRENGTH IN LIMITED WAR

THE elements of strength in limited war are closely analogous to those generally inherent in defence. That is to say, that as a correct use of defence will sometimes enable an inferior force to gain its end against a superior one, so are there instances in which the correct use of the limited form of war has enabled a weak military Power to attain success against a much stronger one, and these instances are too numerous to permit us to regard the results as accidental.

An obvious element of strength is that where the geographical conditions are favourable we are able by the use of our navy to restrict the amount of force our army will have to deal with. We can in fact bring up our fleet to redress the adverse balance of our land force. But apart from this very practical reason there is another, which is rooted in the first principles of strategy.

It is that limited war permits the use of the defensive without its usual drawbacks to a degree that is impossible in unlimited war. These drawbacks are chiefly that it tends to surrender the initiative to the enemy and that it deprives us of the moral exhilaration of the offensive. But in limited war, as we shall see, this need not be the case, and if without making these sacrifices we are able to act mainly on the defensive our position becomes exceedingly strong.

The proposition really admits of no doubt. For even if we be not in whole-hearted agreement with

Clausewitz's doctrine of the strength of defence, still we may at least accept Moltke's modification of it. He held that the strongest form of war—that is, the form which economically makes for the highest development of strength in a given force—is strategic offensive combined with tactical defensive. Now these are in effect the conditions which limited war should give— that is, if the theatre and method be rightly chosen. Let it be remembered that the use of this form of war presupposes that we are able by superior readiness or mobility or by being more conveniently situated to establish ourselves in the territorial object before our opponent can gather strength to prevent us. This done, we have the initiative, and the enemy being unable by hypothesis to attack us at home, must conform to our opening by endeavouring to turn us out. We are in a position to meet his attack on ground of our own choice and to avail ourselves of such opportunities of counter-attack as his distant and therefore exhausting offensive movements are likely to offer. Assuming, as in our own case we always must assume, that the territorial object is sea-girt and our enemy is not able to command the sea, such opportunities are certain to present themselves, and even if they are not used will greatly embarrass the main attack—as was abundantly shown in the Russian nervousness during their advance into the Liaotung Peninsula, due to the fear of a counter-stroke from the Gulf of Pe-chi-li.

The actual situation which this method of procedure sets up is that our major strategy is offensive —that is, our main movement is positive, having for its aim the occupation of the territorial object. The minor strategy that follows should be in its general lines defensive, designed, so soon as the enemy sets

about dislodging us, to develop the utmost energy
of counter-attack which our force and opportunities
justify.

Now if we consider that by universal agreement it is no longer possible in the present conditions of land warfare to draw a line between tactics
and minor strategy, we have in our favour for all
practical purposes the identical position which Moltke
regarded as constituting the strongest form of war.
That is to say, our major strategy is offensive and our
minor strategy is defensive.

If, then, the limited form of war has this element of strength over and above the unlimited form,
it must be correct to use it when we are not strong
enough to use the more exhausting form and when
the object is limited; just as much as it is correct
to use the defensive when our object is negative
and we are too weak for the offensive. The point
is of the highest importance, for it is a direct negation of the current doctrine that in war there can
be but one legitimate object, the overthrow of the
enemy's means of resistance, and that the primary
objective must always be his armed forces. It raises
in fact the whole question as to whether it is not
sometimes legitimate and even correct to aim directly
at the ulterior object of the war.

An impression appears to prevail — in spite of
all that Clausewitz and Jomini had to say on the
point—that the question admits of only one answer.
Von der Goltz, for instance, is particularly emphatic
in asserting that the overthrow of the enemy must
always be the object in modern war. He lays it
down as "the first principle of modern warfare,"
that "the immediate objective against which all our

efforts must be directed is the hostile main army."
Similarly Prince Kraft has the maxim that "the
first aim should be to overcome the enemy's army.
Everything else, the occupation of the country, &c.,
only comes in the second line."

It will be observed that he here admits that the
process of occupying the enemy's territory is an
operation distinct from the overthrow of the enemy's
force. Von der Goltz goes further, and protests
against the common error of regarding the annihilation of the enemy's principal army as synonymous
with the complete attainment of the object. He
is careful to assert that the current doctrine only
holds good "when the two belligerent states are of
approximately the same nature." If, then, there are
cases in which the occupation of territory must be
undertaken as an operation distinct from defeating
the enemy's forces, and if in such cases the conditions
are such that we can occupy the territory with advantage without first defeating the enemy, it is surely
mere pedantry to insist that we should put off till
to-morrow what we can do better to-day. If the
occupation of the enemy's whole territory is involved,
or even a substantial part of it, the German principle
of course holds good, but all wars are not of that
character.

Insistence on the principle of "overthrow," and
even its exaggeration, was of value, in its day, to
prevent a recurrence to the old and discredited
methods. But its work is done, and blind adherence
to it without regard to the principles on which it
rests tends to turn the art of war into mere bludgeon
play.

Clausewitz, at any rate, as General Von Caem-

merer has pointed out,[1] was far too practical a
soldier to commit himself to so abstract a proposition in all its modern crudity. If it were true, it
would never be possible for a weaker Power to make
successful war against a stronger one in any cause
whatever—a conclusion abundantly refuted by historical
experience. That the higher form like the offensive
is the more drastic is certain, if conditions are suitable
for its use, but Clausewitz, it must be remembered,
distinctly lays it down that such conditions pre-
suppose in the belligerent employing the higher
form a great physical or moral superiority or a great
spirit of enterprise—an innate propensity for extreme
hazards. Jomini did not go even so far as this.
He certainly would have ruled out "an innate propensity to extreme hazards," for in his judgment it
was this innate propensity which led Napoleon to
abuse the higher form to his own undoing. So
entirely indeed does history, no less than theory,
fail to support the idea of the one answer, that it
would seem that even in Germany a reaction to
Clausewitz's real teaching is beginning. In expound-
ing it Von Caemmerer says, "Since the majority of
the most prominent military authors of our time
uphold the principle that in war our efforts must
always be directed to their utmost limits and that
a deliberate employment of lower means betrays
more or less weakness, I feel bound to declare that
the wideness of Clausewitz's views have inspired me
with a high degree of admiration."

Now what Clausewitz held precisely was this—that
when the conditions are not favourable for the use of
the higher form, the seizure of a small part of the

[1] *Development of Strategical Science.*

enemy's territory may be regarded as a correct alternative to destroying his armed forces. But he clearly regards this form of war only as a make-shift. His purely continental outlook prevented his considering that there might be cases where the object was actually so limited in character that the lower form of war would be at once the more effective and the more economical to use. In continental warfare, as we have seen, such cases can hardly occur, but they tend to declare themselves strongly when the maritime factor is introduced to any serious extent.

The tendency of British warfare to take the lower or limited form has always been as clearly marked as is the opposite tendency on the Continent. To attribute such a tendency, as is sometimes the fashion, to an inherent lack of warlike spirit is sufficiently contradicted by the results it has achieved. There is no reason indeed to put it down to anything but a sagacious instinct for the kind of war that best accords with the conditions of our existence. So strong has this instinct been that it has led us usually to apply the lower form not only where the object of the war was a well-defined territorial one, but to cases in which its correctness was less obvious. As has been explained in the last chapter, we have applied it, and applied it on the whole with success, when we have been acting in concert with continental allies for an unlimited object—where, that is, the common object has been the overthrow of the common enemy.

The choice between the two forms really depends upon the circumstances of each case. We have to consider whether the political object is in fact limited, whether if unlimited in the abstract it can be reduced to a concrete object that is limited, and finally whether

the strategical conditions are such as lend themselves
to the successful application of the limited form.

What we require now is to determine those conditions with greater exactness, and this will be best
done by changing our method to the concrete and
taking a leading case.

The one which presents them in their clearest and
simplest form is without doubt the recent war between
Russia and Japan. Here we have a particularly striking
example of a small Power having forced her will upon
a much greater Power without "overthrowing" her—
that is, without having crushed her power of resistance.
That was entirely beyond the strength of Japan. So
manifest was the fact that everywhere upon the Continent, where the overthrow of your enemy was regarded
as the only admissible form of war, the action of the
Japanese in resorting to hostilities was regarded as
madness. Only in England, with her tradition and
instinct for what an island Power may achieve by
the lower means, was Japan considered to have any
reasonable chance of success.

The case is particularly striking; for every one felt
that the real object of the war was in the abstract
unlimited, that it was in fact to decide whether Russia
or Japan was to be the predominant power in the Far
East. Like the Franco-German War of 1870 it had
all the aspect of what the Germans call "a trial of
strength." Such a war is one which above all appears
incapable of decision except by the complete overthrow
of the one Power or the other. There was no com-
plication of alliances nor any expectation of them.
The Anglo-Japanese Treaty had isolated the struggle.
If ever issue hung on the sheer fighting force of the
two belligerents it would seem to have been this one.

After the event we are inclined to attribute the result to the moral qualities and superior training and readiness of the victors. These qualities indeed played their part, and they must not be minimised; but who will contend that if Japan had tried to make her war with Russia, as Napoleon made his, she could have fared even as well as he did? She had no such preponderance as Clausewitz laid down as a condition precedent to attempting the overthrow of her enemy—the employment of unlimited war.

Fortunately for her the circumstances did not call for the employment of such extreme means. The political and geographical conditions were such that she was able to reduce the intangible object of asserting her prestige to the purely concrete form of a territorial objective. The penetration of Russia into Manchuria threatened the absorption of Korea into the Russian Empire, and this Japan regarded as fatal to her own position and future development. Her power to maintain Korean integrity would be the outward and visible sign of her ability to assert herself as a Pacific Power. Her abstract quarrel with Russia could therefore be crystallised into a concrete objective in the same way as the quarrel of the Western Powers with Russia in 1854 crystallised into the concrete objective of Sebastopol.

In the Japanese case the immediate political object was exceptionally well adapted for the use of limited war. Owing to the geographical position of Korea and to the vast and undeveloped territories which separate it from the centre of Russian power, it could be practically isolated by naval action. Further than this, it fulfilled the condition to which Clausewitz attached the greatest importance—that is to say, the

seizure of the particular object so far from weakening
the home defence of Japan would have the effect
of greatly increasing the strength of her position.
Though offensive in effect and intention it was also,
like Frederick's seizure of Saxony, a sound piece of
defensive work. So far from exposing her heart, it
served to cover it almost impregnably. The reason
is plain. Owing to the wide separation of the two
Russian arsenals at Port Arthur and Vladivostock, with
a defile controlled by Japan interposed, the Russian
naval position was very faulty. The only way of
correcting it was for Russia to secure a base in the
Straits of Korea, and for this she had been striving by
diplomatic means at Seoul for some time. Strategically the integrity of Korea was for Japan very much
what the integrity of the Low Countries was for us,
but in the case of the Low Countries, since they were
incapable of isolation, our power of direct action was
always comparatively weak. Portugal, with its un-
rivalled strategical harbour at Lisbon, was an analogous
case in our old oceanic wars, and since it was capable
of being in a measure isolated from the strength of
our great rival by naval means we were there almost
uniformly successful. On the whole it must be said
that notwithstanding the success we achieved in our
long series of wars waged on a limited basis, in none of
them were the conditions so favourable for us as in
this case they were for Japan. In none of them did
our main offensive movement so completely secure our
home defence. Canada was as eccentric as possible to
our line of home defence, while in the Crimea so completely did our offensive uncover the British Islands,
that we had to supplement our movement against the
limited object by sending our main fighting fleet to

hold the exit of the Baltic against the danger of an unlimited counter-stroke.[1]

Whether or not it was on this principle that the Japanese conceived the war from the outset matters little. The main considerations are that with so favourable a territorial object as Korea limited war was possible in its most formidable shape, that the war did in fact develop on limited lines, and that it was entirely successful. Without waiting to secure the command of the sea, Japan opened by a surprise seizure of Seoul, and then under cover of minor operations of the fleet proceeded to complete her occupation of Korea. As she faced the second stage, that of making good the defence of her conquest, the admirable nature of her geographical object was further displayed. The theoretical weakness of limited war at this point is the arrest of your offensive action. But in this case such arrest was neither necessary nor possible, and for these reasons. To render the conquest secure not only must the Korean frontier be made inviolable, but Korea must be permanently isolated by sea. This involved the destruction of the Russian fleet, and this in its turn entailed the reduction of Port

---

[1] The strategical object with which the Baltic fleet was sent was certainly to prevent a counter-stroke—that is, its main function in our war plan was negative. Its positive function was minor and diversionary only. It also had a political object as a demonstration to further our efforts to form a Baltic coalition against Russia, which entirely failed. Public opinion mistaking the whole situation expected direct positive results from this fleet, even the capture of St. Petersburg. Such an operation would have converted the war from a limited to an unlimited one. It would have meant the "overthrow of the enemy," a task quite beyond the strength of the allies without the assistance of the Baltic Powers, and even so their assistance would not have justified changing the nature of the war, unless both Sweden and Prussia had been ready to make unlimited war, and nothing was further from their intention.

Arthur by military means. Here, then, in the second
stage Japan found herself committed to two lines of
operation with two distinct objectives, Port Arthur and
the Russian army that was slowly concentrating
in Manchuria—a thoroughly vicious situation. So
fortunate, however, was the geographical conformation of the theatre that by promptitude and the
bold use of an uncommanded sea it could be
reduced to something far more correct. By continuing
the advance of the Korean army into Manchuria and
landing another force between it and the Port Arthur
army the three corps could be concentrated and the
vicious separation of the lines of operations turned to
good account. They could be combined in such a
way as to threaten an enveloping counter-attack on
Liao-yang before the Russian offensive concentration
could be completed. Not only was Liao-yang the
Russian point of concentration, but it also was a sound
position both for defending Korea and covering the
siege of Port Arthur. Once secured, it gave the
Japanese all the advantages of defence and forced
the Russians to exhaust themselves in offensive operations which were beyond their strength. Nor was it
only ashore that this advantage was gained. The
success of the system, which culminated in the fall of
Port Arthur, went further still. Not only did it make
Japan relatively superior at sea, but it enabled her
to assume a naval defensive and so to force the final
naval decision on Russia with every advantage of time,
place, and strength in her own favour.

By the battle of Tsushima the territorial object was
completely isolated by sea, and the position of Japan in
Korea was rendered as impregnable as that of Wellington
at Torres Vedras. All that remained was to proceed

to the third stage and demonstrate to Russia that the acceptance of the situation that had been set up was more to her advantage than the further attempt to break it down. This the final advance to Mukden accomplished, and Japan obtained her end very far short of having overthrown her enemy. The offensive power of Russia had never been so strong, while that of Japan was almost if not quite exhausted.

Approached in this way, the Far Eastern struggle is seen to develop on the same lines as all our great maritime wars of the past, which continental strategists have so persistently excluded from their field of study. It presents the normal three phases—the initial offensive movement to seize the territorial object, the secondary phase, which forces an attenuated offensive on the enemy, and the final stage of pressure, in which there is a return to the offensive "according," as Jomini puts it, "to circumstances and your relative force in order to obtain the cession desired."

It must not of course be asked that these phases shall be always clearly defined. Strategical analysis can never give exact results. It aims only at approximations, at groupings which will serve to guide but will always leave much to the judgment. The three phases in the Russo-Japanese War, though unusually well defined, continually overlapped. It must be so; for in war the effect of an operation is never confined to the limits of its immediate or primary intention. Thus the occupation of Korea had the secondary defensive effect of covering the home country, while the initial blow which Admiral Togo delivered at Port Arthur to cover the primary offensive movement proved, by the demoralisation it caused in the Russian fleet, to be a distinct step in the secondary phase of isolating the conquest. In the later stages of the war the line between what was essential to set up the second phase of perfecting the isolation and the third phase of general pressure seems to have grown very nebulous.

It was at this stage that the Japanese strategy has been most severely criticised, and it was just here they seem to have lost hold of the conception of a limited war, if in fact they had ever securely grasped the conception as the elder Pitt understood it. It has been argued that in their eagerness to deal a blow at the enemy's main army they neglected to devote sufficient force to reduce Port Arthur, an essential step to complete the second phase. Whether or not the exigencies of the case rendered such distribution of force inevitable or whether it was due to miscalculation of difficulties, the result was a most costly set-back. For not only did it entail a vast loss of time and life at Port Arthur itself, but when the sortie of the Russian fleet in June brought home to them their error, the offensive movement on Liao-yang had to be delayed, and the opportunity passed for a decisive counter-stroke at the enemy's concentration ashore.

This misfortune, which was to cost the Japanese so dear, may perhaps be attributed at least in part to the continental influences under which their army had been trained. We at least can trace the unlimited outlook in the pages of the German Staff history. In dealing with the Japanese plan of operations it is assumed that the occupation of Korea and the isolation of Port Arthur were but preliminaries to a concentric advance on Liao-yang, "which was kept in view as the first objective of the operations on land." But surely on every theory of the war the first objective of the Japanese on land was Seoul, where they ex-

pected to have to fight their first important action
against troops advancing from the Yalu; and surely
their second was Port Arthur, with its fleet and arsenal,
which they expected to reduce with little less difficulty
than they had met with ten years before against the
Chinese. Such at least was the actual progression
of events, and a criticism which regards operations
of such magnitude and ultimate importance as mere
incidents of strategic deployment is only to be explained by the domination of the Napoleonic idea of
war, against the universal application of which Clausewitz so solemnly protested. It is the work of men who
have a natural difficulty in conceiving a war plan that
does not culminate in a Jena or a Sedan. It is a view
surely which is the child of theory, bearing no relation
to the actuality of the war in question and affording no
explanation of its ultimate success. The truth is, that
so long as the Japanese acted on the principles of limited
war, as laid down by Clausewitz and Jomini and plainly
deducible from our own rich experience, they progressed
beyond all their expectations, but so soon as they
departed from them and suffered themselves to be
confused with continental theories they were surprised
by unaccountable failure.

The expression "Limited war" is no doubt not
entirely happy. Yet no other has been found to condense the ideas of limited object and limited interest,
which are its special characteristics. Still if the above
example be kept in mind as a typical case, the meaning of the term will not be mistaken. It only remains
to emphasise one important point. The fact that the
doctrine of limited war traverses the current belief
that our primary objective must always be the enemy's
armed forces is liable to carry with it a false inference

that it also rejects the corollary that war means the use of battles. Nothing is further from the conception. Whatever the form of war, there is no likelihood of our ever going back to the old fallacy of attempting to decide wars by manœuvres. All forms alike demand the use of battles. By our fundamental theory war is always "a continuation of political intercourse, in which fighting is substituted for writing notes." However great the controlling influence of the political object, it must never obscure the fact that it is by fighting we have to gain our end.

It is the more necessary to insist on this point, for the idea of making a piece of territory your object is liable to be confused with the older method of conducting war, in which armies were content to manœuvre for strategical positions, and a battle came almost to be regarded as a mark of bad generalship. With such parading limited war has nothing to do. Its conduct differs only from that of unlimited war in that instead of having to destroy our enemy's whole power of resistance, we need only overthrow so much of his active force as he is able or willing to bring to bear in order to prevent or terminate our occupation of the territorial object.

The first consideration, then, in entering on such a war is to endeavour to determine what that force will amount to. It will depend, firstly, on the importance the enemy attaches to the limited object, coupled with the nature and extent of his preoccupations elsewhere, and, secondly, it will depend upon the natural difficulties of his lines of communication and the extent to which we can increase those difficulties by our conduct of the initial operations. In favourable circumstances therefore (and here lies the great value of the limited form) we are able to control the amount of force we shall have to encounter. The most favourable circumstances and the only circumstances by which we ourselves can profit are such as permit the more or less complete isolation of the object by naval action, and such isolation can never be established until we have entirely overthrown the enemy's naval forces.

Here, then, we enter the field of naval strategy. We can now leave behind us the theory of war in general and, in order to pave the way to our final conclusions, devote our attention to the theory of naval warfare in particular.

PART II

THEORY OF NAVAL WAR

CHAPTER I

THE object of naval warfare must always be directly or indirectly either to secure the command of the sea or to prevent the enemy from securing it.

The second part of the proposition should be noted with special care in order to exclude a habit of thought, which is one of the commonest sources of error in naval speculation. That error is the very general assumption that if one belligerent loses the command of the sea it passes at once to the other belligerent. The most cursory study of naval history is enough to reveal the falseness of such an assumption. It tells us that the most common situation in naval war is that neither side has the command; that the normal position is not a commanded sea, but an uncommanded sea. The mere assertion, which no one denies, that the object of naval warfare is to get command of the sea actually connotes the proposition that the command is normally in dispute. It is this state of dispute with which naval strategy is most nearly concerned, for when the command is lost or won pure naval strategy comes to an end.

This truth is so obvious that it would scarcely be worth mentioning were it not for the constant recurrence of such phrases as: " If England were to lose command of the sea, it would be all over with her." The fallacy of the idea is that it ignores the power of the strategical defensive. It assumes that if in the face of some extraordinary hostile coalition or through

some extraordinary mischance we found ourselves without sufficient strength to keep the command, we
should therefore be too weak to prevent the enemy
getting it—a negation of the whole theory of war,
which at least requires further support than it ever
receives.

And not only is this assumption a negation of
theory; it is a negation both of practical experience
and of the expressed opinion of our greatest masters.
We ourselves have used the defensive at sea with
success, as under William the Third and in the War of
American Independence, while in our long wars with
France she habitually used it in such a way that sometimes for years, though we had a substantial preponderance, we could not get command, and for years
were unable to carry out our war plan without serious
interruption from her fleet.

So far from the defensive being a negligible factor
at sea, or even the mere pestilent heresy it is generally
represented, it is of course inherent in all war, and, as
we have seen, the paramount questions of strategy both
at sea and on land turn on the relative possibilities of
offensive and defensive, and upon the relative pro-
portions in which each should enter into our plan of
war. At sea the most powerful and aggressively-
minded belligerent can no more avoid his alternating
periods of defence, which result from inevitable arrests
of offensive action, than they can be avoided on land.
The defensive, then, has to be considered ; but before we
are in a position to do so with profit, we have to proceed with our analysis of the phrase, "Command of the
Sea," and ascertain exactly what it is we mean by it
in war.

In the first place, "Command of the Sea" is not

identical in its strategical conditions with the conquest
of territory. You cannot argue from the one to the
other, as has been too commonly done. Such phrases
as the "Conquest of water territory" and "Making
the enemy's coast our frontier" had their use and
meaning in the mouths of those who framed them, but
they are really little but rhetorical expressions founded
on false analogy, and false analogy is not a secure
basis for a theory of war.

The analogy is false for two reasons, both of which
enter materially into the conduct of naval war. You
cannot conquer sea because it is not susceptible of
ownership, at least outside territorial waters. You
cannot, as lawyers say, "reduce it into possession,"
because you cannot exclude neutrals from it as you
can from territory you conquer. In the second place,
you cannot subsist your armed force upon it as you
can upon enemy's territory. Clearly, then, to make
deductions from an assumption that command of the
sea is analogous to conquest of territory is unscientific,
and certain to lead to error.

The only safe method is to inquire what it is we
can secure for ourselves, and what it is we can deny
the enemy by command of the sea. Now, if we
exclude fishery rights, which are irrelevant to the
present matter, the only right we or our enemy can
have on the sea is the right of passage; in other
words, the only positive value which the high seas
have for national life is as a means of communication.
For the active life of a nation such means may stand
for much or it may stand for little, but to every
maritime State it has some value. Consequently by
denying an enemy this means of passage we check
the movement of his national life at sea in the same

kind of way that we check it on land by occupying
his territory.   So far the analogy holds good, but no
further.

So much for the positive value which the sea has
in national life.   It has also a negative value.   For
not only is it a means of communication, but, unlike
the means of communication ashore, it is ' also a
barrier.   By winning command of the sea we remove
that barrier from our own path, thereby placing
ourselves in position to exert direct military pressure
upon the national life of our enemy ashore, while at
the same time we solidify it against him and prevent
his exerting direct military pressure upon ourselves.

Command of the sea, therefore, means nothing but
the control of maritime communications, whether for
commercial or military purposes.   The object of naval
warfare is the control of communications, and not, as
in land warfare, the conquest of territory.   The
difference is fundamental.   True, it is rightly said that
strategy ashore is mainly a question of communications,
but they are communications in another sense.   The
phrase refers to the communications of the army alone,
and not to the wider communications which are part
of the life of the nation.

But on land also there are communications of a
kind which are essential to national life—the internal
communications which connect the points of distribution.   Here again we touch an analogy between the
two kinds of war.   Land warfare, as the most devoted
adherents of the modern view admit, cannot attain its
end by military victories alone.   The destruction of
your enemy's forces will not avail for certain unless
you have in reserve sufficient force to complete the
occupation of his inland communications and principal

points of distribution. This power is the real fruit of victory, the power to strangle the whole national life. It is not until this is done that a high-spirited nation, whose whole heart is in the war, will consent to make peace and do your will. It is precisely in the same way that the command of the sea works towards peace, though of course in a far less coercive manner, against a continental State. By occupying her maritime communications and closing the points of distribution in which they terminate we destroy the national life afloat, and thereby check the vitality of that life ashore so far as the one is dependent on the other. Thus we see that so long as we retain the power and right to stop maritime communications, the analogy between command of the sea and the conquest of territory is in this aspect very close. And the analogy is of the utmost practical importance, for on it turns the most burning question of maritime war, which it will be well to deal with in this place.

It is obvious that if the object and end of naval warfare is the control of communications it must carry with it the right to forbid, if we can, the passage of both public and private property upon the sea. Now the only means we have of enforcing such control of commercial communications at sea is in the last resort the capture or destruction of sea-borne property. Such capture or destruction is the penalty which we impose upon our enemy for attempting to use the communications of which he does not hold the control. In the language of jurisprudence, it is the ultimate sanction of the interdict which we are seeking to enforce. The current term " Commerce destruction " is not in fact a logical expression of the strategical idea. To make the position clear we should say " Commerce prevention."

The methods of this "Commerce prevention" have no more connection with the old and barbarous idea of plunder and reprisal than orderly requisitions ashore have with the old idea of plunder and ravaging. No form of war indeed causes so little human suffering as the capture of property at sea. It is more akin to process of law, such as distress for rent, or execution of judgment, or arrest of a ship, than to a military operation. Once, it is true, it was not so. In the days of privateers it was accompanied too often, and particularly in the Mediterranean and the West Indies, with lamentable cruelty and lawlessness, and the existence of such abuses was the real reason for the general agreement to the Declaration of Paris by which privateering was abolished.

But it was not the only reason. The idea of privateering was a survival of a primitive and unscientific conception of war, which was governed mainly by a general notion of doing your enemy as much damage as possible and making reprisal for wrongs he had done you. To the same class of ideas belonged the practice of plunder and ravaging ashore. But neither of these methods of war was abolished for humanitarian reasons. They disappeared indeed as a general practice before the world had begun to talk of humanity. They were abolished because war became more scientific. The right to plunder and ravage was not denied. But plunder was found to demoralise your troops and unfit them for fighting, and ravaging proved to be a less powerful means of coercing your enemy than exploiting the occupied country by means of regular requisitions for the supply of your own army and the increase of its offensive range. In short, the reform arose from a desire to husband your enemy's resources for your own use instead of wantonly wasting them.

In a similar way privateering always had a debilitating effect upon our own regular force. It greatly increased the difficulty of manning the navy, and the occasional large profits had a demoralising influence on detached cruiser commanders. It tended to keep alive the mediæval corsair spirit at the expense of the modern military spirit which made for direct operations against the enemy's armed forces. It was inevitable that as the new movement of opinion gathered force it should carry with it a conviction that for operating against sea-borne trade sporadic attack could never be so efficient as an organised system of operations to secure a real strategical control of the enemy's maritime communications. A riper and sounder view of war revealed that what may be called tactical commercial blockade—that is, the blockade of ports—could be extended to and supplemented by a strategical blockade of the great trade routes. In moral principle there is no difference between the two. Admit the principle of tactical or close blockade, and as between belligerents you cannot condemn the principle of strategical or distant blockade. Except in their effect upon neutrals, there is no juridical difference between the two.

Why indeed should this humane yet drastic process of war be rejected at sea if the same thing is permitted on land? If on land you allow contributions and requisitions, if you permit the occupation of towns, ports, and inland communications, without which no conquest is complete and no effective war possible, why should you refuse similar procedure at sea where it causes far less individual suffering? If you refuse the right of controlling communications at sea, you must also refuse the right on land. If you admit the right of contributions on land, you must admit the right of capture at sea. Otherwise you will permit to military Powers the extreme rights of war and leave to the maritime Powers no effective rights at all. Their ultimate argument would be gone.

In so far as the idea of abolishing private capture at sea is humanitarian, and in so far as it rests on a belief that it would strengthen our position as a commercial maritime State, let it be honourably dealt with. But so far as its advocates have as yet expressed themselves, the proposal appears to be based on two fallacies. One is, that you can avoid attack by depriving yourself of the power of offence and resting on defence alone, and the other, the idea that war consists entirely of battles between armies or fleets. It ignores the fundamental fact that battles are only the means of enabling you to do that which really brings wars to an end—that is, to exert pressure on the citizens and their collective life. "After shattering the hostile main army," says Von der Goltz, "we still have the forcing of a peace as a separate and, in certain circumstances, a more difficult task . . . to make the enemy's country feel the burdens of war with such weight that the desire for peace will prevail. This is the point in which Napoleon failed. . . . It may be necessary to seize the harbours, commercial centres, important lines of traffic, fortifications and arsenals, in other words, all important property necessary to the existence of the people and army."

If, then, we are deprived of the right to use analogous means at sea, the object for which we fight battles almost ceases to exist. Defeat the enemy's

fleets as we may, he will be but little the worse.
We shall have opened the way for invasion, but any
of the great continental Powers can laugh at our
attempts to invade single-handed. If we cannot reap
the harvest of our success by deadening his national
activities at sea, the only legitimate means of pressure
within our strength will be denied us. Our fleet,
if it would proceed with such secondary operations
as are essential for forcing a peace, will be driven
to such barbarous expedients as the bombardment
of seaport towns and destructive raids upon the hostile
coasts.

If the means of pressure which follow successful
fighting were abolished both on land and sea there
would be this argument in favour of the change, that
it would mean perhaps for civilised States the entire
cessation of war ; for war would become so impotent,
that no one would care to engage in it.   It would
be an affair between regular armies and fleets, with
which the people had little concern. International
quarrels would tend to take the form of the mediæval
private disputes which were settled by champions
in trial by battle, an absurdity which led rapidly
to the domination of purely legal procedure. If international quarrels could go the same way, humanity
would have advanced a long stride. But the world
is scarcely ripe for such a revolution. Meanwhile to
abolish the right of interference with the flow of
private property at sea without abolishing the corresponding right ashore would only defeat the ends of
humanitarians. The great deterrent, the most powerful check on war, would be gone. It is commerce and
finance which now more than ever control or check
the foreign policy of nations. If commerce and finance

stand to lose by war, their influence for a peaceful solution will be great; and so long as the right of private capture at sea exists, they stand to lose in every maritime war immediately and inevitably whatever the ultimate result may be. Abolish the right, and this deterrent disappears; nay, they will even stand to win immediate gains owing to the sudden expansion of Government expenditure which the hostilities will entail, and the expansion of sea commerce which the needs of the armed forces will create. Any such losses as maritime warfare under existing conditions must immediately inflict will be remote if interference with property is confined to the land. They will never indeed be serious except in the case of complete defeat, and no one enters upon war expecting defeat. It is in the hope of victory and gain that aggressive wars are born. The fear of quick and certain loss is their surest preventive. Humanity, then, will surely beware how in a too hasty pursuit of peaceful ideals it lets drop the best weapon it has for scotching the evil which it has as yet no power to kill.

In what follows, therefore, it is intended to regard the right of private capture at sea as still subsisting. Without it, indeed, naval warfare is almost inconceivable, and in any case no one has any experience of such a truncated method of war on which profitable study can be founded.

The primary method, then, in which we use victory or preponderance at sea and bring it to bear on the enemy's population to secure peace, is by the capture or destruction of the enemy's property, whether public or private. But in comparing the process with the analogous occupation of territory and the levying of contributions and requisitions we have to observe a marked difference. Both processes are what may be called economic pressure. But ashore the economic pressure can only be exerted as the consequence of victory or acquired domination by military success. At sea the process begins at once. Indeed, more often than not, the first act of hostility in maritime wars has been the capture of private property at sea. In a sense this is also true ashore. The first step of an invader after crossing the frontier will be to control to a less or greater extent such private property as he is able to use for his purposes. But such interference with private property is essentially a military act, and does not belong to the secondary phase of economic pressure. At sea it does, and the reason why this should be so lies in certain fundamental differences between land and sea warfare which are implicit in the communication theory of naval war.

To elucidate the point, it must be repeated that maritime communications, which are the root of the idea of command of the sea, are not analogous to military communications in the ordinary use of the term. Military communications refer solely to the army's lines of supply and retreat. Maritime communications have a wider meaning. Though in effect embracing the lines of fleet supply, they correspond in strategical values not to military lines of supply, but to those internal lines of communication by which the flow of national life is maintained ashore. Consequently maritime communications are on a wholly different footing from land communications. At sea the communications are, for the most part, common to both belligerents, whereas ashore each possesses his own in his own territory. The strategical effect is of far-reaching importance, for it means that at sea strategical offence and defence tend to merge in a way that is unknown ashore. Since maritime communications are common, we as a rule cannot attack those of the enemy without defending our own. In military operations the converse is the rule. Normally, an attack on our enemy's communications tends to expose our own.

The theory of common communications will become clear by taking an example. In our wars with France our communications with the Mediterranean, India, and America ran down from the Channel mouth past Finisterre and St. Vincent; and those of France, at least from her Atlantic ports, were identical for almost their entire distance. In our wars with the Dutch the identity was even closer. Even in the case of Spain, her great trade routes followed the same lines as our own for the greater part of their extent. Consequently the opening moves which we generally made to defend our trade by the occupation of those lines placed us in a position to attack our enemy's trade. The same situation arose even when our opening dispositions were designed as defence against home invasion or against attacks upon our colonies, for the positions our fleet had to take up to those ends always lay on or about the terminal and focal points of trade routes. Whether our immediate object were to bring the enemy's main fleets to action or to exercise economic pressure, it made but little difference. If the enemy were equally anxious to engage, it was at one of the terminal or focal areas we were almost certain to get contact. If he wished to avoid a decision, the best way to force him to action was to occupy his trade routes at the same vital points.

Thus it comes about that, whereas on land the process of economic pressure, at least in the modern conception of war, should only begin after decisive victory, at sea it starts automatically from the first. Indeed such pressure may be the only means of forcing the decision we seek, as will appear more clearly when we come to deal with the other fundamental difference between land and sea warfare.

Meanwhile we may note that at sea the use of economic pressure from the commencement is justified for two reasons. The first is, as we have seen, that it is an economy of means to use our defensive positions for attack when attack does not vitiate those positions, and it will not vitiate them if fleet cruisers operate with restraint. The second is, that interference with the enemy's trade has two aspects. It is not only a means of exerting the secondary economic pressure, it is also a primary means towards overthrowing the enemy's power of resistance. Wars are not decided exclusively by military and naval force. Finance is scarcely less important. When other things are equal, it is the longer purse that wins. It has even many times redressed an unfavourable balance of armed force and given victory to the physically weaker Power. Anything, therefore, which we are able to achieve towards crippling our enemy's finance is a direct step to his overthrow, and the most effective means we can employ to this end against a maritime State is to deny him the resources of sea-borne trade.

It will be seen, therefore, that in naval warfare, however closely we may concentrate our efforts on the destruction of our enemy's armed forces as the direct means to his overthrow, it would be folly to stay our hands when opportunities occur, as they will automatically, for undermining his financial position on which the continued vigour of those armed forces so largely depends. Thus the occupation of our enemy's sea communications and the confiscatory operations it connotes are in a sense primary operations, and not, as on land, secondary.

Such, then, are the abstract conclusions at which we arrive in our attempt to analyse the idea of command of the sea and to give it precision as the control of common communications. Their concrete value will appear when we come to deal with the various forms which naval operations may take, such as, "seeking out the enemy's fleet," blockade, attack and defence of trade, and the safeguarding of combined expeditions. For the present it remains to deal with the various kinds of sea command which flow from the communication idea.

If the object of the command of the sea is to control communications, it is obvious it may exist in various degrees. We may be able to control the whole of the common communications as the result either of great initial preponderance or of decisive victory. If we are not sufficiently strong to do this, we may still be able to control some of the communications; that is, our control may be general or local. Obvious as the point is, it needs emphasising, because of a maxim that has become current that "the sea is all one." Like other maxims of the kind, it conveys a truth with a trail of error in its wake. The truth it contains seems to be simply this, that as a rule local control can only avail us temporarily, for so long as the enemy has a sufficient fleet anywhere, it is theoretically in his power to overthrow our control of any special sea area.

It amounts indeed to little more than a rhetorical expression, used to emphasise the high mobility of fleets as contrasted with that of armies and the absence of physical obstacles to restrict that mobility. That this vital feature of naval warfare should be consecrated in a maxim is well, but when it is caricatured into a doctrine, as it sometimes is, that you cannot move a battalion oversea till you have entirely overthrown your enemy's fleet, it deserves gibbeting. It would be as wise to hold that in war you must never risk anything.

It would seem to have been the evil influence of this travestied maxim which had much to do with the cramped and timorous strategy of the Americans in their late war with Spain. They had ample naval force to secure such a local and temporary command of the Gulf of Mexico as to have justified them at once in throwing all the troops they had ready into Cuba to support the insurgents, in accordance with their war plan. They had also sufficient strength to ensure that the communications with the expeditionary force could not be interrupted permanently. And yet, because the Spaniards had an undefeated fleet at sea somewhere, they hesitated, and were nearly lost. The Japanese had no such illusions. Without having struck a naval blow of any kind, and with a hostile fleet actually within the theatre of operations, they started their essential military movement oversea, content that though they might not be able to secure the control of the line of passage, they were in a position to deny effective control to the enemy. Our own history is full of such operations. There are cases in plenty where the results promised by a successful military blow oversea, before permanent command had been obtained, were great enough to justify a risk which, like the Japanese, we knew how to minimise by judicious use of our favourable geographical position, and of a certain system of protection, which must be dealt with later.

For the purpose, then, of framing a plan of war or campaign, it must be taken that command may exist in various states or degrees, each of which has its special possibilities and limitations. It may be general or local, and it may be permanent or temporary. General command may be permanent or temporary, but mere local command, except in very favourable geographical conditions, should scarcely ever be regarded as more than temporary, since normally it is always liable to interruption from other theatres so long as the enemy possesses an effective naval force.

Finally, it has to be noted that even permanent general command can never in practice be absolute. No degree of naval superiority can ensure our communications against sporadic attack from detached cruisers, or even raiding squadrons if they be boldly led and are prepared to risk destruction. Even after Hawke's decisive victory at Quiberon had completed the overthrow of the enemy's sea forces, a British transport was captured between Cork and Portsmouth, and an Indiaman in sight of the Lizard, while Wellington's complaints in the Peninsula of the insecurity of his communications are well known.[1] By general

---

[1] In justice to Wellington it should be said that his complaints were due to false reports which exaggerated a couple of insignificant captures into a serious interruption.

and permanent control we do not mean that the enemy can do nothing, but that he cannot interfere with our maritime trade and oversea operations so seriously as to affect the issue of the war, and that he cannot carry on his own trade and operations except at such risk and hazard as to remove them from the field of practical strategy. In other words, it means that the enemy can no longer attack our lines of passage and communication effectively, and that he cannot use or defend his own.

To complete our equipment for appreciating any situation for which operations have to be designed, it is necessary to remember that when the command is in dispute the general conditions may give a stable or an unstable equilibrium. It may be that the power of neither side preponderates to any appreciable extent. It may also be that the preponderance is with ourselves, or it may be that it lies with the enemy. Such preponderance of course will not depend entirely on actual relative strength, either physical or moral, but will be influenced by the inter-relation of naval positions and the comparative convenience of their situation in regard to the object of the war or campaign. By naval positions we mean, firstly, naval bases and, secondly, the terminals of the greater lines of communication or trade-routes and the focal areas where they tend to converge, as at Finisterre, Gibraltar, Suez, the Cape, Singapore, and many others.

Upon the degree and distribution of this preponderance will depend in a general way the extent to which our plans will be governed by the idea of defence or offence. Generally speaking, it will be to the advantage of the preponderating side to seek a decision as quickly as possible in order to terminate the state of dispute. Conversely, the weaker side will as a rule seek to avoid or postpone a decision in hope of being able by minor operations, the chances of war, or the development of fresh strength, to turn the balance in its favour. Such was the line which France adopted frequently in her wars with us, sometimes legitimately, but sometimes to such an excess as seriously to demoralise her fleet. Her experience has led to a hasty deduction that the defensive at sea for even a weaker Power is an unmixed evil. Such a conclusion is foreign to the fundamental principles of war. It is idle to exclude the use of an expectant attitude because in itself it cannot lead to final success, and because if used to excess it ends in demoralisation and the loss of will to attack. The misconception appears to have arisen from insistence on the drawbacks of defence by writers seeking to persuade their country to prepare in time of peace sufficient naval strength to justify offence from the outset.

Having now determined the fundamental principles which underlie the idea of Command of the Sea, we are in a position to consider the manner in which fleets are constituted in order to fit them for their task.

CHAPTER II

In all eras of naval warfare fighting ships have exhibited a tendency to differentiate into groups in accordance with the primary function each class was designed to serve. These groupings or classifications are what is meant by the constitution of a fleet. A threefold differentiation into battleships, cruisers, and flotilla has so long dominated naval thought that we have come to regard it as normal, and even essential. It may be so, but such a classification has been by no means constant. Other ideas of fleet constitution have not only existed, but have stood the test of war for long periods, and it is unscientific and unsafe to ignore such facts if we wish to arrive at sound doctrine.

The truth is, that the classes of ships which constitute a fleet are, or ought to be, the expression in material of the strategical and tactical ideas that prevail at any given time, and consequently they have varied not only with the ideas, but also with the material in vogue. It may also be said more broadly that they have varied with the theory of war, by which more or less consciously naval thought was dominated. It is true that few ages have formulated a theory of war, or even been clearly aware of its influence; but nevertheless such theories have always existed, and even in their most nebulous and intangible shapes seem to have exerted an ascertainable influence on the constitution of fleets.

Going back to the dawn of modern times, we note that at the opening of the sixteenth century, when galley warfare reached its culmination, the constitution was threefold, bearing a superficial analogy to that which we have come to regard as normal. There were the galeasses and heavy galleys corresponding to our battle-ships, light galleys corresponding to our cruisers, while the flotilla was represented by the small "frigates," "brigantines," and similar craft, which had no slave gang for propulsion, but were rowed by the fighting crew. Such armed sailing ships as then existed were regarded as auxiliaries, and formed a category apart, as fireships and bomb-vessels did in the sailing period, and as mine-layers do now. But the parallel must not be overstrained. The distinction of function between the two classes of galleys was not so strongly marked as that between the lighter craft and the galleys; that is to say, the scientific differentiation between battleships and cruisers had not yet been so firmly developed as it was destined to become in later times, and the smaller galleys habitually took their place in the fighting line.

With the rise of the sailing vessel as the typical ship-of-war an entirely new constitution made its appearance. The dominating classification became two-fold. It was a classification into vessels of subservient movement using sails, and vessels of free movement using oars. It was on these lines that our true Royal Navy was first organised by Henry the Eighth, an expert who, in the science of war, was one of the most advanced masters in Europe. In this constitution there appears even less conception than in that of the galley period of a radical distinction between battleships and cruisers. As Henry's fleet was originally designed, practically the whole of the battleships were sailing vessels, though it is true that when the French brought up galleys from the Mediterranean, he gave some of the smartest of them oars. The constitution was in fact one of battleships and flotilla. Of cruisers there were none as we understand them. Fleet scouting was done by the "Row-barges" and newly introduced "Pinnaces" of the flotilla, while as for commerce protection, merchant vessels had usually to look after themselves, the larger ones being regularly armed for their own defence.

The influence of this twofold constitution continued long after the conditions of its origin had passed away. In ever-lessening degree indeed it may be said to have lasted for two hundred years. During the Dutch wars of the seventeenth century, which finally established the dominant status of the sailing warship, practically all true sailing vessels—that is, vessels that had no auxiliary oar propulsion—took station in the line. The "Frigates" of that time differed not at all from the "Great Ship" in their functions, but only in their design. By the beginning of the eighteenth century, however, the old tendency to a threefold organisation began to reassert itself, but it was not till the middle of the century that the process of development can be regarded as complete.

Down to the end of the War of the Austrian Succession—a period which is usually deemed to be one of conspicuous depression in the naval art—the classification of our larger sailing vessels was purely arbitrary. The "Rates" (which had been introduced during the Dutch wars) bore no relation to any philosophical

conception of the complex duties of a fleet. In the
first rate were 100-gun ships; in the second, 90-gun
ships—all three-deckers. So far the system of rating
was sound enough, but when we come to the third
rate we find it includes 80-gun ships, which were also
of three decks, while the bulk of the rest were 70-gun
two-deckers. The fourth rate was also composed of
two-decked ships—weak battle-units of 60 and 50
guns—and this was far the largest class. All these
four rates were classed as ships-of-the-line. Below
them came the fifth rates, which, though they were
used as cruisers, had no distinct class name. They
differed indeed only in degree from the ship-of-the-line,
being all cramped two-deckers of 44 and 40 guns, and
they must be regarded, in so far as they expressed any
logical idea of naval warfare, as the forerunners of
the " Intermediate " class, represented in the succeeding epochs by 50-gun ships, and in our own time by
armoured cruisers. The only true cruiser is found in
the sixth rate, which comprised small and weakly
armed 20-gun ships, and between them and the
" Forties " there was nothing. Below them, but
again without any clear differentiation, came the unrated sloops representing the flotilla.

In such a system of rating there is no logical distinction either between large and small battleships or
between battleships and cruisers, or between cruisers
and flotilla. The only marked break in the gradual
descent is that between the 40-gun two-deckers and
the 20-gun cruisers. As these latter vessels as well
as the sloops used sweeps for auxiliary propulsion,
we are forced to conclude that the only basis of the
classification was that adopted by Henry the Eighth,
which, sound as it was in his time, had long ceased

to have any real relation to the actuality of naval war.

It was not till Anson's memorable administration that a scientific system of rating was re-established and the fleet at last assumed the logical constitution which it retained up to our own time. In the first two rates appear the fleet flagship class, three-deckers of 100 and 90 guns respectively. All smaller three-deckers are eliminated. In the next two rates we have the rank and file of the battle-line, two-deckers of increased size—namely, seventy-fours in the third rate, and sixty-fours in the fourth. Here, however, is a slight break in the perfection of the system, for the fourth rate also included 50-gun ships of two decks, which, during the progress of the Seven Years' War, ceased to be regarded as ships-of-the-line. War experience was eliminating small battleships, and therewith it called for a type intermediate between battleships and cruisers, with whose functions we shall have to deal directly. In practice these units soon formed a rate by themselves, into which, by the same tendency, 60-gun ships were destined to sink half a century later.

But most pregnant of all Anson's reforms was the introduction of the true cruiser, no longer a small battleship, but a vessel specialised for its logical functions, and distinct in design both from the battle rates and the flotilla. Both 40-gun and 20-gun types were abolished, and in their place appear two cruiser rates, the fifth consisting of 32-gun true frigates, and the sixth of 28-gun frigates, both completely divorced from any battle function. Finally, after a very distinct gap, came the unrated sloops and smaller craft, which formed the flotilla for coastwise and inshore work, despatch service, and kindred duties.

The reforms of the great First Lord amounted in fact to a clearly apprehended threefold constitution, in which the various groups were frankly specialised in accordance with the functions each was expected to perform. Specialisation, it will be observed, is the note of the process of development. We have no longer an endeavour to adapt the fleet to its multifarious duties by multiplying a comparatively weak nature of fighting-ship, which could act in the line and yet be had in sufficient numbers to protect commerce, but which was not well fitted for either service. Instead we note a definite recognition of the principle that battleships should be as powerful as possible, and that in order to permit of their due development they must be relieved of their cruising functions by a class of vessel specially adapted for the purpose. The question we have to consider is, was this specialisation, which has asserted itself down to our own times, in the true line of development? Was it, in fact, a right expression of the needs which are indicated by the theory of naval war?

By the theory of naval war it must be reiterated we mean nothing but an enunciation of the fundamental principles which underlie all naval war. Those principles, if we have determined them correctly, should be found giving shape not only to strategy and tactics, but also to material, whatever method and means of naval warfare may be in use at any given time. Conversely, if we find strategy, tactics, or organisation exhibiting a tendency to reproduce the same forms under widely differing conditions of method and material, we should be able to show that those forms bear a constant and definite relation to the principles which our theory endeavours to express.

In the case of Anson's threefold organisation, the

relation is not far to seek, though it has become obscured by two maxims. The one is, that "the command of the sea depends upon battleships," and the other, that "cruisers are the eyes of the fleet." It is the inherent evil of maxims that they tend to get stretched beyond their original meaning. Both of these express a truth, but neither expresses the whole truth. On no theory of naval warfare can we expect to command the sea with battleships, nor, on the communication theory, can we regard the primary function of cruisers as being to scout for a battle-fleet. It is perfectly true that the control depends ultimately on the battle-fleet if control is disputed by a hostile battle-fleet, as it usually is. It is also true that, so far as is necessary to enable the battle-fleet to secure the control, we have to furnish it with eyes from our cruiser force. But it does not follow that this is the primary function of cruisers. The truth is, we have to withdraw them from their primary function in order to do work for the battle-fleet which it cannot do for itself.

Well established as is the "Eyes of the fleet" maxim, it would be very difficult to show that scouting was ever regarded as the primary function of cruisers by the highest authorities. In Nelson's practice at least their paramount function was to exercise the control which he was securing with his battle-squadron. Nothing is more familiar in naval history than his incessant cry from the Mediterranean for more cruisers, but the significance of that cry has become obscured. It was not that his cruisers were not numerous in proportion to his battleships—they were usually nearly double in number—but it was rather that he was so deeply convinced of their true function, that he used them to exercise control to an extent which sometimes reduced his fleet cruisers below the limit of bare necessity. The result on a memorable occasion was the escape of the enemy's battle-fleet, but the further result is equally important. It was that the escape of that fleet did not deprive him of the control which he was charged to maintain. His judgment may have been at fault, but the strategical distribution of his force was consistent throughout the whole period of his Mediterranean command. Judged by his record, no man ever grasped more clearly than Nelson that the object of naval warfare was to control communications, and if he found that he had not a sufficient number of cruisers to exercise that control and to furnish eyes for his battle-fleet as well, it was the battle-fleet that was made to suffer, and surely this is at least the logical view. Had the French been ready to risk settling the question of the control in a fleet action, it would have been different. He would then have been right to sacrifice the exercise of control for the time in order to make sure that the action should take place and end decisively in his favour. But he knew they were not ready to take such a risk, and he refused to permit a purely defensive attitude on the part of the enemy to delude him from the special function with which he had been charged.

If the object of naval warfare is to control communications, then the fundamental requirement is the means of exercising that control. Logically, therefore, if the enemy holds back from battle decision, we must relegate the battle-fleet to a secondary position, for cruisers are the means of exercising control; the battle-fleet is but the means of preventing their being interfered with in their work. Put it to the test of actual practice. In no case can we exercise control by battleships alone. Their specialisation has rendered them unfit for the work, and has made them too costly ever to be numerous enough. Even, therefore, if our enemy had no battle-fleet we could not make control effective with battleships alone. We should still require cruisers specialised for the work and in sufficient numbers to cover the necessary ground. But the converse is not true. We could exercise control with cruisers alone if the enemy had no battle-fleet to interfere with them.

If, then, we seek a formula that will express the practical results of our theory, it would take some such shape as this. On cruisers depends our exercise of control; on the battle-fleet depends the security of control. That is the logical sequence of ideas, and it shows us that the current maxim is really the conclusion of a logical argument in which the initial steps must not be ignored. The maxim that the command of the sea depends on the battle-fleet is then perfectly sound so long as it is taken to include all the other facts on which it hangs. The true function of the battle-fleet is to protect cruisers and flotilla at their special work. The best means of doing this is of course to destroy the enemy's power of interference. The doctrine of destroying the enemy's armed forces as the paramount object here reasserts itself, and reasserts itself so strongly as to permit for most practical purposes the rough generalisation that the command depends upon the battle-fleet.

Of what practical use then, it may be asked, is all this hair-splitting? Why not leave untainted the conviction that our first and foremost business is to crush the enemy's battle-fleet, and that to this end our whole

effort should be concentrated? The answer is to point
to Nelson's dilemma. It was a dilemma which, in the
golden age of naval warfare, every admiral at sea had
had to solve for himself, and it was always one of the
most difficult details of every naval war plan. If we
seek to ensure the effective action of the battle-fleet
by giving it a large proportion of cruisers, by so much
do we weaken the actual and continuous exercise of
control. If we seek to make that control effective by
devoting to the service a large proportion of cruisers,
by so much do we prejudice our chance of getting
contact with and defeating the enemy's battle-fleet,
which is the only means of perfecting control.

The correct solution of the dilemma will of course
depend upon the conditions of each case—mainly upon
the relative strength and activity of the hostile battle-
fleet and our enemy's probable intentions. But no
matter how completely we have tabulated all the
relevant facts, we can never hope to come to a sound
conclusion upon them without a just appreciation of
all the elements which go to give command, and without
the power of gauging their relative importance. This,
and this alone, will ultimately settle the vital question
of what proportion of our cruiser force it is right to
devote to the battle-fleet.

If the doctrine of cruiser control be correct, then
every cruiser attached to the battle-fleet is one withdrawn from its true function. Such withdrawals are
inevitable. A squadron of battleships is an imperfect
organism unable to do its work without cruiser
assistance, and since the performance of its work is
essential to cruiser freedom, some cruisers must be
sacrificed. But in what proportion? If we confine
ourselves to the view that command depends on the

battle-fleet, then we shall attach to it such a number as its commander may deem necessary to make contact with the enemy absolutely certain and to surround himself with an impenetrable screen. If we knew the enemy was as anxious for a decision as ourselves, such a course might be justified. But the normal condition is that if we desire a decision it is because we have definite hopes of success, and consequently the enemy will probably seek to avoid one on our terms. In practice this means that if we have perfected our arrangements for the destruction of his main fleet he will refuse to expose it till he sees a more favourable opportunity. And what will be the result? He remains on the defensive, and theoretically all the ensuing period of inaction tends to fall into his scale. Without stirring from port his fleet is doing its work. The more closely he induces us to concentrate our cruiser force in face of his battle-fleet, the more he frees the sea for the circulation of his own trade, and the more he exposes ours to cruiser raids.

Experience, then, and theory alike dictate that as a general principle cruisers should be regarded as primarily concerned with the active occupation of communications, and that withdrawals for fleet purposes should be reduced to the furthest margin of reasonable risk. What that margin should be can only be decided on the circumstances of each case as it arises, and by the personal characteristics of the officers who are responsible. Nelson's practice was to reduce fleet cruisers lower than perhaps any other commander. So small indeed was the margin of efficiency he left, that in the campaign already cited, when his judgment was ripest, one stroke of ill-luck—a chance betrayal of his position by a neutral—availed to deprive him of the decision he sought, and to let the enemy's fleet escape.

We arrive, then, at this general conclusion. The object of naval warfare is to control maritime communications. In order to exercise that control effectively we must have a numerous class of vessels specially adapted for pursuit. But their power of exercising control is in proportion to our degree of command, that is, to our power of preventing their operations being interfered with by the enemy. Their own power of resistance is in inverse proportion to their power of exercising control; that is to say, the more numerous and better adapted they are for preying on commerce and transports, the weaker will be their individual fighting power. We cannot give them as a whole the power of resisting disturbance without at the same time reducing their power of exercising control. The accepted solution of the difficulty during the great period of Anson's school was to provide them with a covering force of battle units specially adapted for fighting. But here arises a correlative difficulty. In so far as we give our battle units fighting power we deny them scouting power, and scouting is essential to their effective operation. The battle-fleet must have eyes. Now, vessels adapted for control of communications are also well adapted for "eyes." It becomes the practice, therefore, to withdraw from control operations a sufficient number of units to enable the battle-fleet to cover effectively the operations of those that remain.

Such were the broad principles on which the inevitable dilemma always had to be solved, and on which Anson's organisation was based. They flow naturally from the communication theory of maritime war, and it was this theory which then dominated naval thought, as is apparent from the technical use of such phrases as "lines of passage and communication." The war plans of the great strategists from Anson and Barham can always be resolved into these simple elements, and where we find the Admiralty grip of them loosened, we have the confusion and quite unnecessary failures of the War of American Independence. In that mismanaged contest the cardinal mistake was that we suffered the enemy's battle-fleets to get upon and occupy the vital lines of "passage and communication" without first bringing them to action, an error partly due to the unreadiness of a weak administration, and partly to an insufficient allocation of cruisers to secure contact at the right places.

So far, then, the principles on which our naval supremacy was built up are clear. For the enemies with whom we had to deal Anson's system was admirably conceived. Both Spain and France held the communication theory so strongly, that they were content to count as success the power of continually disturbing our control without any real attempt to secure it for themselves. To defeat such a policy Anson's constitution and the strategy it connoted were thoroughly well adapted and easy to work. But it by no means follows that his doctrine is the last word. Even in his own time complications had begun to develop which tended to confuse the precision of his system. By the culminating year of Trafalgar there were indications that it was getting worn out, while the new methods and material used by the Americans in 1812 made a serious rent in it. The disturbances then inaugurated have continued to develop, and it is necessary to consider how seriously they have confused the problem of fleet constitution.

Firstly, there is the general recognition, always patent to ourselves, that by far the most drastic, economical, and effective way of securing control is to destroy the enemy's means of interfering with it. In our own service this "overthrow" idea always tended to assert itself so strongly, that occasionally the means became for a time more important than the end; that is to say, circumstances were such that on occasions it was considered advisable to sacrifice the exercise of control for a time in order quickly and permanently to deprive the enemy of all means of interference. When there was reasonable hope of the enemy risking a decision this consideration tended to override all others; but when, as in Nelson's case in the Mediterranean, the hope was small, the exercise of control tended to take the paramount place.

The second complexity arose from the fact that however strong might be our battleship cover, it is impossible for it absolutely to secure cruiser control from disturbance by sporadic attack. Isolated heavy ships, taking advantage of the chances of the sea, could elude even the strictest blockade, and one such ship, if she succeeded in getting upon a line of communication, might paralyse the operations of a number of weaker units. They must either run or concentrate, and in either case the control was broken. If it were a squadron of heavy ships that caused the disturbance, the practice was to detach against it a division of the covering battle-fleet. But it was obviously highly inconvenient and contrary to the whole idea on which the constitution of the fleet was based to allow every slight danger to cruiser control to loosen the cohesion of the main fleet.

It was necessary, then, to give cruiser lines some power of resistance. This necessity once admitted, there seemed no point at which you could stop increasing the fighting power of your cruisers, and sooner or later, unless some means of checking the process were found, the distinction between cruisers and battleships would practically disappear. Such a means was found in what may be called the "Intermediate" ship. Frigates did indeed continue to increase in size and fighting power throughout the remainder of the sailing era, but it was not only in this manner that the power of resistance was gained. The evil results of the movement were checked by the introduction of a supporting ship, midway between frigates and true ships-of-the-line. Sometimes classed as a battleship, and taking her place in the line, the 50-gun ship came to be essentially a type for stiffening cruiser squadrons. They most commonly appear as the flagships of cruiser commodores, or stationed in terminal waters or at focal points where sporadic raids were likely to fall and be most destructive. The strategical effect of the presence of such a vessel in a cruiser line was to give the whole line in some degree the strength of the intermediate ship; for any hostile cruiser endeavouring to disturb the line was liable to have to deal with the supporting ship, while if a frigate and a 50-gun ship got together they were a match even for a small ship-of-the-line.

In sailing days, of course, this power of the supporting ship was weak owing to the imperfection of the means of distant communication between ships at sea and the non-existence of such means beyond

extreme range of vision. But as wireless telegraphy
develops it is not unreasonable to expect that the
strategic value of the supporting or intermediate ship
will be found greater than it ever was in sailing days,
and that for dealing with sporadic disturbance the
tendency will be for a cruiser line to approximate more
and more in power of resistance to that of its strongest
unit.

For fleet service a cruiser's power of resistance was
hardly less valuable; for though we speak of fleet
cruisers as the eyes of the fleet, their purpose is almost
equally to blindfold the enemy. Their duty is not
only to disclose the movements of the enemy, but also
to act as a screen to conceal our own. The point was
specially well marked in the blockades, where the old
50-gun ships are almost always found with the inshore
cruiser squadron, preventing that squadron being forced
by inquisitive frigates. Important as this power of
resistance in the screen was in the old days, it is
tenfold more important now, and the consequent difficulty of keeping cruisers distinct from battleships is
greater than ever. The reason for this is best considered under the third and most serious cause of
complexity.

The third cause is the acquisition by the flotilla of
battle power. It is a feature of naval warfare that is
entirely new.[1] For all practical purposes it was unknown until the full development of the mobile
torpedo. It is true that the fireship as originally
conceived was regarded as having something of the
same power. During the Dutch wars—the heyday of

[1] But not without analogous precedent. In the later Middle Ages
small craft were assigned the function in battle of trying to wedge up
the rudders of great ships or bore holes between wind and water. See
Fighting Instructions (Navy Record Society), p. 12.

its vogue—its assigned power was on some occasions actually realised, as in the burning of Lord Sandwich's flagship at the battle of Solebay, and the destruction of the Spanish-Dutch fleet at Palermo by Duquesne. But as the "nimbleness" of great-ships increased with the ripening of seamanship and naval architecture, the fire-ship as a battle weapon became almost negligible, while a fleet at anchor was found to be thoroughly defensible by its own picket - boats. Towards the middle of the eighteenth century indeed the occasions on which the fireship could be used for its special purpose were regarded as highly exceptional, and though the type was retained till the end of the century, its normal functions differed not at all from those of the rest of the flotilla of which it then formed part.

Those functions, as we have seen, expressed the cruising idea in its purest sense. It was numbers and mobility that determined flotilla types rather than arma-ment or capacity for sea-endurance. Their primary purpose was to control communications in home and colonial waters against weakly armed privateers. The type which these duties determined fitted them ade-quately for the secondary purpose of inshore and despatch work with a fleet. It was, moreover, on the ubiquity which their numbers gave them, and on their power of dealing with unarmed or lightly armed vessels, that we relied for our first line of defence against invasion. These latter duties were of course excep-tional, and the Navy List did not carry as a rule suffi-cient numbers for the purpose. But a special value of the class was that it was capable of rapid and almost indefinite expansion from the mercantile marine. Anything that could carry a gun had its use, and during the period of the Napoleonic threat the defence flotilla rose all told to considerably over a thousand units.

Formidable and effective as was a flotilla of this type for the ends it was designed to serve, it obviously in no way affected the security of a battle-fleet. But so soon as the flotilla acquired battle power the whole situation was changed, and the old principles of cruiser design and distribution were torn to shreds. The battle-fleet became a more imperfect organism than ever. Formerly it was only its offensive power that required supplementing. The new condition meant that unaided it could no longer ensure its own defence. It now required screening, not only from observation, but also from flotilla attack. The theoretical weakness of an arrested offensive received a practical and concrete illustration to a degree that war had scarcely ever known. Our most dearly cherished strategical traditions were shaken to the bottom. The "proper place" for our battle-fleet had always been "on the enemy's coasts," and now that was precisely where the enemy would be best pleased to see it. What was to be done? So splendid a tradition could not lightly be laid aside, but the attempt to preserve it involved us still deeper in heresy. The vital, most difficult, and most absorbing problem has become not how to increase the power of a battle-fleet for attack, which is a comparatively simple matter, but how to defend it. As the offensive power of the flotilla developed, the problem pressed with an almost bewildering intensity. With every increase in the speed and sea-keeping power of torpedo craft, the problem of the screen grew more exacting. To keep the hostile flotilla out of night range the screen must be flung out wider and wider, and this meant more and more cruisers withdrawn

from their primary function.   And not only this.   The
screen must not only be far flung, but it must be
made as far as possible impenetrable.   In other words,
its own power of resistance must be increased all along
the line.   Whole squadrons of armoured cruisers had
to be attached to battle-fleets to support the weaker
members of the screen.   The crying need for this type
of ship set up a rapid movement for increasing their
fighting power, and with it fell with equal rapidity the
economic possibility of giving the cruiser class its
essential attribute of numbers.

As an inevitable result we find ourselves involved
in an effort to restore to the flotilla some of its old
cruiser capacity, by endowing it with gun armament,
higher sea-keeping power, and facilities for distant
communication, all at the cost of specialisation and
of greater economic strain.   Still judged by past experience, some means of increasing numbers in the
cruising types is essential, nor is it clear how it is
possible to secure that essential in the ranks of the
true cruiser.   No point has been found at which it
was possible to stop the tendency of this class of vessel
to increase in size and cost, or to recall it to the
strategical position it used to occupy.   So insecure is
the battle-squadron, so imperfect as a self-contained
weapon has it become, that its need has overridden the
old order of things, and the primary function of the
cruising ship inclines to be no longer the exercise of
control under cover of the battle-fleet.   The battle-
fleet now demands protection by the cruising ship, and
what the battle-fleet needs is held to be the first
necessity.

Judged by the old naval practice, it is an anomalous
position to have reached.   But the whole naval art has

suffered a revolution beyond all previous experience, and it is possible the old practice is no longer a safe guide. Driven by the same necessities, every naval Power is following the same course. It may be right, it may be wrong; no one at least but the ignorant or hasty will venture to pass categorical judgment. The best we can do is to endeavour to realise the situation to which, in spite of all misgivings, we have been forced, and to determine its relations to the developments of the past.

It is undoubtedly a difficult task. As we have seen, there have prevailed in the constitution of fleets at various times several methods of expressing the necessities of naval war. The present system differs from them all. On the one hand, we have the fact that the latest developments of cruiser power have finally obliterated all logical distinction between cruisers and battleships, and we thus find ourselves hand in hand with the fleet constitution of the old Dutch wars. On the other, however, we have armoured cruisers organised in squadrons and attached to battle-fleets not only for strategical purposes, but also with as yet undeveloped tactical functions in battle. Here we come close to the latest development of the sailing era, when "Advanced" or "Light" squadrons began to appear in the organisation of battle-fleets.

The system arose towards the end of the eighteenth century in the Mediterranean, where the conditions of control called for so wide a dispersal of cruisers and so great a number of them, that it was almost imperative for a battle-squadron in that sea to do much of its own scouting. It was certainly for this purpose that the fastest and lightest ships-of-the-line were formed into a separate unit, and the first designation

it received was that of "Observation Squadron." It
remained for Nelson to endeavour to endow it with a
tactical function, but his idea was never realised either
by himself or any of his successors.

Side by side with this new element in the organisation of a battle-fleet, which perhaps is best designated
as a "Light Division," we have another significant
fact. Not only was it not always composed entirely
of ships-of-the-line, especially in the French service,
but in 1805, the year of the full development, we have
Sir Richard Strachan using the heavy frigates attached
to his battle-squadron as a "Light Division," and
giving them a definite tactical function. The collapse
of the French Navy put a stop to further developments
of either idea. Whither they would have led we
cannot tell. But it is impossible to shut our eyes
to the indication of a growing tendency towards the
system that exists at present. It is difficult at least
to ignore the fact that both Nelson and Strachan in
that culminating year found the actuality of war calling
for something for which there was then no provision in
the constitution of the fleet, but which it does contain
to-day. What Nelson felt for was a battleship of
cruiser speed. What Strachan desired was a cruiser
fit to take a tactical part in a fleet action. We have
them both, but with what result? Anson's specialisation of types has almost disappeared, and our present
fleet constitution is scarcely to be distinguished from
that of the seventeenth century. We retain the threefold nomenclature, but the system itself has really gone.
Battleships grade into armoured cruisers, armoured
cruisers into protected cruisers. We can scarcely detect any real distinction except a twofold one between
vessels whose primary armament is the gun and

vessels whose primary armament is the torpedo. But even here the existence of a type of cruiser designed to act with flotillas blurs the outline, while, as we have seen, the larger units of the flotilla are grading up to cruiser level.

We are thus face to face with a situation which has its closest counterpart in the structureless fleets of the seventeenth century. That naval thought should have so nearly retraced its steps in the course of two centuries is curious enough, but it is still more striking when we consider how widely the underlying causes differ in each case. The pressure which has forced the present situation is due most obviously to two causes. One is the excessive development of the "intermediate" ship originally devised for purposes of commerce protection, and dictated by a menace which the experience of the American War had taught us to respect. The other is the introduction of the torpedo, and the consequent vulnerability of battle-squadrons that are not securely screened. Nothing of the kind had any influence on the fleet constitution of the seventeenth century. But if we seek deeper, there is a less obvious consideration which for what it is worth is too striking to be ignored.

It has been suggested above that the constitution of fleets appears to have some more or less recognisable relation to the prevalent theory of war. Now, amongst all our uncertainty we can assert with confidence that the theory which holds the field at the present day bears the closest possible resemblance to that which dominated the soldier-admirals of the Dutch war. It was the "Overthrow" theory, the firm faith in the decisive action as the key of all strategical problems. They carried it to sea with them from the battlefields of the New Model Army, and the Dutch met them squarely. In the first war at least their commerce had to give place to the exigencies of throwing into the battle everything that could affect the issue. It is not of course pretended that this attitude was dictated by any clearly conceived theory of absolute war. It was due rather to the fact that, owing to the relative geographical conditions, all attempts to guard trade communications were useless without the command of the home waters in the North Sea, and the truth received a clinching moral emphasis from the British claim to the actual dominion of the Narrow Seas. It was, in fact, a war which resembled rather the continental conditions of territorial conquest than the naval procedure that characterised our rivalry with France.

Is it then possible, however much we may resist the conclusion in loyalty to the eighteenth-century tradition, that the rise of a new naval Power in the room of Holland must bring us back to the drastic, if crude, methods of the Dutch wars, and force us to tread under foot the nicer ingenuity of Anson's system? Is it this which has tempted us to mistrust any type of vessel which cannot be flung into the battle? The recurrence of a formidable rival in the North Sea was certainly not the first cause of the reaction. It began before that menace arose. Still it has undoubtedly forced the pace, and even if it be not a cause, it may well be a justification.

CHAPTER III

THEORY OF THE METHOD—CONCENTRATION AND DISPERSAL OF FORCE

FROM the point of view of the method by which its ends are obtained, strategy is often described as the art of assembling the utmost force at the right time and place; and this method is called "Concentration."

At first sight the term seems simple and expressive enough, but on analysis it will be found to include several distinct ideas, to all of which the term is applied indifferently. The result is a source of some confusion, even to the most lucid writers. "The word concentration," says one of the most recent of them, "evokes the idea of a grouping of forces. We believe, in fact, that we cannot make war without grouping ships into squadrons and squadrons into fleets."[1] Here in one sentence the word hovers between the formation of fleets and their strategical distribution. Similar looseness will embarrass the student at every turn. At one time he will find the word used to express the antithesis of division or dispersal of force; at another, to express strategic deployment, which implies division to a greater or less extent. He will find it used of the process of assembling a force, as well as of the state of a force when the process is complete. The truth is that the term, which is one of the most common and most necessary in strategical discussion, has never

[1] Daveluy, *L'Esprit de la Guerre Navale*, vol. i. p. 26, note.

acquired a very precise meaning, and this lack of pre-cision is one of the commonest causes of conflicting opinion and questionable judgments. No strategical term indeed calls more urgently for a clear determina-tion of the ideas for which it stands.

Military phraseology, from which the word is taken, employs " concentration" in three senses. It is used for assembling the units of an army after they have been mobilised. In this sense, concentration is mainly an administrative process ; logically, it means the com-plement of the process of mobilisation, whereby the army realises its war organisation and becomes ready to take the field. In a second sense it is used for the process of moving the army when formed, or in process of formation, to the localities from which operations can best begin. This is a true strategical stage, and it culminates in what is known as strategic deployment. Finally, it is used for the ultimate stage when the army so deployed is closed up upon a definite line of operations in immediate readiness for tactical deployment—gathered up, that is, to deal a concentrated blow.

Well as this terminology appears to serve on land, where the processes tend to overlap, something more exact is required if we try to extend it to the sea. Such extension magnifies the error at every step, and clear thinking becomes difficult. Even if we set aside the first meaning, that is, the final stage of mobilisation, we have still to deal with the two others which, in a great measure, are mutually contradictory. The essential distinction of strategic deployment, which contemplates dispersal with a view to a choice of combinations, is flexibility and free movement. The characteristic of an army massed for a blow is rigidity and restricted mobility. In the one sense of concentration we contemplate a disposal of force which will conceal our intention from the enemy and will permit us to adapt our movements to the plan of operations he develops. In the other, strategic concealment is at an end. We have made our choice, and are committed to a definite operation. Clearly, then, if we would apply the principles of land concentration to naval warfare it is desirable to settle which of the two phases of an operation we mean by the term.

Which meaning, then, is most closely connected with the ordinary use of the word? The dictionaries define concentration as "the state of being brought to a common point or centre," and this coincides very exactly with the stage of a war plan which intervenes between the completion of mobilisation and the final massing or deployment for battle. It is an incomplete and continuing act. Its ultimate consequence is the mass. It is a method of securing mass at the right time and place. As we have seen, the essence of the state of strategic deployment to which it leads is flexibility. In war the choice of time and place will always be influenced by the enemy's dispositions and movements, or by our desire to deal him an unexpected blow. The merit of concentration, then, in this sense, is its power of permitting us to form our mass in time at one of the greatest number of different points where mass may be required.

It is for this stage that the more recent text-books incline to specialise concentration—qualifying it as "strategic concentration." But even that term scarcely meets the case, for the succeeding process of gathering up the army into a position for tactical deployment is also a strategical concentration. Some further specialisation is required. The analytical difference between the two processes is that the first is an operation of major strategy and the other of minor, and if they are to be fully expressed, we have to weight ourselves with the terms "major and minor strategic concentration."

Such cumbrous terminology is too forbidding to use. It serves only to mark that the middle stage differs logically from the third as much as it does from the first. In practice it comes to this. If we are going to use concentration in its natural sense, we must regard it as something that comes after complete mobilisation and stops short of the formation of mass.

In naval warfare at least this distinction between concentration and mass is essential to clear appreciation. It leads us to conclusions that are of the first importance. For instance, when once the mass is formed, concealment and flexibility are at an end. The further, therefore, from the formation of the ultimate mass we can stop the process of concentration the better designed it will be. The less we are committed to any particular mass, and the less we indicate what and where our mass is to be, the more formidable our concentration. To concentration, therefore, the idea of division is as essential as the idea of connection. It is this view of the process which, at least for naval warfare, a weighty critical authority has most strongly emphasised. "Such," he says, "is concentration reasonably understood—not huddled together like a drove of sheep, but distributed with a regard to a common purpose, and linked together by the effectual energy of a single will." [1] Vessels in a state of concentration he

[1] Mahan, *War of 1812*, i. 316.

compares to a fan that opens and shuts. In this view concentration connotes not a homogeneous body, but a compound organism controlled from a common centre, and elastic enough to permit it to cover a wide field without sacrificing the mutual support of its parts.

If, then, we exclude the meaning of mere assembling and the meaning of the mass, we have left a signification which expresses coherent disposal about a strategical centre, and this it will be seen gives for naval warfare just the working definition that we want as the counterpart of strategic deployment on land. The object of a naval concentration like that of strategic deployment will be to cover the widest possible area, and to preserve at the same time elastic cohesion, so as to secure rapid condensations of any two or more of the parts of the organism, and in any part of the area to be covered, at the will of the controlling mind ; and above all, a sure and rapid condensation of the whole at the strategical centre.

Concentration of this nature, moreover, will be the expression of a war plan which, while solidly based on an ultimate central mass, still preserves the faculty of delivering or meeting minor attacks in any direction. It will permit us to exercise control of the sea while we await and work for the opportunity of a decision which shall permanently secure control, and it will permit this without prejudicing our ability of bringing the utmost force to bear when the moment for the decision arrives. Concentration, in fact, implies a continual conflict between cohesion and reach, and for practical purposes it is the right adjustment of those two tensions—ever shifting in force—which constitutes the greater part of practical strategy.

In naval warfare this concentration stage has a

peculiar significance in the development of a campaign, and at sea it is more clearly detached than ashore. Owing to the vast size of modern armies, and the restricted nature of their lines of movement, no less than their lower intrinsic mobility as compared with fleets, the processes of assembly, concentration, and forming the battle mass tend to grade into one another without any demarcation of practical value. An army frequently reaches the stage of strategic deployment direct from the mobilisation bases of its units, and on famous occasions its only real concentration has taken place on the battlefield. In Continental warfare, then, there is less difficulty in using the term to cover all three processes. Their tendency is always to overlap. But at sea, where communications are free and unrestricted by obstacles, and where mobility is high, they are susceptible of sharper differentiation. The normal course is for a fleet to assemble at a naval port; thence by a distinct movement it proceeds to the strategical centre and reaches out in divisions as required. The concentration about that centre may be very far from a mass, and the final formation of the mass will bear no resemblance to either of the previous movements, and will be quite distinct.

But free as a fleet is from the special fetters of an army, there always exist at sea peculiar conditions of friction which clog its freedom of disposition. One source of this friction is commerce protection. However much our war plan may press for close concentration, the need of commerce protection will always be calling for dispersal. The other source is the peculiar freedom and secrecy of movements at sea. As the sea knows no roads to limit or indicate our own lines of operation, so it tells little about those of the enemy. The most distant and widely dispersed points must be kept in view as possible objectives of the enemy. When we add to this that two or more fleets can act in conjunction from widely separated bases with far greater certainty than is possible for armies, it is obvious that the variety of combinations is much higher at sea than on land, and variety of combination is in constant opposition to the central mass.

It follows that so long as the enemy's fleet is divided, and thereby retains various possibilities of either concentrated or sporadic action, our distribution will be dictated by the need of being able to deal with a variety of combinations and to protect a variety of objectives. Our concentrations must therefore be kept as open and flexible as possible. History accordingly shows us that the riper and fresher our experience and the surer our grip of war, the looser were our concentrations. The idea of massing, as a virtue in itself, is bred in peace and not in war. It indicates the debilitating idea that in war we must seek rather to avoid than to inflict defeat. True, advocates of the mass entrench themselves in the plausible conception that their aim is to inflict crushing defeats. But this too is an idea of peace. War has proved to the hilt that victories have not only to be won, but worked for. They must be worked for by bold strategical combinations, which as a rule entail at least apparent dispersal. They can only be achieved by taking risks, and the greatest and most effective of these is division.

The effect of prolonged peace has been to make "concentration" a kind of shibboleth, so that the division of a fleet tends almost to be regarded as a sure mark of bad leadership. Critics have come to lose sight of the old war experience, that without division no strategical combinations are possible. In truth they must be founded on division. Division is bad only when it is pushed beyond the limits of well-knit deployment. It is theoretically wrong to place a section of the fleet in such a position that it may be prevented from falling back on its strategical centre when it is encountered by a superior force. Such retreats of course can never be made certain; they will always depend in some measure on the skill and resource of the opposing commanders, and on the chances of weather: but risks must be taken. If we risk nothing, we shall seldom perform anything. The great leader is the man who can measure rightly to what breadth of deployment he can stretch his concentration. This power of bold and sure adjustment between cohesion and reach is indeed a supreme test of that judgment which in the conduct of war takes the place of strategical theory.

In British naval history examples of faulty division are hard to find. The case most commonly cited is an early one. It occurred in 1666 during the second Dutch war. Monk and Rupert were in command of the main fleet, which from its mobilisation bases in the Thames and at Spithead had concentrated in the Downs. There they were awaiting De Ruyter's putting to sea in a position from which they could deal with him whether his object was an attack on the Thames or to join hands with the French. In this position a rumour reached them that the Toulon squadron was on its way to the Channel to co-operate with the Dutch. Upon this false intelligence the fleet was divided, and Rupert went back to Portsmouth to

cover that position in case it might be the French objective. De Ruyter at once put to sea with a fleet greatly
superior to Monk's division. Monk, however, taking advantage of thick weather that had supervened, surprised
him at anchor, and believing he had a sufficient tactical
advantage attacked him impetuously. Meanwhile the
real situation became known. There was no French
fleet, and Rupert was recalled. He succeeded in
rejoining Monk after his action with De Ruyter had
lasted three days. In the course of it Monk had
been very severely handled and forced to retreat to
the Thames, and it was generally believed that it was
only the belated arrival of Rupert that saved us from
a real disaster.

The strategy in this case is usually condemned out
of hand and made to bear the entire blame of the
reverse. Monk, who as a soldier had proved himself
one of the finest strategists of the time, is held to have
blundered from sheer ignorance of elementary principles. It is assumed that he should have kept his fleet
massed; but his critics fail to observe that at least in
the opinion of the time this would not have met the
case. Had he kept the whole to deal with De Ruyter,
it is probable that De Ruyter would not have put to
sea, and it is certain Portsmouth and the Isle of Wight
would have lain open to the French had they come.
If he had moved his mass to deal with the French, he
would have exposed the Thames to De Ruyter. It
was a situation that could not be solved by a simple
application of what the French call the *masse
centrale*. The only way to secure both places from
attack was to divide the fleet, just as in 1801 Nelson
in the same theatre was compelled to divide his defence
force. In neither case was division a fault, because it

was a necessity. The fault in Monk's and Rupert's case was that they extended their reach with no proper provision to preserve cohesion. Close cruiser connection should have been maintained between the two divisions, and Monk should not have engaged deeply till he felt Rupert at his elbow. This we are told was the opinion of most of his flag-officers. They held that he should not have fought when he did. His correct course, on Kempenfelt's principle, would have been to hang on De Ruyter so as to prevent his doing anything, and to have slowly fallen back, drawing the Dutch after him till his loosened concentration was closed up again. If De Ruyter had refused to follow him through the Straits, there would have been plenty of time to mass the fleet. If De Ruyter had followed, he could have been fought in a position from which there would have been no escape. The fault, in fact, was not strategical, but rather one of tactical judgment. Monk over-estimated the advantage of his surprise and the relative fighting values of the two fleets, and believed he saw his way to victory single-handed. The danger of division is being surprised and forced to fight in inferiority. This was not Monk's case. He was not surprised, and he could easily have avoided action had he so desired. To judge such a case simply by using concentration as a touchstone can only tend to set up such questionable habits of thought as have condemned the more famous division which occurred in the crisis of the campaign of 1805, and with which we must deal later.

Apart from the general danger of using either words or maxims in this way, it is obviously specially unwise in the case of concentration and division. The current rule is that it is bad to divide unless you have a great superiority; yet there have been numerous occasions when, being at war with an inferior enemy, we have found our chief embarrassment in the fact that he kept his fleet divided, and was able thereby to set up something like a deadlock. The main object of our naval operations would then be to break it down. To force an inferior enemy to concentrate is indeed the almost necessary preliminary to securing one of those crushing victories at which we must always aim, but which so seldom are obtained. It is by forcing the enemy to attempt to concentrate that we get our opportunity by sagacious dispersal of crushing his divisions in detail. It is by inducing him to mass that we simplify our problem and compel him to choose between leaving to us the exercise of command and putting it to the decision of a great action.

Advocates of close concentration will reply that that is true enough. We do often seek to force our enemy to concentrate, but that does not show that concentration is sometimes a disadvantage, for we ourselves must concentrate closely to force a similar concentration on the enemy. The maxim, indeed, has become current that concentration begets concentration, but it is not too much to say that it is a maxim which history flatly contradicts. If the enemy is willing to hazard all on a battle, it is true. But if we are too superior, or our concentration too well arranged for him to hope for victory, then our concentration has almost always had the effect of forcing him to disperse for sporadic action. So certain was this result, that in our old wars, in which we were usually superior, we always adopted the loosest possible concentrations in order to prevent sporadic action. True, the tendency of the French to adopt this mode of warfare is usually set down to some constitutional ineptitude that is outside strategical theory, but this view is due rather to the irritation which the method caused us, than to sober reasoning. For a comparatively weak belligerent sporadic action was better than nothing, and the only other alternative was for him to play into our hands by hazarding the decision which it was our paramount interest to obtain. Sporadic action alone could never give our enemy command of the sea, but it could do us injury and embarrass our plans, and there was always hope it might so much loosen our concentration as to give him a fair chance of obtaining a series of successful minor decisions.

Take, now, the leading case of 1805. In that campaign our distribution was very wide, and was based on several concentrations. The first had its centre in the Downs, and extended not only athwart the invading army's line of passage, but also over the whole North Sea, so as to prevent interference with our trade or our system of coast defence either from the Dutch in the Texel or from French squadrons arriving north-about. The second, which was known as the Western Squadron, had its centre off Ushant, and was spread over the whole Bay of Biscay by means of advanced squadrons before Ferrol and Rochefort. With a further squadron off the coast of Ireland, it was able also to reach far out into the Atlantic in order to receive our trade. It kept guard, in fact, not only over the French naval ports, but over the approaches to the Channel, where were the home terminals of the great southern and western trade-routes. A third concentration was in the Mediterranean, whose centre under Nelson was at Sardinia. It had outlying sub-centres at Malta and Gibraltar, and covered

the whole ground from Cape St. Vincent outside the
Straits to Toulon, Trieste, and the Dardanelles. When
war broke out with Spain in 1804, it was considered
advisable to divide this command, and Spanish waters
outside the Straits were held by a fourth concentration,
whose centre was off Cadiz, and whose northern limit
was Cape Finisterre, where it joined the Ushant concentration. For reasons which were personal rather
than strategical this arrangement was not continued
long, nor indeed after a few months was there the
same need for it, for the Toulon squadron had changed
its base to Cadiz. By this comprehensive system the
whole of the European seas were controlled both for
military and trade purposes. In the distant terminal
areas, like the East and West Indies, there were
nucleus concentrations with the necessary connective
machinery permanently established, and to render
them effective, provision was made by which the
various European squadrons could throw off detachments to bring up their force to any strength which
the movements of the enemy might render necessary.

Wide as was this distribution, and great as its
reach, a high degree of cohesion was maintained not
only between the parts of each concentration, but
between the several concentrations themselves. By
means of a minor cruiser centre at the Channel Islands,
the Downs and Ushant concentrations could rapidly
cohere. Similarly the Cadiz concentration was linked
up with that of Ushant at Finisterre, and but for
personal friction and repulsion, the cohesion between
the Mediterranean and Cadiz concentrations would
have been equally strong. Finally, there was a
masterly provision made for all the concentrations to
condense into one great mass at the crucial point off

Ushant before by any calculable chance a hostile mass could gather there.

For Napoleon's best admirals, " who knew the craft of the sea," the British fleet thus disposed was in a state of concentration that nothing but a stroke of luck beyond the limit of sober calculation could break. Decrès and Bruix had no doubt of it, and the knowledge overpowered Villeneuve when the crisis came. After he had carried the concentration which Napoleon had planned so far as to have united three divisions in Ferrol, he knew that the outlying sections of our Western Squadron had disappeared from before Ferrol and Rochefort.   In his eyes, as well as those of the British Admiralty, this squadron, in spite of its dispersal in the Bay of Biscay, had always been in a state of concentration.   It was not this which caused his heart to fail.   It was the news that Nelson had reappeared at Gibraltar, and had been seen steering northward. It meant for him that the whole of his enemy's European fleet was in a state of concentration.   " Their concentration of force," he afterwards wrote, " was at the moment more serious than in any previous disposition, and such that they were in a position to meet in superiority the combined forces of Brest and Ferrol," and for that reason, he explained, he had given up the game as lost.   But to Napoleon's unpractised eye it was impossible to see what it was he had to deal with.   Measuring the elasticity of the British naval distribution by the comparatively cumbrous and restricted mobility of armies, he saw it as a rash and unwarlike dispersal.   Its looseness seemed to indicate so great a tenderness for the distant objectives that lay open to his scattered squadrons, that he believed by a show of sporadic action he could further disperse ourfleet, and then by a close concentration crush the essential part in detail. It was a clear case of the enemy's dispersal forcing us to adopt the loosest concentration, and of our comparative dispersal tempting the enemy to concentrate and hazard a decision. It cannot be said we forced the fatal move upon him intentionally. It was rather the operation of strategical law set in motion by our bold distribution. We were determined that his threat of invasion, formidable as it was, should not force upon us so close a concentration as to leave our widespread interests open to his attack. Neither can it be said that our first aim was to prevent his attempting to concentrate. Every one of his naval ports was watched by a squadron, but it was recognised that this would not prevent concentration. The escape of one division might well break the chain. But that consideration made no difference. The distribution of our squadrons before his naval ports was essential for preventing sporadic action. Their distribution was dictated sufficiently by the defence of commerce and of colonial and allied territory, by our need, that is, to exercise a general command even if we could not destroy the enemy's force.

The whole of Nelson's correspondence for this period shows that his main object was the protection of our Mediterranean trade and of Neapolitan and Turkish territory. When Villeneuve escaped him, his irritation was caused not by the prospect of a French concentration, which had no anxieties for him, for he knew counter-concentrations were provided for. It was caused rather by his having lost the opportunity which the attempt to concentrate had placed within his reach. He followed Villeneuve to the West Indies, not to prevent concentration, but, firstly, to protect the local trade and Jamaica, and, secondly, in hope of another chance of dealing the blow he had missed. Lord Barham took precisely the same view. When on news of Villeneuve's return from the West Indies he moved out the three divisions of the Western Squadron, that is, the Ushant concentration, to meet him, he expressly stated, not that his object was to prevent concentration, but that it was to deter the French from attempting sporadic action. " The interception of the fleet in question," he wrote, " on its return to Europe would be a greater object than any I know. It would damp all future expeditions, and would show to Europe that it might be advisable to relax in the blockading system occasionally for the express purpose of putting them in our hands at a convenient opportunity."

Indeed we had no reason for preventing the enemy's concentration. It was our best chance of solving effectually the situation we had to confront. Our true policy was to secure permanent command by a great naval decision. So long as the enemy remained divided, no such decision could be expected. It was not, in fact, till he attempted his concentration, and its last stage had been reached, that the situation was in our hands. The intricate problem with which we had been struggling was simplified down to closing up our own concentration to the strategical centre off Ushant. But at the last stage the enemy could not face the formidable position we held. His concentration was stopped. Villeneuve fell back on Cadiz, and the pro- blem began to assume for us something of its former intricacy. So long as we held the mass off Ushant which our great concentration had produced, we were safe from invasion. But that was not enough. It left

the seas open to sporadic action from Spanish ports.
There were convoys from the East and West Indies at
hand, and there was our expedition in the Mediterranean in jeopardy, and another on the point of sailing
from Cork. Neither Barham at the Admiralty nor
Cornwallis in command off Ushant hesitated an hour.
By a simultaneous induction they both decided the
mass must be divided. The concentration must be
opened out again, and it was done. Napoleon called
the move an *insigne betise*, but it was the move that
beat him, and must have beaten him, whatever the skill
of his admirals, for the two squadrons never lost touch.
He found himself caught in a situation from which
there was nothing to hope. His fleet was neither concentrated for a decisive blow nor spread for sporadic
action. He had merely simplified his enemy's problem.
Our hold was surer than ever, and in a desperate
attempt to extricate himself he was forced to expose
his fleet to the final decision we required.

The whole campaign serves well to show what was
understood by concentration at the end of the great
naval wars. To Lord Barham and the able admirals
who interpreted his plans it meant the possibility of
massing at the right time and place. It meant, in
close analogy to strategic deployment on land, the
disposal of squadrons about a strategical centre from
which fleets could condense for massed action in any
required direction, and upon which they could fall back
when unduly pressed. In this case the ultimate centre
was the narrows of the Channel, where Napoleon's army
lay ready to cross, but there was no massing there.
So crude a distribution would have meant a purely
defensive attitude. It would have meant waiting to
be struck instead of seeking to strike, and such an

attitude was arch-heresy to our old masters of war.

So far we have only considered concentration as applied to wars in which we have a preponderance of naval force, but the principles are at least equally valid when a coalition places us in inferiority. The leading case is the home campaign of 1782. It was strictly on defensive lines. Our information was that France and Spain intended to end the war with a great combined effort against our West Indian islands, and particularly Jamaica. It was recognised that the way to meet the threat was to concentrate for offensive action in the Caribbean Sea everything that was not absolutely needed for home defence. Instead, therefore, of trying to be strong enough to attempt the offensive in both areas, it was decided to make sure of the area that was most critical. To do this the home fleet had to be reduced so low relatively to what the enemy had in European waters, that offence was out of the question.

While Rodney took the offensive area, Lord Howe was given the other. His task was to prevent the coalition obtaining such a command of home waters as would place our trade and coasts at their mercy, and it was not likely to prove a light one. We knew that the enemy's plan was to combine their attack on the West Indies with an attempt to control the North Sea, and possibly the Straits of Dover, with a Dutch squadron of twelve to fifteen of the line, while a combined Franco-Spanish fleet of at least forty sail would occupy the mouth of the Channel. It was also possible that these two forces would endeavour to form a junction. In any case the object of the joint operations would be to paralyse our trade and annoy our coasts, and thereby force us to neglect the West Indian area and the two Spanish objectives, Minorca and Gibraltar. All told we had only about thirty of the line on the home station, and though a large proportion of these were three-deckers, a good many could not be ready for sea till the summer.

Inferior as was the available force, there was no thought of a purely passive defence. It would not meet the case. Something must be done to interfere with the offensive operations of the allies in the West Indies and against Gibraltar, or they would attain the object of their home campaign. It was resolved to effect this by minor counterstrokes on their line of communications to the utmost limit of our defensive reach. It would mean a considerable stretch of our concentration, but we were determined to do what we could to prevent reinforcements from reaching the West Indies from Brest, to intercept French trade as occasion offered, and, finally, at almost any risk to relieve Gibraltar.

In these conditions the defensive concentration was based on a central mass or reserve at Spithead, a squadron in the Downs to watch the Texel for the safety of the North Sea trade, and another to the westward to watch Brest and interrupt its transatlantic communications. Kempenfelt in command of the latter squadron had just shown what could be done by his great exploit of capturing Guichen's convoy of military and naval stores for the West Indies. Early in the spring he was relieved by Barrington, who sailed on April 5th to resume the Ushant position. His instructions were not to fight a superior enemy unless in favourable circumstances, but to retire on Spithead. He was away three weeks, and returned with a French

East India convoy with troops and stores, and two of
the ships of-the-line which formed its escort.

Up to this time there had been no immediate sign
of the great movement from the south. The Franco-
Spanish fleet which had assembled at Cadiz was occupied ineffectually in trying to stop small reliefs reaching
Gibraltar and in covering their own homeward-bound
trade. The Dutch, however, were becoming active, and
the season was approaching for our Baltic trade to come
home. Ross in the North Sea had but four of the line
to watch the Texel, and was in no position to deal with
the danger. Accordingly early in May the weight of
the home concentration was thrown into the North
Sea. On the 10th Howe sailed with Barrington and
the bulk of the fleet to join Ross in the Downs, while
Kempenfelt again took the Ushant position. Only
about half the Brest squadron had gone down to join
the Spaniards at Cadiz, and he was told his first duty
was to intercept the rest if it put to sea, but, as in
Barrington's instructions, if he met a superior squadron
he was to retire up Channel under the English coast and
join hands with Howe. In spite of the fact that influenza was now raging in the fleet, he succeeded in
holding the French inactive. Howe with the same
difficulty to face was equally successful. The Dutch
had put to sea, but returned immediately they knew of
his movement, and cruising off the Texel, he held them
there, and kept complete command of the North Sea till
our Baltic trade was safe home.

By the end of May it was done, and as our intelligence indicated that the great movement from Cadiz
was at last about to begin, Howe, to whom a certain
discretion had been left, decided it was time to shift the
weight to his other wing and close on Kempenfelt.

The Government, however, seemed to think that he ought to be able to use his position for offensive operations against Dutch trade, but in the admiral's opinion this was to lose hold of the design and sacrifice cohesion too much to reach. He informed them that he had not deemed it advisable to make detachments from his squadron against the trade, "not knowing how suddenly there might be a call, for the greater part of it at least, to the westward." In accordance, therefore, with his general instructions he left with Ross a strong squadron of nine of the line, sufficient to hold in check, and even "to take and destroy," the comparatively weak ships of the Dutch, and with the rest returned to the westward.[1] His intention was to proceed with all possible expedition to join Kempenfelt on the coast of France, but this, owing to the ravages of the influenza, he was unable to do. Kempenfelt was forced to come in, and on June 5th the junction was made at Spithead.

For three weeks, so severe was the epidemic, they could not move. Then came news that the Cadiz fleet under Langara had sailed the day Howe had reached Spithead, and he resolved to make a dash with every ship fit to put to sea to cut it off from Brest. He was too late. Before he could get into position the junction between Langara and the Brest squadron was made, and in their full force the allies had occupied the mouth of the Channel. With the addition of the Brest ships the combined fleet numbered forty of the line, while all Howe could muster was twenty-two, but amongst them were seven three-deckers and three eighties, and he would soon be reinforced. Three of

---

[1] The Dutch were believed to have sixteen of the line—one seventy-four, seven sixty-eights, and the rest under sixty guns. In Ross's squadron were one three-decker and two eighties.

Ross's smallest ships were recalled, and five others were nearly ready, but for these Howe could not wait. The homeward-bound Jamaica convoy was at hand, and at all hazards it must be saved.

What was to be done? So soon as he sighted the enemy he realised that a successful action was out of the question. Early in the morning of July 12th, "being fifteen leagues S.S.E. from Scilly," Langara with thirty-six of the line was seen to the westward. "As soon," wrote Howe, "as their force had been ascertained, I thought proper to avoid coming to battle with them as then circumstanced, and therefore steered to the north to pass between Scilly and the Land's End. My purpose therein was to get to the westward of the enemy, both for protecting the Jamaica convoy and to gain the advantage of situation for bringing them to action which the difference in our numbers renders desirable."

By a most brilliant effort of seamanship the dangerous movement was effected safely that night, and it proved an entire success. Till Howe was met with and defeated, the allies would not venture into the Channel, and his unprecedented feat had effectually thrown them off. Assuming apparently that he must have passed round their rear to seaward, they sought him to the southward, and there for a month beat up and down in ineffective search. Meanwhile Howe, sending his cruisers ahead to the convoy's rendezvous off the south-west coast of Iceland, had taken his whole fleet about two hundred miles west of the Skelligs to meet it. Northerly winds prevented his reaching the right latitude in time, but it mattered little. The convoy passed in between him and the south of Ireland, and as the enemy had taken a cast

down to Ushant, it was able to enter the Channel in
safety without sighting an enemy's sail. Ignorant of
what had happened, Howe cruised for a week practis-
ing the ships " in connected movements so particularly
necessary on the present occasion." Then with his
fleet in fine condition to carry out preventive tactics in
accordance with Kempenfelt's well-known exposition,[1]
he returned to seek the enemy to the eastward, in order
to try to draw them from their station at Scilly and
open the Channel. On his way he learnt the convoy
had passed in, and with this anxiety off his mind he
bore up for the Lizard, where his reinforcements were
awaiting him. There he found the Channel was free.
From lack of supplies the enemy had been forced to
retire to port, and he returned to Spithead to make
preparations for the relief of Gibraltar. While this
work was going on, the North Sea squadron was again
strengthened that it might resume the blockade of the
Texel and cover the arrival of the autumn convoys
from the Baltic. It was done with complete success.
Not a single ship fell into the enemy's hands, and the
campaign, and indeed the war, ended by Howe taking
the mass of his force down to Gibraltar and perform-
ing his remarkable feat of relieving it in the face of
the Spanish squadron. For the power and reach of
a well-designed concentration there can be no finer
example.

If, now, we seek from the above and similar examples for principles to serve as a guide between concentration and division we shall find, firstly, this one.
The degree of division we shall require is in proportion
to the number of naval ports from which the enemy
can act against our maritime interests and to the

[1] See *post*, pp. 222–4.

extent of coastline along which they are spread. It is a principle which springs from the soul of our old tradition that we must always seek, not merely to prevent the enemy striking at our heart, but also to strike him the moment he attempts to do anything. We must make of his every attempt an opportunity for a counterstroke. The distribution this aim entailed varied greatly with different enemies. In our wars with France, and particularly when Spain and Holland were in alliance with her, the number of the ports to be dealt with was very considerable and their distribution very wide. In our wars with the Dutch alone, on the other hand, the number and distribution were comparatively small, and in this case our concentration was always close.

This measure of distribution, however, will never stand alone. Concentration will not depend solely upon the number and position of the enemy's naval ports. It will be modified by the extent to which the lines of operation starting from those ports traverse our own home waters. The reason is plain. Whatever the enemy opposed to us, and whatever the nature of the war, we must always keep a fleet at home. In any circumstances it is essential for the defence of our home trade terminals, and it is essential as a central reserve from which divisions can be thrown off to reinforce distant terminals and to seize opportunities for counterstrokes. It is "the mainspring," as Lord Barham put it, "from which all offensive operations must proceed." This squadron, then, being permanent and fixed as the foundation of our whole system, it is clear that if, as in the case of the French wars, the enemy's lines of operation do not traverse our home waters, close concentration upon it will not serve our turn. If, on the other hand, as in the case of the Dutch wars, the lines do traverse home waters, a home concentration is all that is required. Our division will then be measured by the amount of our surplus strength, and by the extent to which we feel able to detach squadrons for offensive action against the enemy's distant maritime interests without prejudicing our hold on the home terminals of his lines of operation and our power of striking directly he moves. These remarks apply, of course, to the main fleet operations. If such an enemy has distant colonial bases from which he can annoy our trade, minor concentrations must naturally be arranged in those areas.

Next we have to note that where the enemy's squadrons are widely distributed in numerous bases, we cannot always simplify the problem by leaving some of them open so as to entice him to concentrate and reduce the number of ports to be watched. For if we do this, we leave the unwatched squadrons free for sporadic action. Unless we are sure he intends to concentrate with a view to a decisive action, our only means of simplifying the situation is to watch every port closely enough to interfere effectually with sporadic action. Then, sporadic action being denied him, the enemy must either do nothing or concentrate.

The next principle is flexibility. Concentration should be so arranged that any two parts may freely cohere, and that all parts may quickly condense into a mass at any point in the area of concentration. The object of holding back from forming the mass is to deny the enemy knowledge of our actual distribution or its intention at any given moment, and at the same time to ensure that it will be adjusted to meet any dangerous movement that is open to him. Further than this our aim should be not merely to prevent any part being overpowered by a superior force, but to regard every detached squadron as a trap to lure the enemy to destruction. The ideal concentration, in short, is an appearance of weakness that covers a reality of strength.

PART III
CONDUCT OF NAVAL WAR

CHAPTER I

INTRODUCTORY

I

INHERENT DIFFERENCES IN THE CONDITIONS OF WAR ON LAND AND ON SEA

BEFORE attempting to apply the foregoing general principles in a definite manner to the conduct of naval war, it is necessary to clear the ground of certain obstacles to right judgment. The gradual elucidation of the theory of war, it must be remembered, has been almost entirely the work of soldiers, but so admirable is the work they have done, and so philosophical the method they have adopted, that a very natural tendency has arisen to assume that their broad-based conclusions are of universal application. That the leading lines which they have charted are in a certain sense those which must govern all strategy no one will deny. They are the real pioneers, and their methods must be in the main our methods, but what we have to remember is that the country we have to travel is radically different from that in which they acquired their skill.

A moment's consideration will reveal how far-reaching the differences are. Let us ask ourselves what are the main ideas around which all the military lore turns. It may be taken broadly that the general principles are three in number. Firstly, there is the idea of concentration of force, that is, the idea of over-

throwing the enemy's main strength by bringing to bear
upon it the utmost accumulation of weight and energy
within your means; secondly, there is the idea that
strategy is mainly a question of definite lines of communication; and thirdly, there is the idea of concentration of
effort, which means keeping a single eye on the force
you wish to overthrow without regard to ulterior objects.
Now if we examine the conditions which give these
principles so firm a footing on land, we shall find that
in all three cases they differ at sea, and differ materially.

Take the first, which, in spite of all the deductions
we have to make from it in the case of limited wars,
is the dominating one. The pithy maxim which
expresses its essence is that our primary objective is
the enemy's main force. In current naval literature
the maxim is applied to the sea in some such form as
this: "The primary object of our battle-fleet is to seek
out and destroy that of the enemy." On the surface
nothing could look sounder, but what are the conditions which underlie the one and the other?

The practical value of the military maxim is based
upon the fact that in land warfare it is always theoretically possible to strike at your enemy's army, that is,
if you have the strength and spirit to overcome the
obstacles and face the risks. But at sea this is not
so. In naval warfare we have a far-reaching fact
which is entirely unknown on land. It is simply this
—that it is possible for your enemy to remove his fleet
from the board altogether. He may withdraw it into
a defended port, where it is absolutely out of your reach
without the assistance of an army. No amount of
naval force, and no amount of offensive spirit, can avail
you. The result is that in naval warfare an embarrassing dilemma tends to assert itself. If you are in a

superiority that justifies a vigorous offensive and prompts you to seek out your enemy with a view to a decision, the chances are you will find him in a position where you cannot touch him. Your offence is arrested, and you find yourself in what, at least theoretically, is the weakest general position known to war.

This was one of our earliest discoveries in strategy. It followed indeed immediately and inevitably upon our discovery that the most drastic way of making war was to concentrate every effort on the enemy's armed forces. In dealing with the theory of war in general a caveat has already been entered against the too common assumption that this method was an invention of Napoleon's or Frederick's, or that it was a foreign importation at all. In the view at least of our own military historians the idea was born in our Civil Wars with Cromwell and the New Model Army. It was the conspicuous feature that distinguished our Civil War from all previous wars of modern times. So astonishing was its success—as foreign observers remarked—that it was naturally applied by our soldier-admirals at sea so soon as war broke out with the Dutch. Whatever may be the claims of the Cromwellian soldiers to have invented for land warfare what is regarded abroad as the chief characteristic of the Napoleonic method, it is beyond doubt that they deserve the credit of it at sea. All three Dutch wars had a commercial object, and yet after the first campaign the general idea never was to make the enemy's commerce a primary objective. That place was occupied throughout by their battle-fleets, and under Monk and Rupert at least those objectives were pursued with a singleness of purpose and a persistent vehemence that was entirely Napoleonic.

But in the later stages of the struggle, when we began to gain a preponderance, it was found that the method ceased to work. The attempt to seek the enemy with a view to a decisive action was again and again frustrated by his retiring to his own coasts, where either we could not reach him or his facilities for retreat made a decisive result impossible. He assumed, in fact, a defensive attitude with which we were powerless to deal, and in the true spirit of defence he sprang out from time to time to deal us a counter-stroke as he saw his opportunity.

It was soon perceived that the only way of dealing with this attitude was to adopt some means of forcing the enemy to sea and compelling him to expose himself to the decision we sought. The most cogent means at hand was to threaten his commerce. Instead, therefore, of attempting to seek out his fleet directly, our own would sit upon the fairway of his homeward-bound trade, either on the Dogger Bank or elsewhere, thereby setting up a situation which it was hoped would cost him either his trade or his battle-fleet, or possibly both. Thus in spite of the fact that with our increasing preponderance our preoccupation with the idea of battle decision had become stronger than ever, we found ourselves forced to fall back upon subsidiary operations of an ulterior strategical character. It is a curious paradox, but it is one that seems inherent in the special feature of naval war, which permits the armed force to be removed from the board altogether.

The second distinguishing characteristic of naval warfare which relates to the communication idea is not so well marked, but it is scarcely less important. It will be recalled that this characteristic is concerned with lines of communication is so far as they tend to

determine lines of operation. It is a simple question
of roads and obstacles. In land warfare we can determine with some precision the limits and direction of
our enemy's possible movements. We know that they
must be determined mainly by roads and obstacles.
But afloat neither roads nor obstacles exist. There is
nothing of the kind on the face of the sea to assist us
in locating him and determining his movements. True
it is that in sailing days his movements were to some
extent limited by prevailing winds and by the elimination
of impossible courses, but with steam even these de-
terminants have gone, and there is practically nothing
to limit the freedom of his movement except the exigencies of fuel. Consequently in seeking to strike our
enemy the liability to miss him is much greater at sea
than on land, and the chances of being eluded by the
enemy whom we are seeking to bring to battle become
so serious a check upon our offensive action as to
compel us to handle the maxim of "Seeking out the
enemy's fleet" with caution.

The difficulty obtruded itself from the moment the
idea was born. It may be traced back—so far at
least as modern warfare is concerned—to Sir Francis
Drake's famous appreciation in the year of the Armada.
This memorable despatch was written when an acute
difference of opinion had arisen as to whether it were
better to hold our fleet back in home waters or to send
it forward to the coast of Spain. The enemy's objective was very uncertain. We could not tell whether
the blow was to fall in the Channel or Ireland or
Scotland, and the situation was complicated by a
Spanish army of invasion ready to cross from the
Flemish coast, and the possibility of combined action
by the Guises from France. Drake was for solving

the problem by taking station off the Armada's port
of departure, and fully aware of the risk such a move
entailed, he fortified his purely strategical reasons with
moral considerations of the highest moment. But the
Government was unconvinced, not as is usually assumed
out of sheer pusillanimity and lack of strategical insight, but because the chances of Drake's missing
contact were too great if the Armada should sail before
our own fleet could get into position.

Our third elementary principle is the idea of
concentration of effort, and the third characteristic of
naval warfare which clashes with it is that over and
above the duty of winning battles, fleets are charged
with the duty of protecting commerce. In land warfare, at least since laying waste an undefended part of
your enemy's country ceased to be a recognised strategical operation, there is no corresponding deflection
of purely military operations. It is idle for purists
to tell us that the deflection of commerce protection
should not be permitted to turn us from our main
purpose. We have to do with the hard facts of war,
and experience tells us that for economic reasons alone,
apart from the pressure of public opinion, no one has
ever found it possible to ignore the deflection entirely.
So vital indeed is financial vigour in war, that more
often than not the maintenance of the flow of trade
has been felt as a paramount consideration. Even in
the best days of our Dutch wars, when the whole plan
was based on ignoring the enemy's commerce as an
objective, we found ourselves at times forced to protect
our own trade with seriously disturbing results.

Nor is it more profitable to declare that the only
sound way to protect your commerce is to destroy the
enemy's fleet. As an enunciation of a principle it is

a truism—no one would dispute it. As a canon of practical strategy, it is untrue; for here our first deflection again asserts itself. What are you to do if the enemy refuses to permit you to destroy his fleets? You cannot leave your trade exposed to squadronal or cruiser raids while you await your opportunity, and the more you concentrate your force and efforts to secure the desired decision, the more you will expose your trade to sporadic attack. The result is that you are not always free to adopt the plan which is best calculated to bring your enemy to a decision. You may find yourself compelled to occupy, not the best positions, but those which will give a fair chance of getting contact in favourable conditions, and at the same time afford reasonable cover for your trade. Hence the maxim that the enemy's coast should be our frontier. It is not a purely military maxim like that for seeking out the enemy's fleet, though the two are often used as though they were interchangeable. Our usual positions on the enemy's coast were dictated quite as much by the exigencies of commerce protection as by primary strategical reasons. To maintain a rigorous watch close off the enemy's ports was never the likeliest way to bring him to decisive action—we have Nelson's well-known declaration on the point—but it was the best way, and often the only way, to keep the sea clear for the passage of our own trade and for the operations of our cruisers against that of the enemy.

For the present these all-important points need not be elaborated further. As we proceed to deal with the methods of naval warfare they will gather force and lucidity. Enough has been said to mark the shoals and warn us that, admirably constructed as is the craft which the military strategists have provided for our use, we must be careful with our navigation.

But before proceeding further it is necessary to simplify what lies before us by endeavouring to group the complex variety of naval operations into manageable shape.

II

TYPICAL FORMS OF NAVAL OPERATIONS

In the conduct of naval war all operations will be found to relate to two broad classes of object. The one is to obtain or dispute the command of the sea, and the other to exercise such control of communications as we have, whether the complete command has been secured or not.

It was on the logical and practical distinction between these two kinds of naval object, as we have seen, that the constitution of fleets was based in the fulness of the sailing period, when maritime wars were nearly incessant and were shaping the existing distribution of power in the world. During that period at any rate the dual conception lay at the root of naval methods and naval policy, and as it is also the logical outcome of the theory of war, we may safely take it as the basis of our analysis of the conduct of naval operations.

Practically, of course, we can seldom assert categorically that any operation of war has but one clearly defined object. A battle-squadron whose primary function was to secure command was often so placed as to enable it to exercise control; and, *vice versa*, cruiser lines intended primarily to exercise control upon the trade routes were regarded as outposts of the battle-fleet to give it warning of the movements of hostile squadrons. Thus Cornwallis during his blockade of Brest had sometimes to loosen his hold in order to cover the arrival of convoys against raiding squadrons; and thus also when Nelson was asked by Lord Barham for his views on cruiser patrol lines, he expressed himself as follows: " Ships on this service would not only prevent the depredations of privateers, but be in the way to watch any squadron of the enemy should they pass on their track. . . . Therefore intelligence will be quickly conveyed, and the enemy never, I think, lost sight of."[1] Instructions in this sense were issued by Lord Barham to the commodores concerned. In both cases, it will be seen, the two classes of operation overlapped. Still for purposes of analysis the distinction holds good, and is valuable for obtaining a clear view of the field.

Take, first, the methods of securing command, by which we mean putting it out of the enemy's power to use effectually the common communications or materially to interfere with our use of them. We find the means employed were two : decision by battle, and blockade. Of the two, the first was the less frequently attainable, but it was the one the British service always preferred. It was only natural that it should be so, seeing that our normal position was one of preponderance over our enemy, and so long as the policy of preponderance is maintained, the chances are the preference will also be maintained.

But further than this, the idea seems to be rooted in the oldest traditions of the Royal Navy. As we have seen, the conviction of the sea service that war is primarily a question of battles, and that battles once joined on anything like equal terms must be pressed

[1] Nelson to Barham, August 29, 1805.

to the last gasp, is one that has had nothing to learn from more recent continental discoveries. The Cromwellian admirals handed down to us the memory of battles lasting three, and even four, days. Their creed is enshrined in the robust article of war under which Byng and Calder were condemned; and in the apotheosis of Nelson the service has deified the battle idea.

It is true there were periods when the idea seemed to have lost its colour, but nevertheless it is so firmly embedded in the British conception of naval warfare, that there would be nothing left to say but for the unavoidable modification with which we have to temper the doctrine of overthrow. "Use that means," said its best-known advocate, "when you can and when you must." Devoutly as we may hold the battle faith, it is not always possible or wise to act upon it. If we are strong, we press to the issue of battle when we can. If we are weak, we do not accept the issue unless we must. If circumstances are advantageous to us, we are not always able to effect a decision; and if they are disadvantageous, we are not always obliged to fight. Hence we find the apparently simple doctrine of the battle was almost always entangled in two of the most difficult problems that beset our old admirals. The most thorny questions they had to decide were these. In the normal case of strength, it was not how to defeat the enemy, but how to bring him to action; and in casual cases of temporary weakness, it was not how to sell your life dearly, but how to maintain the fleet actively on the defensive so as at once to deny the enemy the decision he sought and to prevent his attaining his ulterior object.

From these considerations it follows that we are able to group all naval operations in some such way as this. Firstly, on the only assumption we can permit ourselves, namely, that we start with a preponderance of force or advantage, we adopt methods for securing command. These methods, again, fall under two heads. Firstly, there are operations for securing a decision by battle, under which head, as has been explained, we shall be chiefly concerned with methods of bringing an unwilling enemy to action, and with the value to that end of the maxim of "Seeking out the enemy's fleet." Secondly, there are the operations which become necessary when no decision is obtainable and our war plan demands the immediate control of communications. Under this head it will be convenient to treat all forms of blockade, whether military or commercial, although, as we shall see, certain forms of military, and even commercial, blockade are primarily concerned with forcing the enemy to a decision.

Our second main group covers operations to which we have to resort when our relative strength is not adequate for either class of operations to secure command. In these conditions we have to content ourselves with endeavouring to hold the command in dispute; that is, we endeavour by active defensive operations to prevent the enemy either securing or exercising control for the objects he has in view. Such are the operations which are connoted by the true conception of "A fleet in being." Under this head also should fall those new forms of minor counter-attack which have entered the field of strategy since the introduction of the mobile torpedo and offensive mining.

In the third main group we have to deal with the methods of exercising control of passage and communication. These operations vary in character according to the several purposes for which the control is desired, and they will be found to take one of three general forms. Firstly, the control of the lines of passage of an invading army; secondly, the control of trade routes and trade terminals for the attack and defence of commerce; and thirdly, the control of passage and communication for our own oversea expeditions, and the control of their objective area for the active support of their operations.

For clearness we may summarise the whole in tabulated analysis, thus:—

1. Methods of securing command :
   (*a*) By obtaining a decision.
   (*b*) By blockade.
2. Methods of disputing command :
   (*a*) Principle of " the fleet in being."
   (*b*) Minor counter-attacks.
3. Methods of exercising command :
   (*a*) Defence against invasion.
   (*b*) Attack and defence of commerce.
   (*c*) Attack, defence, and support of military expeditions.

CHAPTER II

METHODS OF SECURING COMMAND

I

ON OBTAINING A DECISION

WHATEVER the nature of the war in which we are engaged, whether it be limited or unlimited, permanent and general command of the sea is the condition of ultimate success. The only way of securing such a command by naval means is to obtain a decision by battle against the enemy's fleet. Sooner or later it must be done, and the sooner the better. That was the old British creed. It is still our creed, and needs no labouring. No one will dispute it, no one will care even to discuss it, and we pass with confidence to the conclusion that the first business of our fleet is to seek out the enemy's fleet and destroy it.

No maxim can so well embody the British spirit of making war upon the sea, and nothing must be permitted to breathe on that spirit. To examine its claim to be the logical conclusion of our theory of war will even be held dangerous, yet nothing is so dangerous in the study of war as to permit maxims to become a substitute for judgment. Let us examine its credentials, and as a first step put it to the test of the two most modern instances.

Both of them, it must be noted, were instances of Limited War, the most usual form of our own activities, and indeed the only one to which our war organisation, with its essential preponderance of the naval element, has ever been really adapted. The first instance is the Spanish-American War, and the second that between Russia and Japan.

In the former case the Americans took up arms in order to liberate Cuba from Spanish domination— a strictly limited object. There is no evidence that the nature of the war was ever clearly formulated by either side, but in just conformity with the general political conditions the American war plan aimed at opening with a movement to secure the territorial object. At the earliest possible moment they intended to establish themselves in the west of Cuba in support of the Colonial insurgents. Everything depended on the initiative being seized with decision and rapidity. Its moral and physical importance justified the utmost risk, and such was the conformation of the sea which the American army had to pass, that a strictly defensive or covering attitude with their fleet could reduce the risk almost to security. Yet so unwisely dominated were the Americans by recently rediscovered maxims, that when on the eve of executing the vital movement they heard a Spanish squadron was crossing the Atlantic, their own covering force was diverted from its defensive position and sent away to " seek out the enemy's fleet and destroy it."

Puerto Rico was the most obvious point at which to seek it, and thither Admiral Sampson was permitted to go, regardless of the elementary truth that in such cases what is obvious to you is also usually obvious to your enemy. The result was that not only did the Americans fail to get contact, but they also uncovered their own army's line of passage and paralysed the initial movement. In the end it was only pure chance that permitted them to retrieve the mistake they had made. Had the Spanish squadron put into a Cuban port in railway communication with the main Royalist army, such as Cienfuegos or Havana, instead of hurrying into Santiago, the whole campaign must have been lost. "It appears now," wrote Admiral Mahan, in his *Lessons of the War with Spain*, "not only that the eastward voyage of our Havana division was unfortunate, but it should have been seen beforehand to be a mistake, because inconsistent with a well and generally accepted principle of war, the non-observance of which was not commanded by the conditions. The principle is that which condemns eccentric movements. By the disregard of rule in this case we uncovered both Havana and Cienfuegos, which it was our object to close to the enemy's division."

Whether or not we regard Admiral Mahan's exposition of the error as penetrating to the real principle that was violated, the movement was in fact not only eccentric, but unnecessary. Had the Americans been content to keep their fleet concentrated in its true defensive position, not only would they have covered their army's line of passage and their blockade of the territorial objective, but they would have had a far better chance of bringing the Spaniards to action. The Spaniards were bound to come to them or remain outside the theatre of operations where they could in no way affect the issue of the war except adversely to themselves by sapping the spirit of their own Cuban garrison. It is a clear case of the letter killing the spirit, of an attractive maxim being permitted to shut the door upon judgment. Strategical offence in this case was not the best defence. "Seeking out the enemy's fleet" was almost bound to end in a blow in the air, which not only would fail to gain any offensive result, but would sacrifice the main defensive plank in the American war plan upon which their offensive relied for success. To stigmatise such a movement as merely eccentric is to pass very lenient censure.

In the Russo-Japanese War we have a converse case, in which judgment kept the aphorism silent. It is true that during the earlier stage of the naval operations the Japanese did in a sense seek out the enemy's fleet, in so far as they advanced their base close to Port Arthur; but this was done, not with any fixed intention of destroying the Russian fleet—there was small hope of that at sea—but rather because by no other means could they cover the army's lines of passage, which it was the function of the fleet to secure, the true offensive operations being on land. Never except once, under express orders from Tokio, did either Admiral Togo or Admiral Kamimura press offensive movements in such a way as to jeopardise the preventive duty with which the war plan charged them. Still less in the later stage, when everything depended on the destruction of the Baltic fleet, did Admiral Togo " seek it out." He was content, as the Americans should have been content, to have set up such a situation that the enemy must come and break it down if they were to affect the issue of the war. So he waited on the defensive, assured his enemy must come to him, and thereby he rendered it, as certain as war can be, that when the moment for the tactical offensive came his blow should be sure and sudden, in overwhelming strength of concentration, and decisive beyond all precedent.

Clearly, then, the maxim of " seeking out" for all its moral exhilaration, for all its value as an expression of high and sound naval spirit, must not be permitted to displace well-reasoned judgment. Trusty servant as it is, it will make a bad master, as the Americans found to their serious jeopardy. Yet we feel instinctively that it expresses, as no other aphorism does, the secret of British success at sea. We cannot do without it; we cannot do with it in its nakedness. Let us endeavour to clothe it with its real meaning, with the true principles that it connotes. Let us endeavour to determine the stuff that it is made of, and for this purpose there is no better way than to trace its gradual growth from the days when it was born of the crude and virile instinct of the earliest masters.

The germ is to be found in the despatch already mentioned which Drake wrote from Plymouth at the end of March in 1588. His arguments were not purely naval, for it was a combined problem, a problem of defence against invasion, that had to be solved. What he wished to persuade the Government was, that the kernel of the situation was not so much Parma's army of invasion in Flanders, as the fleet that was preparing in Spain to clear its passage. The Government appeared to be acting on the opposite view. Howard with the bulk of the fleet was at the base in the Medway within supporting distance of the light squadron that was blockading the Flemish ports in concert with the Dutch. Drake himself with another light squadron had been sent to the westward with some indeterminate idea of his serving as an observation squadron, or being used in the mediæval fashion for an eccentric counter-stroke. Being invited to give his opinion on this disposition, he pronounced it vicious. In his eyes, what was demanded was an offensive movement against the enemy's main fleet. "If there may be such a stay

or stop made," he urged, "by any means of this fleet
in Spain, so that they may not come through the seas
as conquerors, then shall the Prince of Parma have
such a check thereby as were meet." What he had
in his mind is clearly not so much a decision in the
open as an interruption of the enemy's incomplete
mobilisation, such as he had so brilliantly effected
the previous year. For later on he says that "Next
under God's mighty protection the advantage of time
and place will be the only and chief means for our
good, wherein I most humbly beseech your good
lordships to persevere as you have begun, for with
fifty sail of shipping we shall do more upon their own
coast than a great many more will do here at home;
and the sooner we are gone, the better we shall be
able to impeach them." He does not say "destroy."
"Impeach" meant "to prevent."

Clearly, then, what he had in his mind was a repetition of the previous year's strategy, whereby he had
been able to break up the Spanish mobilisation and
"impeach" the Armada from sailing. He did not even
ask for a concentration of the whole fleet for the purpose,
but only that his own squadron should be reinforced
as was thought convenient. The actual reasons he
gave for his advice were purely moral—that is, he
dwelt on the enheartening effect of striking the first
blow, and attacking instead of waiting to be attacked.
The nation, he urged, "will be persuaded that the
Lord will put into Her Majesty and her people courage
and boldness not to fear invasion, but to seek God's
enemies and Her Majesty's where they may be found."

Here is the germ of the maxim. The consequence
of his despatch was a summons to attend the Council.
The conference was followed, not by the half measure,

which was all he had ventured to advise in his despatch, but by something that embodied a fuller expression of his general idea, and closely resembled what was to be consecrated as our regular disposition in such cases. The whole of the main fleet, except the squadron watching the Flemish coast, was massed to the westward to cover the blockade of Parma's transports, but the position assigned to it was inside the Channel instead of outside, which tactically was bad, for it was almost certain to give the Armada the weather gage. No movement to the coast of Spain was permitted — not necessarily, be it remembered, out of pusillanimity or failure to grasp Drake's idea, but for fear that, as in the recent American case, a forward movement was likely to result in a blow in the air, and to uncover the vital position without bringing the enemy to action.

When, however, the sailing of the Armada was so long delayed Drake's importunity was renewed, with that of Howard and all his colleagues to back it. It brought eventually the desired permission. The fleet sailed for Coruña, where it was known the Armada, after an abortive start from Lisbon, had been driven by bad weather, and something like what the Government feared happened. Before it could reach its destination it met southerly gales, its offensive power was exhausted, and it had to return to Plymouth impotent for immediate action as the Armada finally sailed. When the Spaniards appeared it was still in port refitting and victualling. It was only by an unprecedented feat of seamanship that the situation was saved, and Howard was able to gain the orthodox position to seaward of his enemy.

So far, then, the Government's cautious clinging to

a general defensive attitude, instead of seeking out the enemy's fleet, was justified, but it must be remembered that Drake from the first had insisted it was a question of time as well as place.   If he had been permitted to make the movement when he first proposed it, there is good reason to believe that the final stages of the Spanish mobilisation could not have been carried out that year; that is to say, the various divisions of the Armada could not have been assembled into a fleet. But information as to its condition was at the time very uncertain, and in view of the negotiations that were on foot, there were, moreover, high political reasons for our not taking too drastic an offensive if a reasonable alternative existed.

The principles, then, which we distil from this, the original case of "seeking out," are, firstly, the moral value of seizing the initiative, and, secondly, the importance of striking before the enemy's mobilisation is complete.   The idea of overthrow by a great fleet action is not present, unless we find it in a not clearly formulated idea of the Elizabethan admirals of striking a fleet when it is demoralised, as the Armada was by its first rebuff, or immediately on its leaving port before it had settled down.

In our next naval struggle with the Dutch in the latter half of the seventeenth century the principle of overthrow, as we have seen, became fully developed. It was the keynote of the strategy which was evolved, and the conditions which forced it to recognition also emphasised the principles of seeking out and destroying.   It was a case of a purely naval struggle, in which there were no military considerations to deflect naval strategy.   It was, moreover, a question of narrow seas, and the risk of missing contact which had cramped the Elizabethans in their oceanic theatre was a negligible factor. Yet fresh objections to using the "seeking out" maxim as a strategical panacea soon declared themselves.

The first war opened without any trace of the new principle. The first campaign was concerned in the old fashion entirely with the attack and defence of trade, and such indecisive actions as occurred were merely incidental to the process. No one appears to have realised the fallacy of such method except, perhaps, Tromp. The general instructions he received were that "the first and principal object was to do all possible harm to the English," and to that end "he was given a fleet in order to sail to the damage and offence of the English fleet, and also to give convoy to the west." Seeing at once the incompatibility of the two functions, he asked for more definite instructions. What, for instance, was he to do if he found a chance of blockading the main English fleet at its base? Was he to devote himself to the blockade and "leave the whole fleet of merchantmen to be a prey to a squadron of fast-sailing frigates," or was he to continue his escort duty? Full as he was of desire to deal with the enemy's main fleet, he was perplexed with the practical difficulty—too often forgotten—that the mere domination of the enemy's battle strength does not solve the problem of control of the sea. No fresh instructions were forthcoming to clear his perplexity, and he could only protest again. " I could wish," he wrote, " to be so fortunate as to have only one of these two duties—to seek out the enemy, or to give convoy, for to do both is attended with great difficulties."

The indecisive campaign which naturally resulted from this lack of strategical grip and concentration of

effort came to an end with Tromp's partial defeat of
Blake off Dungeness on 30th November 1652. Though
charged in spite of his protests with a vast convoy, the
Dutch admiral had sent it back to Ostend when he
found Blake was in the Downs, and then, free from all
preoccupation, he had gone to seek out his enemy.

It was the effect which this unexpected blow had
upon the strong military insight of the Cromwellian
Government that led to those famous reforms which
made this winter so memorable a landmark in British
naval history. Monk, the most finished professional
soldier in the English service, and Deane, another
general, were joined in the command with Blake, and
with their coming was breathed into the sea service
the high military spirit of the New Model Army. To
that winter we owe not only the Articles of War, which
made discipline possible, and the first attempt to
formulate Fighting Instructions, in which a regular
tactical system was conceived, but also two other
conceptions that go to make up the modern idea of
naval warfare. One was the conviction that war upon
the sea meant operations against the enemy's armed
fleets in order to destroy his power of naval resistance
as distinguished from operations by way of reprisal
against his trade; and the other, that such warfare
required for its effective use a fleet of State-owned ships
specialised for war, with as little assistance as possible
from private-owned ships. It was not unnatural that
all four ideas should have taken shape together, so
closely are they related. The end connotes the means.
Discipline, fleet tactics, and a navy of warships were
indispensable for making war in the modern sense of
the term.

The results were seen in the three great actions of

the following spring, the first under the three Generals, and the other two under Monk alone. In the last, he carried the new ideas so far as to forbid taking possession of disabled vessels, that nothing might check the work of destruction. All were to be sunk with as much tenderness for human life as destruction would permit. In like manner the second war was characterised by three great naval actions, one of which, after Monk had resumed command, lasted no less than four days. The new doctrine was indeed carried to ex-aggeration. So entirely was naval thought centred on the action of the battle-fleets, that no provision was made for an adequate exercise of control. In our own case at least, massing for offensive action was pressed so far that no thought was given to sustaining it by reliefs. Consequently our offensive power suffered periods of exhaustion when the fleet had to return to its base, and the Dutch were left sufficient freedom not only to secure their own trade, but to strike severely at ours. Their counterstrokes culminated in the famous attack upon Sheerness and Chatham. That such an opportunity was allowed them can be traced directly to an exaggeration of the new doctrine. In the belief of the British Government the " St. James's Fight" —the last of the three actions — had settled the question of command. Negotiations for peace were opened, and they were content to reap the fruit of the great battles in preying on Dutch trade. Having done its work, as was believed, the bulk of the battle-fleet for financial reasons was laid up, and the Dutch seized the opportunity to demonstrate the limitations of the abused doctrine. The lesson is one we have never forgotten, but its value is half lost if we attribute the disaster to lack of grasp of the battle-fleet doctrine rather than to an exaggeration of its possibilities.

The truth is, that we had not obtained a victory sufficiently decisive to destroy the enemy's fleet. The most valuable lesson of the war was that such victories required working for, and particularly in cases where the belligerents face each other from either side of a narrow sea. In such conditions it was proved that owing to the facility of retreat and the restricted possibilities of pursuit a complete decision is not to be looked for without very special strategical preparation. The new doctrine in fact gave that new direction to strategy which has been already referred to. It was no longer a question of whether to make the enemy's trade or his fleet the primary objective, but of how to get contact with his fleet in such a way as to lead to decisive action. Merely to seek him out on his own coasts was to ensure that no decisive action would take place. Measures had to be taken to force him to sea away from his own bases. The favourite device was to substitute organised strategical operations against his trade in place of the old sporadic attacks ; that is, the fleet took a position calculated to stop his trade altogether, not on his own coasts, but far to sea in the main fairway. The operations failed for lack of provision for enabling the fleet by systematic relief to retain its position, but nevertheless it was the germ of the system which after-wards, under riper organisation, was to prove so effective, and to produce such actions as the " Glorious First of June."

In the third war, after this device had failed again and again, a new one was tried. It was Charles the Second's own conception. His idea was to use the threat of a military expedition. Some 15,000 men in transports were brought to Yarmouth in the hope that the Dutch would come out to bar their passage across the open North Sea, and would thus permit our fleet to cut in behind them. There was, however, no proper co-ordination of the two forces, and the project failed.

This method of securing a decision was not lost sight of; Anson tried to use it in the Seven Years' War. For two years every attempt to seek out the enemy's fleet had led to nothing but the exhaustion of our own. But when Pitt began his raids on the French coast, Anson, who had little faith in their value for military purposes, thought he saw in them definite naval possibilities. Accordingly when, in 1758, he was placed in command of the Channel Fleet to cover the expedition against St. Malo, he raised the blockade of Brest, and took up a position near the Isle of Batz between the enemy's main fleet and the army's line of passage. The Brest fleet, however, was in no condition to move, and again there was no result. It was not till 1805 that there was any clear case of the device succeeding, and then it was not used deliberately. It was a joint Anglo-Russian expedition in the Mediterranean that forced from Napoleon his reckless order for Villeneuve to put to sea from Cadiz, and so solved the problem out of which Nelson had seen no issue. Lissa may be taken as an analogous case. But there the Italians, treating the territorial attack as a real attack instead of as a strategical device, suffered themselves to be surprised by the Austrian fleet and defeated.

This instance serves well to introduce the important fact, that although our own military expeditions have seldom succeeded in leading to a naval decision, the converse was almost always true. The attempt of the

enemy to use his army against our territory has been
the most fertile source of our great naval victories.
The knowledge that our enemy intends to invade these
shores, or to make some serious expedition against our
oversea dominions or interests, should always be wel-
comed. Unless History belie herself, we know that such
attempts are the surest means of securing what we want.
We have the memories of La Hogue, Quiberon, and the
Nile to assure us that sooner or later they must lead to
a naval decision, and the chance of a real decision is all
we can ask of the Fortune of War.

Enough has now been said to show that " seeking
out the enemy's fleet " is not in itself sufficient to secure
such a decision. What the maxim really means is that
we should endeavour from the first to secure contact in
the best position for bringing about a complete decision
in our favour, and as soon as the other parts of our war
plan, military or political, will permit. If the main
offensive is military, as it was in the Japanese and
American cases, then if possible the effort to secure
such control must be subordinated to the movement of
the army, otherwise we give the defensive precedence
of the offensive. If, however, the military offensive
cannot be ensured until the naval defensive is perfected,
as will be the case if the enemy brings a fleet up to our
army's line of passage, then our first move must be to
secure naval contact.

The vice of the opposite method of procedure is
obvious. If we assume the maxim that the first duty
of our fleet is to seek out the enemy wherever he may
be, it means in its nakedness that we merely conform to
the enemy's dispositions and movements. It is open to
him to lead us wherever he likes. It was one of the fallacies that underlay all Napoleon's naval combinations,

that he believed that our hard-bitten admirals would
behave in this guileless manner. But nothing was
further from their cunning. There is a typical order of
Cornwallis's which serves well to mark their attitude.
It was one he gave to Admiral Cotton, his second in
command, in July 1804 on handing over to his charge
the Western Squadron off Ushant : " If the French put
to sea," he says, " without any of your vessels seeing
them, do not follow them, unless you are absolutely
sure of the course they have taken. If you leave the
entrance of the Channel without protection, the enemy
might profit by it, and assist the invasion which threatens
His Majesty's dominions, the protection of which is
your principal object."

It is indeed a common belief that Nelson never
permitted himself but a single purpose, the pursuit
of the enemy's fleet, and that, ignoring the caution
which Cornwallis impressed upon Cotton, he fell into
the simple trap. But it has to be noted that he never
suffered himself to be led in pursuit of a fleet away
from the position he had been charged to maintain,
unless and until he had made that position secure
behind him. His famous chase to the West Indies is
the case which has led to most misconception on the
point from an insufficient regard to the surrounding
circumstances. Nelson did not pursue Villeneuve with
the sole, or even the primary, object of bringing him to
action. His dominant object was to save Jamaica from
capture. If it had only been a question of getting
contact, he would certainly have felt in a surer position
by waiting for Villeneuve's return off St. Vincent or
closing in to the strategical centre off Ushant. Further,
it must be observed that Nelson by his pursuit did
not uncover what it was his duty to defend. The

Mediterranean position was rendered quite secure before he ventured on his eccentric movement. Finally, we have the important fact that though the moral effect of Nelson's implacable persistence and rapidity was of priceless value, it is impossible to show that as a mere strategical movement it had any influence on the course of the campaign. His appearance in the West Indies may have saved one or two small islands from ransom and a good deal of trade from capture. It may also have hastened Villeneuve's return by a few days, but that was not to our advantage. Had he returned even a week later there would have been no need to raise the Rochefort blockade. Barham would have had enough ships at his command to preserve the whole of his blockades, as he had intended to do till the *Curieux's* news of Villeneuve's precipitate return forced his hand before he was ready.

If we desire a typical example of the way the old masters used the doctrine of seeking out, it is to be found, not in Nelson's magnificent chase, but in the restrained boldness of Barham's orders to Cornwallis and Calder. Their instructions for seeking out Villeneuve were to move out on his two possible lines of approach for such a time and such a distance as would make decisive action almost certain, and at the same time, if contact were missed, would ensure the preservation of the vital defensive positions. Barham was far too astute to play into Napoleon's hands, and by blindly following his enemy's lead to be jockeyed into sacrificing the position which his enemy wished to secure. If our maxim be suffered to usurp the place of instructed judgment, the almost inevitable result will be that it will lead us into just the kind of mistake which Barham avoided.

II

BLOCKADE

Under the term blockade we include operations which vary widely in character and in strategical intention. In the first place, blockade may be either naval or commercial. By naval blockade we seek either to prevent an enemy's armed force leaving port, or to make certain it shall be brought to action before it can carry out the ulterior purpose for which it puts to sea. That armed force may be purely naval, or it may consist wholly or in part of a military expedition. If it be purely naval, then our blockade is a method of securing command. If it be purely military, it is a method of exercising command, and as such will be dealt with when we come to consider defence against invasion. But in so far as military expeditions are normally accompanied by a naval escort, operations to prevent their sailing are not purely concerned with the exercise of command. Naval blockade, therefore, may be regarded for practical purposes as a method of securing command and as a function of battle-squadrons. Commercial blockade, on the other hand, is essentially a method of exercising command, and is mainly an affair of cruisers. Its immediate object is to stop the flow of the enemy's sea-borne trade, whether carried in his own or neutral bottoms, by denying him the use of trade communications.

From the point of view of the conduct of war, therefore, we have two well-defined categories of blockade, naval and commercial. But our classification must go further; for naval blockade itself is equally varied in intention, and must be subdivided. Strictly speaking, the term implies a desire to close the blockaded

port and to prevent the enemy putting to sea.
But this was not always the intention. As often as
not our wish was that he should put to sea that we
might bring him to action, and in order to do this,
before he could effect his purpose, we had to watch the
port with a fleet more or less closely. For this operation there was no special name. Widely as it differed
in object from the other, it was also usually called
blockade, and Nelson's protest against the consequent
confusion of thought is well known. "It is not my
intention," he said, "to close-watch Toulon"; and
again, "My system is the very contrary of blockading.
Every opportunity has been offered the enemy to put
to sea." It is desirable, therefore, to adopt terms to
distinguish the two forms. "Close" and "open"
express the antithesis suggested by Nelson's letter,
and the two terms serve well enough to mark the
characteristic feature of each operation. Close blockade, it is true, as formerly conceived, is generally
regarded as no longer practicable; but the antithetical
ideas, which the two forms of blockade connote, can
never be eliminated from strategical consideration. It
must always be with the relations of these two forms,
whatever shape they may take in future, that the strategy
of naval blockade is chiefly concerned.

   With regard to commercial blockade, in strict
analysis it should be eliminated from an inquiry that
concerns methods of securing command and postponed to that section of exercising command which
deals with the attack and defence of trade. It is,
however, necessary to treat certain of its aspects in
conjunction with naval blockade for two reasons:
one, that as a rule naval blockade is indissolubly
united to a subordinate commercial blockade; and

the other, that the commercial form, though its immediate object is the exercise of control, has almost invariably an ulterior object which is concerned with securing control; that is to say, while its immediate object was to keep the enemy's commercial ports closed, its ulterior object was to force his fleet to sea.

Commercial blockade, therefore, has an intimate relation with naval blockade in its open form. We adopt that form when we wish his fleet to put to sea, and commercial blockade is usually the most effective means we have of forcing upon him the movement we leave him free to attempt. By closing his commercial ports we exercise the highest power of injuring him which the command of the sea can give us. We choke the flow of his national activity afloat in the same way that military occupation of his territory chokes it ashore. He must, therefore, either tamely submit to the worst which a naval defeat can inflict upon him, or he must fight to release himself. He may see fit to choose the one course or the other, but in any case we can do no more by naval means alone to force our will upon him.

In the long run a rigorous and uninterrupted blockade is almost sure to exhaust him before it exhausts us, but the end will be far and costly. As a rule, therefore, we have found that where we had a substantial predominance our enemy preferred to submit to commercial blockade in hope that by the chances of war or the development of fresh force he might later on be in a better position to come out into the open. That he should come out and stake the issue in battle was nearly always our wish, and it was obvious that too rigorous a naval blockade was not the way to achieve the desired end, or to reap the strategical result which we might expect from paralysing his commerce. Consequently where the desire for a decision at sea was not crossed by higher military considerations, as in the case of imminent invasion, or where we ourselves had an important expedition in hand, it was to our interest to incline the enemy's mind towards the bolder choice.

The means was to tempt him with a prospect of success, either by leading him to believe the blockading force was smaller than it was, or by removing it to such a distance as would induce him to attempt to evade it, or both. A leading case of such an open blockade was Nelson's disposition of his fleet off Cadiz when he was seeking to bring Villeneuve to action in 1805. But merely to leave a port open does not fulfil the idea of open blockade, and in this case to opportunity and temptation Nelson added the pressure of a commercial blockade of the adjacent ports in hope of starving Villeneuve into the necessity of taking to the sea.

Finally, in a general comparison of the two forms, we have to observe that close blockade is characteristically a method of securing local and temporary command. Its dominating purpose will usually be to prevent the enemy's fleet acting in a certain area and for a certain purpose. Whereas open blockade, in that it aims at the destruction of an enemy's naval force, is a definite step towards securing permanent command.

Enough has now been said to show that the question of choice between close and open blockade is one of extreme complexity. Our naval literature, it is true, presents the old masters as divided into two schools on the subject, implying that one was in favour of the close form always, and the other of the open form. We are even led to believe that the choice depended on the military spirit of the officer concerned. If his military spirit was high, he chose the close and more exacting form; if it were low, he was content with the open and less exacting form. True, we are told that men of the latter school based their objections to close blockade on the excessive wear and tear of a fleet that it involved, but it is too often suggested that this attitude was no more than a mask for a defective spirit. Seldom if ever are we invited to compare their decisions with the attendant strategical intention, with the risks which the conditions justified, or with the expenditure of energy which the desired result could legitimately demand. Yet all these considerations must enter into the choice, and on closer examination of the leading cases it will be found that they bear a striking and almost constant relation to the nature of the blockade employed.

In considering open blockade, three postulates must be kept in mind. Firstly, since our object is to get the enemy to sea, our position must be such as will give him an opportunity of doing so. Secondly, since we desire contact for a decisive battle, that position must be no further away from his port than is compatible with bringing him to action before he can effect his purpose. Thirdly, there is the idea of economy—that is, the idea of adopting the method which is least exhausting to our fleet, and which will best preserve its battle fitness. It is on the last point that the greatest difference of opinion has existed. A close blockade alway tended to exhaust a fleet, and always must do so. But, on the other hand, it was contended that the

exhaustion is compensated by the high temper and
moral domination which the maintenance of a close
blockade produces in a good fleet, whereas the comparative ease of distant and secure watch tended to
deterioration.   Before considering these opposed views,
one warning is necessary.   It is usually assumed that
the alternative to close blockade is watching the enemy
from one of our own ports, but this is not essential.
What is required is an interior and, if possible, a secret
position which will render contact certain; and with
modern developments in the means of distant communication, such a position is usually better found at
sea than in port.   A watching position can in fact be
obtained free from the strain of dangerous navigation
and incessant liability to attack without sacrifice of
sea training.   With this very practical point in mind,
we may proceed to test the merits of the two forms on
abstract principles.

It was always obvious that a close naval blockade
was one of the weakest and least desirable forms of
war.   Here again when we say "weakest" we do not
mean "least effective," but that it was exhausting, and
that it tended to occupy a force greater than that
against which it was acting.   This was not because a
blockading fleet, tempered and toughened by its watch,
and with great advantage of tactical position, could not
be counted on to engage successfully a raw fleet of
equal force issuing from port, but because in order to
maintain its active efficiency it required large reserves
for its relief.   So severe was the wear and tear both to
men and ships, that even the most strenuous exponents
of the system considered that at least a fifth of the force
should always be refitting, and in every case two
admirals were employed to relieve one another.   In

1794 one of the highest authorities in the service considered that to maintain an effective close blockade of Brest two complete sets of flag-officers were necessary, and that no less than one-fourth of the squadron should always be in port.[1]

Now these weaknesses, being inherent in close blockade, necessarily affected the appreciation of its value. The weight of the objection tended of course to decrease as seamanship, material, or organisation improved, but it was always a factor. It is true also that it seems to have had more weight with some men than with others, but it will appear equally true, if we endeavour to trace the movement of opinion on the subject, that it was far from being the sole determinant.

It was in the Seven Years' War under Anson's administration that continuous and close blockade was first used systematically, but it was Hawke who originated it. In the first three campaigns the old system of watching Brest from a British western port had been in vogue, but it had twice failed to prevent a French concentration in the vital Canadian theatre. In the spring of 1759 Hawke was in command of the Channel Fleet with the usual instructions for watching, but being directed to stand over and look into Brest, he intimated his intention, unless he received orders to the contrary, to remain off the port instead of returning to Torbay. His reason was that he had found there a squadron which he believed was intended for the West Indies, and he considered it better to prevent its sailing than to let it put to sea and try to catch it. In other

---

[1] Captain Philip Patton to Sir Charles Middleton, June 2, 1794. *Barham Papers*, ii. 393. Patton had probably wider war experience than any officer then living. He was regarded as possessing a very special knowledge of personnel, and as Vice-Admiral became Second Sea Lord under Barham in 1804.

words, he argued that none of the usual western watching ports afforded a position interior to the usual French route from Brest to the West Indies.

Since rumours of invasion were in the air, it was obviously the better course to deal with the enemy's squadrons in home waters and avoid dispersal of the fleet in seeking them out. In spite of extraordinarily bad weather, therefore, he was permitted to act as he advised. With Boscawen as relief, the new form of blockade was kept up thenceforward, and with entire success. But it must be noted that this success was rather due to the fact that the French made no further effort to cross the Atlantic, than to the fact that the blockade was maintained with sufficient strictness to prevent their doing so. In certain states of weather our fleet was forced to raise the blockade and run to Torbay or Plymouth. Such temporary reversions to the open form nearly always afforded an opportunity for the French to get away to the southward with two or three days' start. Against any attempt, however, to get to the east or the north in order to dispute command of the Channel or other home waters the system was thoroughly efficient, and was unaffected by the intervals of the open form.

It may have been these considerations which in the War of American Independence induced so fine an officer as Howe to be strongly in favour of a reversion to the old system. The vital theatre was then again across the Atlantic, and there was no serious preparation for invasion. It should also be borne in mind in judging Howe against Hawke, that in the Seven Years' War we had such a preponderance at sea as permitted ample reserves to nourish a close blockade, whereas in the latter war we were numerically inferior to the hostile coalition. Since it was impossible to prevent the French reaching the West Indies and North America if they so determined, our policy was to follow them with equal fleets and reduce the home force as low as that policy demanded and as was consistent with a reasonable degree of safety. The force required might well be inferior to the enemy, since it was certain that all attempts upon the Channel would be made with an unwieldy and ill-knit force composed of Spanish and French units.

In Howe's opinion this particular situation was not to be solved by attempting to close Brest, and nothing can be more misleading than to stretch such an opinion beyond the circumstances it was intended to meet. He did not consider it was in his power to close the port. The enemy, he held, could always be in readiness to escape after a gale of wind by which the blockading squadron would be drawn off or dispersed, the ships much damaged, and the enemy enheartened. " An enemy," he said, " is not to be restrained from putting to sea by a station taken off their port with a barely superior squadron." The experience of 1805 appears to contradict him. Then a barely superior squadron did succeed in preventing Ganteaume's exit, but though the squadron actually employed was barely superior, it had ample fleet reserves to sustain its numbers in efficiency. It was, moreover, only for a short time that it had to deal with any real effort to escape. After May 20th, Ganteaume was forbidden to put to sea. There were certainly several occasions during that famous blockade when he could have escaped to the southward had Napoleon wished it.

This case, then, cannot be taken to condemn Howe's judgment. His special function in the war plan was, with a force reduced to defensive strength, to prevent the enemy obtaining command of our home waters. It was certainly not his duty to undertake operations to which his force was not equal. His first duty was to keep it in being for its paramount purpose. To this end he decided on open blockade based on a general reserve at Spithead or St. Helen's, where he could husband the ships and train his recruits, while at the same time he protected our trade and communications and harassed those of the enemy. Kempenfelt, than whom there was no warmer advocate of activity, entirely approved the policy at least for the winter months, and in his case no one will be found to suggest that the idea was prompted by lack of spirit or love of ease. So far as the summer was concerned there was really little difference of opinion as to whether the fleet should be kept at sea or not, for sea-training during summer more than compensated for the exhaustion of material likely to be caused by intermittent spells of bad weather. Even for the winter the two policies came to much the same thing. Thus in Hawke's blockade at the end of 1759, during the critical month from mid-October to mid-November, he was unable to keep his station for nearly half the time, and when he did get contact with Conflans it was from Torbay and not Ushant. Still it may be doubted if without the confidence bred of his stormy vigil the battle of Quiberon would have been fought as it was.

With all this experience fresh in his mind Kempenfelt frankly advocated keeping the fleet in port for the winter. "Suppose," he wrote from Torbay in November 1779, "the enemy should put to sea with their fleet (that is, from Brest)—a thing much to be wished for by us—let us act wisely and keep ours in port,

Leave them to the mercy of long nights and hard
gales. They will do more in favour of you than your
fleet can." Far better he thought to devote the winter
to preparing the fleet for the next campaign so as to
have "the advantage of being the first in the field."
"Let us," he concluded, "keep a stout squadron to
the westward ready to attend the motions of the
enemy. I don't mean to keep them at sea, disabling
themselves in buffeting the winds, but at Torbay ready
to act as intelligence may suggest."[1] It will be seen,
therefore, that the conclusion that close blockade was
always the best means of rendering the fleet most
efficient for the function it had to perform must not
be accepted too hastily. The reasons which induced
Howe and Kempenfelt to prefer open blockade were
mainly based on this very consideration. Having in
mind the whole of the surrounding conditions, in their
highly experienced opinion careful preparation in the
winter and tactical evolutions in the summer were the
surest road to battle fitness in the force available.

On the other hand, we have the fact that during
the War of American Independence the open system
was not very successful. But before condemning it
out of hand, it must be remembered that the causes
of failure were not all inherent in the system. In the
first place, the need of relieving Gibraltar from time to
time prevented the Western Squadron devoting itself
entirely to its watch. In the next place, owing to
defective administration the winters were not devoted
with sufficient energy to preparing the fleet to be first
in the field in the spring. Finally, we have to recognise that the lack of success was due not so much to
permitting the French to cross the Atlantic, as to the

[1] *Barham Papers*, i. 302.

failure to deal faithfully with them when contact was obtained at their destination. Obviously there is nothing to be said for the policy of " seeking out " as against that of preventing exit unless you are determined when you find to destroy or to be destroyed. It was here that Rodney and his fellows were found wanting. The system failed from defective execution quite as much as from defective design.

In the next war Howe was still in the ascendant and in command of the Channel fleet. He retained his system. Leaving Brest open he forced the French by operating against their trade to put to sea, and he was rewarded with the battle of the First of June. No attempt was made to maintain a close blockade during the following winter. The French were allowed to sail, and their disastrous cruise of January 1795 fully justified Kempenfelt's anticipations. So great was the damage done that they abandoned all idea of using their fleet as a whole. Howe's system was continued, but no longer with entirely successful results. In 1796 the French were able to make descents upon Ireland, and Howe in consequence has come in for the severest castigations. His method is contemptuously contrasted with that which St. Vincent adopted four years later, without any regard to the situation each admiral had to meet, and again on the assumption that the closing of Brest would have solved the one problem as well as it did the other.

In 1796 we were not on the defensive as we were in 1800. The French fleet had been practically destroyed. No invasion threatened. With a view to forcing peace our policy was directed to offensive action against French trade and territory in order by general pressure to back our overtures for a settlement.

The policy may have been mistaken, but that is not the question. The question is, whether or not the strategy fitted the policy. We were also, it must be remembered, at war with Holland and expecting war with Spain, an eventuality which forced us to keep an eye on the defence of Portugal. In these circumstances nothing was further from our desire than to keep what was left of the Brest fleet in port. Our hope was by our offensive action against French maritime interests to force it to expose itself for their defence. To devote the fleet to the closing of Brest was to cripple it for offensive action and to play the enemy's game. The actual disposition of the home fleet was designed so as to preserve its offensive activity, and at the same time to ensure superiority in any part of the home waters in which the enemy might attempt a counterstroke. It was distributed in three active squadrons, one in the North Sea, one before Brest, and one cruising to the westward, with a strong reserve at Portsmouth. It is the location of the reserve that has been most lightly ridiculed, on the hasty assumption that it was merely the reserve of the squadron before Brest; whereas in truth it was a general reserve designed to act in the North Sea or wherever else it might be needed. At the same time it served as a training and depot squadron for increasing our power at sea in view of the probable addition of the Spanish fleet to Napoleon's naval force. To have exhausted our fleet merely to prevent raids leaving Brest which might equally well leave the Texel or Dunkirk was just what the enemy would have desired. The disposition was in fact a good example of concentration— that is, disposal about a strategical centre to preserve flexibility for offence without risking defensive needs,

and yet it is by the most ardent advocates of concentration and the offensive that Howe's dispositions
at this time have been most roundly condemned.

In the end the disposition did fail to prevent the
landing of part of the force intended for Ireland, but
it made the venture so difficult that it had to be
deferred till mid-winter, and then the weather which
rendered evasion possible broke up the expedition and
denied it all chance of serious success. It was, in
fact, another example of the working of Kempenfelt's
rule concerning winter weather. So far as naval defence can go, the disposition was all that was required.
The Irish expedition was seen leaving Brest by our
inshore cruiser squadron. It was reported to Colpoys,
who had the battle-squadron outside, and it was only
a dense fog that enabled it to escape. It was, in fact,
nothing more than the evasion of a small raiding force
—an eventuality against which no naval defence can
provide certain guarantee, especially in winter.

It was under wholly different conditions that at the
end of 1800 Hawke's system was revived. St. Vincent's
succession to the control of the fleet coincided with
Napoleon's definite assumption of the control of the
destinies of France. Our great duel with him had
begun. The measures he was taking made it obvious
we were once more facing the old life and death struggle
for naval supremacy; we were openly threatened with
invasion, and we had a distinct preponderance at sea.
In short, we have to recognise the fact that the methods
of the Seven Years' War were revived when the problems
and factors of that war were renewed. As those
problems grew more intense, as they did after the
Peace of Amiens, and the threat of invasion became
really formidable, so did the rigour of the close blockade

increase. Under Cornwallis and Gardner it was maintained in such a way as to deny, so far as human effort could go, all possibility of exit without fighting. In spite of the importance of dealing with the enemy's squadrons in detail no risks were taken to bring Ganteaume to decisive action. Our first necessity was absolute local command. The acuteness of the invasion crisis demanded that the Brest fleet should be kept in port, and every time Ganteaume showed a foot the British admiral flew at him and drove him back. Once only during the continuation of the crisis was the rigour of this attitude relaxed, and that was to deal with what for the moment was the higher object. It was to meet Villeneuve on his return from the West Indies, but even then so nicely was the relaxation calculated, that Ganteaume was given no time to take advantage of it.

The analogy between the conditions of the blockade which St. Vincent inaugurated and those of the Seven Years' War becomes all the more significant when we note that while Cornwallis and Gardner in home waters were pressing close blockade to its utmost limit of rigour, Nelson in the Mediterranean was not using it at all. Yet with him also the chief concern was to prevent an invasion. His main function, as he and his Government saw it, was to prevent a descent from Southern France upon Neapolitan or Levantine territory. Why, then, did he not employ close blockade? It is usually assumed that it was because of his overpowering desire to bring the Toulon squadron to action. Occasional expressions in his letters give colour to such a view, but his dispositions show clearly that his desire to bring the fleet to action was kept in scientific subordination to the defensive

duty with which he was charged. Close blockade was
the most effectual means of securing this end, but in
his case one of the conditions, which we have found
always accompanying successful close blockade, was
absent. He had no such preponderance of force as
would enable him to nourish it up to the point of
perfect continuity. In the circumstances the close
form was too weak or exhausting for him to use with
the force at his disposal.

If this case be not considered conclusive as to
Nelson's views, we have a perfectly clear endorsement
from his pen in 1801. It is a particularly strong
testimony, for he was at the time actually charged with
defence against the invasion of England. With several
cruiser squadrons he had to prevent the enemy's force
issuing from a number of ports extending from Flush-
ing to Dieppe, and he was directing the operations from
the Downs. On the approach of winter he was impressed with the inexpediency of attempting to continue
a close blockade, and wrote to the Admiralty as follows :
"I am of opinion, and submit to their Lordships'
better judgment, that care should be taken to keep our
squadrons compact and in good order . . . under
Dungeness to be their principal station. . . . In fine
weather our squadrons to go out and show themselves,
but never to risk either being crippled or drawn into
the North Sea; thus we shall always be sure of an
effective force, ready to act as occasion calls for it." [1]

The case of course is not entirely in point, for it
concerns the question of direct resistance to invasion
and not to securing general command. Its value is
that it gives Nelson's views on the broad question of
balancing the risks—that is, the risk of relaxing close

[1] To Evan Nepean, Sept. 4, 1801. Nicolas, *Nelson Despatches*, iv. 484.

watch against the risk of destroying the efficiency of the ships by maintaining it too rigorously.

With Nelson holding this view, it is not surprising to find that as late as 1804 naval opinion was not quite settled on the relative advantages of close and open blockade even in the case of threatened invasion. Just a year before Trafalgar was fought, Cornwallis pressed the Admiralty for more strength to enable him to keep his blockade efficient. Lord Melville, who at this time had Barham at his elbow, replied recommending the " policy of relaxing the strictness of blockade, formerly resorted to." He protested the means available were insufficient for "sustaining the necessary extent of naval force, if your ships are to be torn to pieces by an eternal conflict with the elements during the tempestuous months of winter." [1] Melville was craving for a decisive action to end the insupportable strain. "Allow me to remind you," he added, " that the occasions when we have been able to bring our enemy to battle and our fleets to victory have generally been when we were at a distance from the blockading station." In the end, as we know, Cornwallis had his way, and the verdict of history has been to approve the decision for its moral effect alone. Such conflicts must always arise. "War," as Wolfe said, "is an option of difficulties," and the choice must sway to the one side or the other as the circumstances tend to develop the respective advantages of each form. We can never say that close blockade is better than open, or the reverse. It must always be a matter of judgment.

Are there, then, no principles which we can deduce from the old practice for the strengthening of judgment? Certain broad lines of guidance at least are to

---

[1] For Barham's final views, 1805, see *Barham Papers*, iii. 90–3.

be traced. The main question will be, is it to our advantage, in regard to all the strategical conditions, to keep the enemy in and get him to sea for a decision? Presumably it will always be our policy to get a decision as soon as possible. Still that desire may be over-ridden by the necessity or special advantage of closely blockading one or more of his squadrons. This situa-tion may arise in two ways. Firstly, it may be essential to provide for the local and temporary command of a certain theatre of operations, as when an invasion threatens in that area, or when we wish to pass a military expedition across it, or from special exigencies in regard to the attack or defence of commerce. Secondly, even where we are seeking a great decision, we may blockade one squadron closely in order to induce a decision at the point most advantageous to ourselves; that is to say, we may blockade one or more squadrons in order to induce the enemy to attempt with one or more other squadrons to break that blockade. In this way we may lead him either to expose himself to be struck in detail, or to concentrate where we desire his concentration.

For any of these reasons we may decide that the best way of realising our object is to use close block-ade, but the matter does not end there. We have still to consider whether close blockade is within the limit of the force we have available, and whether it is the best method of developing the fullest potentialities of that force. Close blockade being the more exhausting form will require the greater strength; we cannot blockade closely for any length of time without a force relatively superior; but if by open blockade of a squadron we permit it to put to sea with contact assured, we know that, even with a slightly inferior force, we can so deal with it as to prevent its getting local control sufficient to break down our mobile flotilla defence or to interfere seriously with our trade.

Finally, there is the question of risk. In the old days, before free movement and wireless telegraphy, and before the flotilla had acquired battle power, there was always to be faced the risk of not getting contact in time to prevent mischief. This consideration was specially dominant where the enemy had a squadron within or near the critical theatre of operations. Therefore when invasion threatened, our developed policy was to blockade Brest closely at almost any sacrifice. There was always a vague possibility that by evasion or chance of wind a squadron so close to the line of invasion might get sufficient temporary command in the vital area before it could be brought to action. It was a possibility that was never realised in the Narrow Seas, and since mobility of fleets and means of distant communication have so greatly increased in range and certainty, and since the power of resistance in the flotilla has become so high, the risk is probably much less than ever, and the field for open blockade is consequently less restricted.

There is no need, however, to accept these principles as incontrovertible. Even if we take the great blockade of 1803-5, which has most firmly dominated thought on the subject ever since, it may be argued with some plausibility that the situation could have been solved more quickly and effectually by letting Ganteaume get out from Brest into the open, at least as far as Admiral Togo was forced to permit the Russians to emerge from Port Arthur, though his reasons for keeping them in were even stronger than ours in 1805. But in any case, the whole trend of the evidence will admit no doubt as to the inherent weakness of close blockade as a form of war. As under modern developments the possibilities of open blockade have increased, so the difficulties and dangers of close blockade have certainly not decreased. It is also probable that certain advantages which in the sailing era went far to compensate for its weakness have lost much of their force. A sailing fleet cooped up in port not only rapidly lost its spirit, but, being barred from sea-training, could not be kept in a condition of efficiency, whereas the blockading fleet was quickly raised to the highest temper by the stress of vigilance and danger that was its incessant portion. So long as the strain did not pass the limit of human endurance, it was all to the good. In the old days, with very moderate reliefs, the limit was never reached, and the sacrifices that were made to those exhausting vigils were rewarded twentyfold in exuberant confidence on the day of battle. Can we expect the same compensation now? Will the balance of strength and weakness remain as it used to be? In the face of the vast change of conditions and the thinness of experience, it is to general principles we must turn for the answer.

What, in fact, is the inherent weakness of close blockade? Strategical theory will at once reply that it is an operation which involves " an arrest of the offensive," a situation which is usually taken to exhibit every kind of drawback. Close blockade is essentially an offensive operation, although its object is usually negative; that is, it is a forward movement to prevent the enemy carrying out some offensive operation either direct or by way of counterstroke. So far the common tendency to confuse " Seeking out the

enemy's fleet" with "Making the enemy's coast your
frontier" may be condoned. But the two operations
are widely different in that they have different
objectives. In "seeking out," our objective is the
enemy's armed force. In "making the enemy's coast
our frontier," the objective is inseparable from the
ulterior object of the naval war. In this case the
objective is the common communications. By establishing a blockade we operate offensively against those
communications. We occupy them, and then we can
do no more. Our offensive is arrested; we cannot
carry it on to the destruction of the enemy's fleet.
We have to wait in a defensive attitude, holding
the communications we have seized, till he choses to
attack in order to break our hold; and during that
period of arrest the advantage of surprise—the all-
important advantage in war—passes by a well recognised rule to our enemy. We, in fact, are held upon
the defensive, with none of the material advantages of
the defensive. The moral advantage of having taken
the initiative remains, but that is all. The advantage
which we thus gain will of course have the same kind
of depressing effect upon the blockaded fleet as it had
of old, but scarcely in so high a degree. The degradation of a steam fleet in port can scarcely be so rapid or
debilitating as it was when nine-tenths of seamanship
lay in the smart handling of sails. For the blockading
fleet it is also true that the effects of weather, which
formerly were the main cause of wear and tear, can
scarcely be so severe. But, on the other hand, the
physical strain to officers and men, and the difficulty of
supply, will be far greater, so long at least as coal is
the chief fuel. The wind no longer sets a measure on
the enemy's movements. Vigilance close and unremit-

ting beyond all our predecessors knew is the portion of the blockaders to prevent surprise. Furthermore, in the old days surprise meant at worst the enemy's escape ; now it may mean our own destruction by mine or torpedo. It is unnecessary to labour the point. It is too obvious that a close blockade of the old type exhibits under present conditions the defects of "arrested offence" in so high a degree as practically to prohibit its use.

What, then, can be done? Must we rest content in all situations with Howe's system, which riper experience condemned for cases of extreme necessity? Cannot the old close blockade be given a modern form? Assuredly it can. In old days the shoreward limit of the blockading fleet was just beyond the range of the coast batteries, and this position it held continuously by means of an inshore squadron. In these days of mobile defence that limit is by analogy the night range of destroyers and the day range of submarines, that is, half the distance they can traverse between dark and dawn or dawn and dark respectively, unless within that limit a torpedo-proof base can be established. A blockade of this nature will correspond in principle to a close blockade of the old type ; nor in practice, as was proved in the Japanese blockade of Port Arthur, will its incidents be materially different. The distance at which the battle-squadron must keep will seem at first sight to deny it certainty of immediate contact— the essence of close blockade. But in truth other new factors already noticed will reduce that distance relatively. Quicker and more certain means of com-munication between the admiral and his scouts, the absolute freedom of movement and the power of delaying the enemy's actual exit by mining, may go far to bring things back to their old relations. At Port Arthur they did so entirely. If then, as in that case, our paramount object is to keep the enemy in, there seems still no reason why we should not make our dispositions on the principle of close blockade. Distances will be greater, but that is all.

Nor must it be forgotten that for a squadron to take station off a port in the old manner is not the only means of close blockade. It may still effect its purpose, at least temporarily, by supporting mining vessels or block ships—" sinkers," as they used to be called. The latter expedient, it is true, had little success in the latest experiments, but even in the Russo-Japanese War its possibilities were by no means exhausted. We have therefore to conclude that where the strategical conditions call obviously for close blockade, our plan of operations will be modified in that direction with the means still at our disposal.

If, however, our object is not so sharply defined, if in spite of our desire to deny the enemy the sea we are ready to take risks in order to bring about a decision, the case is not so clear. It will be observed that the looseness which the new conditions force upon close blockade—increasing as they are in intensity year by year—must tend more and more to approximate it in practice to open blockade. The question will therefore present itself whether it would not be more in accordance with the fundamental elements of strength to adopt open blockade frankly for all purposes. We should thus substitute a true defensive disposition for an arrested offence, and, theoretically, that in itself is a great advantage. The practical benefits, whatever the correlative drawbacks, are equally clear, nor are they less great now than they appeared to Howe and Kempenfelt. We avoid exhaustion of machinery, coal, and men, and this, at least for the necessary flotilla screen, will be greater than anything that had to be faced in former days. We have at least the opportunity of occupying a position secure from surprise, and of keeping the fleet continually up to its highest striking energy. Finally, assuming the geographical conditions give reasonable promise of contact, a quick decision, which modern war demands with ever greater insistence, is more probable. In such a disposition of course contact can rarely be made certain. The enemy, whom the hypothesis of blockade assumes to be anxious to avoid action, will always have a chance of evasion, but this will always be so, even with the closest blockade now possible. We may even go further and claim for open blockade that in favourable conditions it may give the better chance of contact. For by adopting the principle of open blockade we shall have, in accordance with the theory of defence, the further advantages of being able the better to conceal our dispositions, and consequently to lay traps for our enemy, such as that which Nelson prepared for Ville-neuve in the Gulf of Lyons in 1805.

The objection to such a course which appears to have the most weight with current opinion is the moral one, which is inseparable from all deliberate choices of the defensive. If the watching fleet remains in a home fortified base, it may be assumed that the usual moral degradation will set in. But the method does not entail the inglorious security of such a base. A sound position may well be found at a spot such as Admiral Togo occupied while waiting for the Baltic fleet, and in that case there was no observable degradation of any kind. Nor is there much evidence that this

objection weighed materially with the opponents of
Howe's view. Their objection was of a purely physical
kind. Open blockade left the enemy too much freedom
to raid our trade routes. The watching system might
be sufficient to keep an unwilling battle-fleet in port
or to bring a more adventurous one to action, but it
could not control raiding squadrons. This was certainly
Barham's objection. " If," he wrote to Pitt in 1794,
" the French should have any intention of sending
their fleet to sea with this easterly wind, and Lord
Howe continues at Torbay, our Mediterranean and
Jamaica convoys are in a very critical situation. Both
fleets must by this time be drawing near the Channel,
and cannot enter it while the easterly wind holds."
This danger must always be with us, especially in narrow
waters such as the North Sea. In more open theatres
the difficulty is not so obtrusive, for with sufficient sea
room trade may take naturally or by direction a course
which our watching dispositions will cover. Thus
with Nelson in the case of Toulon, his normal positions
on the Sardinian coast covered effectually the flow of
our trade to the Levant and the Two Sicilies, which
was all there was at the time.

The truth is, that in endeavouring to decide between
open and close blockade we find ourselves confronted
with those special difficulties which so sharply distinguish naval warfare from warfare on land. We
cannot choose on purely naval considerations. In
naval warfare, however great may be our desire to concentrate our effort on the enemy's main forces, the
ulterior object will always obtrude itself. We must
from the first do our best to control sea communications, and since those communications are usually
common, we cannot refrain from occupying those of

the enemy without at the same time neglecting and exposing our own. Thus in the case of Brest a close blockade was always desirable, and especially at convoy seasons, because the great trade routes which passed within striking distance of the port were all common, whereas in the region of Toulon the main lines were not common except along the coasts of Africa and Southern Italy, and these Nelson's open blockade amply secured.

The general conclusion, then, is that however high may be the purely naval and strategical reasons for adopting open blockade as the best means of securing a decision against the enemy's fleet, yet the inevitable intrusion of the ulterior object in the form of trade protection or the security of military expeditions will seldom leave us entirely free to use the open method. We must be prepared, in fact, to find ourselves at least at times faced with the necessity of using a form of blockade as nearly modelled on the old close blockade as changed conditions will permit.

CHAPTER III

METHODS OF DISPUTING COMMAND

I

DEFENSIVE FLEET OPERATIONS—"A FLEET IN BEING"

In dealing with the theory of sea command, attention was called to the error of assuming that if we are unable to win the command we therefore lose it. It was pointed out that this proposition, which is too often implied in strategical discussion, denies in effect that there can be such a thing as strategical defensive at sea, and ignores the fact that the normal condition in war is for the command to be in dispute. Theory and history are at one on the point. Together they affirm that a Power too weak to win command by offensive operations may yet succeed in holding the command in dispute by assuming a general defensive attitude.

That such an attitude in itself cannot lead to any positive result at sea goes without saying, but nevertheless even over prolonged periods it can prevent an enemy securing positive results, and so give time for the other belligerent to dominate the situation by securing his ends ashore.

It is seldom that we have been forced even for a time to adopt such an attitude, but our enemies have done so frequently to our serious annoyance and loss. In the Seven Years' War, for instance, the French by avoiding offensive operations likely to lead to a decision, and confining themselves to active defence, were able for five campaigns to prevent our reducing Canada, which was the object of the war. Had they staked the issue on a great fleet action in the first campaign, and had the result been against them, we could certainly have achieved our object in half the time. In the end, of course, they failed to prevent the conquest, but during all the time the catastrophe was postponed France had abundant opportunity of gaining offensively elsewhere territory which, as she at all events believed, would have compelled us to give up our conquest at the peace.

Again, in our last great naval war Napoleon by avoiding general actions was able to keep the command in dispute till by alliances and otherwise he had gathered force which he deemed sufficient to warrant a return to the offensive. Eventually that force proved unequal to the task, yet when it failed and the command passed to his enemy, he had had time to consolidate his power so far that the loss of his fleet seemed scarcely to affect it, and for nine years more he was able to continue the struggle.

Such examples—and there are many of them— serve to show how serious a matter is naval defence in the hands of a great military Power with other means of offence. They tell us how difficult it is to deal with, and how serious therefore for even the strongest naval Power is the need to give it careful study.

And not for this reason only, but also because the strongest naval Power, if faced with a coalition, may find it impossible to exert a drastic offensive any-where without temporarily reducing its force in certain areas to a point relatively so low as to permit of nothing higher than the defensive. The leading case of such a state of affairs, which we must further consider presently, was our own position in the War of American Independence, when, as we have seen, in order to secure an adequate concentration for offence in the West Indies we were forced to reduce our home fleet to defensive level.

What, then, do we mean by naval defence? To arrive at a right answer we must first clear our mind of all confusing shadows cast by the accidents of land defence. Both on land and at sea defence means of course taking certain measures to defer a decision until military or political developments so far redress the balance of strength that we are able to pass to the offensive. In the operations of armies the most usual means employed are the holding of positions and forcing our superior enemy to exhaust his strength in attacking them. Consequently the idea of military defence is dominated by the conception of entrenched positions and fortresses.

In naval warfare this is not so. At sea the main conception is avoiding decisive action by strategical or tactical activity, so as to keep our fleet in being till the situation develops in our favour. In the golden age of our navy the keynote of naval defence was mobility, not rest. The idea was to dispute the control by harassing operations, to exercise control at any place or at any moment as we saw a chance, and to prevent the enemy exercising control in spite of his superiority by continually occupying his attention. The idea of mere resistance was hardly present at all. Everything was counter-attack, whether upon the enemy's force or his maritime communications. On land, of course, such methods of defence are also well known, but they belong much more to guerilla warfare than to regular operations. In regular warfare

with standing armies, however brilliantly harassing
operations and counter-attack are used, the fundamental
conception is the defended or defensible position.

Similarly at sea, although the essence of defence
is mobility and an untiring aggressive spirit rather than
rest and resistance, yet there also defended and defensible positions are not excluded.   But they are only
used in the last resort.   A fleet may retire temporarily
into waters difficult of access, where it can only be
attacked at great risk, or into a fortified base, where
it is practically removed from the board and cannot be
attacked at all by a fleet alone.   But the occasions on
which such expedients can be used at sea are far rarer
than on land.   Indeed except for the most temporary
purposes they can scarcely be regarded as admissible
at sea, however great their value on land.   The reason
is simple.   A fleet withdrawing to such a position
leaves open to the enemy the ulterior object, which is
the control of sea communications, whereas on land
an army in a good position may even for a prolonged
period cover the ulterior object, which is usually territory.   An army in position, moreover, is always doing
something to exhaust its opponent and redress the
unfavourable balance, but a fleet in inactivity is too
often permitting the enemy to carry on operations which
tend to exhaust the resources of its own country.

For a maritime Power, then, a naval defensive means
nothing but keeping the fleet actively in being—not
merely in existence, but in active and vigorous life.
No phrase can better express the full significance of
the idea than " A fleet in being," if it be rightly understood.   Unfortunately it has come to be restricted, by
a misunderstanding of the circumstances in which it
was first invented, to one special class of defence.   We

speak of it as though it were essentially a method of defence against invasion, and so miss its fuller meaning. If, however, it be extended to express defence against any kind of maritime attack, whether against territory or sea communications, its broad truth will become apparent, and it will give us the true conception of the idea as held in the British service.

The occasion on which it was first used was one that well exhibits the special possibilities of a naval defensive. It was in the year 1690, when, in alliance with the Dutch, we were at war with France, and though really superior, had been caught in a situation which placed us temporarily at a great disadvantage in home waters. The French by a surprising rapidity of mobilisation and concentration had stolen a march on us before either our mobilisation or our concentration was complete. King William, with the best of the army, was in Ireland dealing with a French invasion in support of James, and a squadron of seven sail under Sir Cloudesley Shovel had been detached into the Irish Sea to guard his communications. Another squadron, consisting of sixteen of the line, British and Dutch, had been sent to Gibraltar under Admiral Killigrew to take down the trade and to keep an eye on Chateaurenault, who with a slightly inferior squadron was at Toulon. It was assumed he would probably make a push for Brest, where the French main fleet was mobilising under the Comte de Tourville, and Killigrew had orders to follow him if he got through the Straits. Chateaurenault did get through ; Killigrew failed to bring him to action, and instead of following him immediately, he went into Cadiz to complete his arrangements for forwarding his outward-bound convoy and escorting the one he was to bring home. What of

course he should have done, according to the practice
of more experienced times, was to have left this work to
a cruiser detachment, and failing contact with Chateaurenault, should have closed at once to the strategical
centre with his battle-squadron.

Meanwhile the home fleet, which Lord Torrington
was to command, was still unformed. It lay in
three divisions, at the Downs, Portsmouth, and Plymouth, while a considerable part of the promised Dutch
contingent had not made its appearance. It was a
splendid chance for the French to seize the command
of the Channel before the concentration could take
place and to crush the British in detail. Accordingly,
on June 13th, as soon as Chateaurenault had arrived,
Tourville put to sea with some seventy of the line.
The day before, however, Torrington, having hoisted his
flag in the Downs, had massed his two main divisions
at Portsmouth, and by the time Tourville appeared off
the Isle of Wight he had with later arrivals, both
Dutch and British, about fifty-six of the line in St.
Helen's Road. Not knowing that the Toulon contingent had joined, he put to sea intending to fight,
but on discovering the great superiority of the French,
he decided in concert with his council of war to act
on the defensive, and before offering battle to endeavour to secure a concentration with Killigrew and
Shovel and the Plymouth division by getting to the
westward. If he found this course impossible without
fighting an action, his plan was to retire before Tourville " even to the Gunfleet," where amidst the shoals
of the Thames estuary he felt he would have a good
chance of repelling an attack with success. There, too,
he counted on being reinforced not only by the ships
still at Chatham, but also possibly by ships from the

westward which might steal along the coast and join him "over the flats" by channels unknown to the French. To fight as he was he considered to be only playing the enemy's game. "If we are beaten," he said in communicating his plan to the Government, "they being absolute masters of the sea will be at great liberty of doing many things which they dare not do whilst we observe them and are in a possibility of joining Admiral Killigrew and our ships to the westward."

It was a plan conceived on the best principles of defence—waiting till the acquisition of fresh force justified a return to the offensive. It is further interesting as a pure case of naval defence, with no ulterior object other than control of home waters. In the minds of the Government there was no apprehension of any definite attempt to invade across the Channel, but the invasion of Ireland was in full progress, and all nourishment of it must be stopped and our own communications kept free. There was, moreover, serious anxiety lest the French should extend their operations to Scotland, and there was Killigrew's homeward-bound convoy approaching. The situation was one that obviously could not be solved effectually except by winning a general command of the sea, but in Torrington's judgment it could be rendered innocuous by holding the command in dispute. His design, therefore, was to act upon the defensive and prevent the enemy achieving any positive result until he was in a position to fight them with a fair chance of victory. A temporary defensive he considered was the only way to win the command, while to hazard a decision in inferior strength was the best way to lose it.

Nothing could be in closer harmony with the

principles of good strategy as we understand them
now. It was undoubtedly in advance of anything that
had been done up to that time, and it was little wonder
if the Government, as is usually said, failed to appreciate
the design. Their rejection of it has come in for very
severe criticism. But it would seem that they misunderstood rather than failed to appreciate. The
Earl of Nottingham, who was at the head of the
Government, believed, as his reply to the admiral
clearly shows, that Torrington meant to retire to the
Gunfleet at once; whereas it is equally clear to us
that the Gunfleet was to be his extreme point, and
that he did not mean to retire so far unless the French
forced him. The Minister failed, as others have done
since, to grasp what the admiral meant by " A fleet
in being." He thought that in Torrington's view a
fleet safe in port and not in contact with the enemy
was " in being," whereas Torrington had no such idea.
As Nottingham conceived the admiral's intention he
saw that although it might preserve the fleet, it would
expose everything else to destruction ; that is, he was
oppressed with the special characteristic of naval warfare which always permits action against the ulterior
object when the enemy denies you any chance of acting
against his armed force.

Under this misapprehension, which indeed was not
justified by the words of Torrington's despatch, he
procured from the Queen an order in these terms :
" We apprehend," it ran, " the consequences of your
retiring to the Gunfleet to be so fatal, that we choose
rather you should upon any advantage of the wind
give battle to the enemy than retreat farther than is
necessary to get an advantage upon the enemy." It
was, however, left to his discretion to proceed to the

westward to complete his concentration that way, provided, it said, "you by no means ever lose sight of the French fleet whereby they may have opportunity of making attempts upon the shore or in the rivers of Medway or Thames, or get away without fighting."

This order has been very hardly dealt with by modern critics, although it clearly contemplates true preventive observation, and even, as the last words suggest, the idea contained in Nelson's well-known saying, "that by the time the enemy had beat our fleet soundly they would do us no more harm this year." It is true that Nelson could rely on the proved superiority of the British at that time unit for unit, but it is also true that Nottingham and his colleagues in the Government had information which led them greatly to underestimate Tourville's strength. This was evident on the face of Nottingham's despatch which covered the order, so evident indeed that Torrington might well perhaps have suspended the execution of an order so obviously based on incorrect information. But knowing probably what intrigues were going on against him at Court, he chose to regard it as a peremptory command to engage whenever he found himself to windward.

Much as a more scientific view of naval strategy may admire Torrington's conception, there seems no reason for losing temper over the Government's plan. It was certainly one way of solving the problem, and seeing how large were our reserves, a defeat need not have meant disaster. Still, it was doubtless dictated by an inability to grasp the strategical strength of Torrington's novel plan, a plan which was not only safer, but was calculated to achieve greater positive results in the end. The real fallacy of the

Government's plan was that although it had a specious appearance of a bold offensive, it could have achieved nothing but a negative result. The most a battle could have given in the circumstances could only have left the command in dispute, and the worst would have given the enemy a positive result, which must have gravely compromised William's campaign in Ireland.

On these lines Torrington replied to the Government. Dealing with their anxiety for the ships to the westward and the Mediterranean convoy, whose danger was their expressed reason for forbidding him the Gunfleet, he pointed out that they could not run much hazard if they took care of themselves. For, as he repeated, "while we observe the French, they cannot make any attempt on ships or shore without running great hazard, and if we are beaten, all is exposed to their mercy." Thus without specially noticing the Minister's misinterpretation of his despatch, he intimated that his intention was observation, and not simple retreat.

By the time Torrington sent this reply he had been pressed back as far as Beachy Head; it was no longer possible to get to the westward; and the following day, finding himself to windward, he attacked. But still confirmed in his idea of defence, and carrying it on to his tactics, he refused to give the French the chance of a real decision, and disengaged as soon as a drop in the wind permitted. So far he felt justified in interpreting orders which he knew were founded on false information. He was sure, as he said in justification of the way he fought the action, " that the Queen could not have been prevailed with to sign an order for it, had not both our weakness and the strength of the enemy been disguised to her."

So severely was his fleet crippled that he believed his plan could no longer act. "What the consequences of this unfortunate battle may be," he wrote in his Journal, "God Almighty only knows, but this I dare be positive in, had I been left to my liberty I had prevented any attempt upon the land, and secured the western ships, Killigrew, and the merchantmen." Actually in all this he was successful. Slowly retiring eastward he drew the French after him as far as Dover before he ran to the Nore; and Tourville was unable to get back to the westward, till all the endangered ships were safe in Plymouth. In spite of Torrington's being forced to fight an action at the wrong time and place, his design had so far succeeded. Not only had he prevented the French doing anything that could affect the issue of the war, but he had completely foiled Tourville's plan of destroying the British fleet in detail. That he had done, but retribution by passing to the offensive was no longer in his power.

That Tourville or his Government was impressed with the efficacy of the method was demonstrated the following year, when he in his turn found himself in an inferiority that denied him hope of a successful battle decision. During the summer he kept his fleet hovering off the mouth of the Channel without giving the British admiral a chance of contact. His method, however, differed from that of Torrington, and he only achieved his negative object by keeping out of sight of his enemy altogether. In his opinion, if a fleet remained at sea in close observation of an active enemy an action could not be avoided. "If (the admiral)," he wrote in his memorandum on the subject, "be ordered to keep the sea to try to amuse the enemy and to let them know we are in a position to attack in case they attempt a descent, I think it my duty to say that in that case we must make up our mind to have to fight them in the end; for if they have really sought an action, they will have been able to fight, seeing that it is impossible to pirouette so long near a fleet without coming to grips."[1] This is as much as to say that a sure point of temporary retreat is necessary to "a fleet in being," and this was an essential part of Torrington's idea.

In Torrington's and Tourville's time, when ships were unhandy and fleet tactics in their infancy, the difficulty of avoiding action, when a determined enemy had once got contact, were undoubtedly great, unless a port of retreat was kept open. But as the art of naval warfare developed, the possibilities of "a fleet in being" were regarded as much wider, at least in the British service. It was nearly a hundred years before we were again forced to use the same device on a large scale, and then it was believed that superior speed and tactical precision were factors that could be counted on to an almost unlimited extent. In the darkest days of the War of American Independence we have a memorandum of the subject by Kempenfelt, which not only gives the developed idea of "a fleet in being" and the high aggressive spirit that is its essence, but also explains its value, not merely as a defensive expedient, but as a means of permitting a drastic offensive even when you are as a whole inferior. "When you know the enemy's designs," he says, " in order to do something effectual you must endeavour to be superior to them in some part where they have designs to execute, and where, if they succeed, they

---

[1] Delarbre, *Tourville et la marine de son temps*, p. 339.

would most injure you. If your fleet is divided as to
be in all places inferior to the enemy, they will have a
fair chance of succeeding everywhere in their attempts.
If a squadron cannot be formed sufficient to face the
enemy's at home, it would be more advantageous to
let your inferiority be still greater in order by it to gain
the superiority elsewhere."

" When inferior to the enemy, and you have only a
squadron of observation to watch and attend upon their
motions, such a squadron should be composed of two-
decked ships only [that is, ships of the highest mobility]
as to assure it purpose. It must have the advantage
of the enemy in sailing, else under certain circumstances it will be liable to be forced to battle or to give
up some of its heavy sailers. It is highly necessary to
have such a flying squadron to hang on the enemy's
large fleet, as it will prevent their dividing into separate
squadrons for intercepting your trade or spreading their
ships for a more extensive view. You will be at hand
to profit from any accidental separation or dispersion
of their fleet from hard gales, fogs, or other causes.
You may intercept supplies, intelligence, &c., sent to
them. In fine, such a squadron will be a check and
restraint upon their motions, and prevent a good deal
of the mischief they might otherwise do."

Three years before, when first called to be Chief of
the Staff in the Channel, he had emphasised the same
points. " Much," he wrote in July 1779, " I may say
all, depends upon this fleet. 'Tis an inferior against a
superior fleet. Therefore the greatest skill and address
is requisite to counteract the designs of the enemy, to
watch and seize the favourable opportunity for action,
and to catch the advantage of making the effort at
some or other feeble part of the enemy's line; or if

such opportunities don't offer, to hover near the enemy, keep him at bay, and prevent his attempting anything but at risk and hazard; to command their attention, and oblige them to think of nothing but being on their guard against your attack." [1]

It was on these lines the war was conducted. The West Indian area, in which lay the enemy's principal object, was treated as the offensive theatre and the home waters as the defensive. Inferior as was the Channel fleet to the home fleet of the allies, its defensive operations proved adequate to prevent their achieving any success. Nor was this all, for Kempenfelt was able to demonstrate the positive side of his theory in the most brilliant and convincing manner. In dealing with concentration we have seen how, in command of such a flying squadron as he postulated, he was able off Ushant to seize a favourable opportunity for action, which resulted in his capturing a convoy of military stores essential to the French operations in the West Indies under the nose of De Guichen with an escort of nearly twice his force.

Nelson certainly shared Kempenfelt's views as to the possibilities of an inferior fleet kept actively in being. " As to our fleet," he wrote from the Mediterranean in 1796, " under such a commander-in-chief as Sir John Jervis nobody has any fear . . . We are now twenty-two sail of the line. The combined fleet will not be above thirty-five. . . . I will venture my life Sir John Jervis defeats them. I do not mean by a regular battle, but by the skill of our admiral and the activity and spirit of our officers and seamen. This country is the most favourable possible for that skill with an inferior fleet; for the winds are so variable,

[1] *Barham Papers*, i. 292.

that some one time in twenty-four hours you must be able to attack a part of a large fleet, and the other will be becalmed or have a contrary wind. Therefore I hope the Government will not be alarmed for our safety."

Such a conception of the defensive may indeed be said to have become current in the British service. It was part of the reasoning which in 1805, after Villeneuve's escape from the Mediterranean, decided Sir John Orde to fall back on Ushant instead of entering the Straits. "I dare believe," he wrote, "Lord Nelson will be found in condition with his twelve of the line and numerous frigates to act on the defensive without loss and even to hang on to the skirts of the enemy's fleet should it attempt any material service, especially when encumbered with troops."[1]

In all this consideration of the potentialities of "a fleet in being" operating defensively it must never be forgotten that we are dealing with its possibilities in relation to a general command of the sea—to its general power of holding such command in dispute, as Torrington used it. Its power of preventing a particular operation, such as oversea invasion, is another matter, which will always depend upon the local conditions. If the "fleet in being" can be contained in such a way that it is impossible for it to reach the invading line of passage, it will be no bar to invasion. In 1690, so far as Torrington's fleet was concerned, the French, had they been so minded, might have made a descent, say, at Portsmouth while Torrington was at the Nore. But Torrington's fleet was not the only factor. His retreat forced Tourville to leave behind him unfought the squadrons of

[1] *Campaign of Trafalgar*, p. 65.

Shovel and Killigrew, and so far as commanding a line of invasion passage was concerned Tourville was himself as well contained as Torrington. The conditions of naval defence against invasion are in fact so complex compared with those of general naval defence that they must be treated later as a special branch of the subject.

The doctrine of the " Fleet in being " as formulated and practised by Torrington and developed by Kempenfelt goes no further than this, that where the enemy regards the general command of a sea area as necessary to his offensive purposes, you may be able to prevent his gaining such command by using your fleet defensively, refusing what Nelson called a regular battle, and seizing every opportunity for a counterstroke. To use it as it was used by the French in the case of Tourville's famous deterrent cruise, where the whole object of the French was offensive and could not be obtained except by offence, is quite another thing.

It is indeed difficult to understand the admiration with which his *campagne au large* has been treated in France. He kept the sea off the mouth of the Channel for fifty days in the summer of 1691, and for forty of those days our Channel fleet was making no systematic effort to seek him out. He had been sent to sea in hope of intercepting our great " Smyrna convoy," which was then the backbone of our oversea trade. Russell with the British main fleet simply took positions to cover its approach until it was safe, knowing presumably that Tourville must come to him if he wished to accomplish his purpose. When the convoy was safe Russell proceeded off Ushant, that is, between the enemy and his base.

Tourville's communications were thus cut, his line of
retreat threatened, and he seized the first opportunity
to elude Russell and to return into port. Beyond
taking a few ships from one of the West India convoys,
he accomplished nothing. The central French offensive
in Ireland was broken at the battle of the Boyne,
and the prestige of England at sea was restored.
It is true our trade suffered in the North Sea, but
this was not directly due to the concentration which
Tourville's cruise forced upon us, but rather to the
failure of the Dutch—apparently by a misunderstanding—to provide for an effective blockade of
Dunkirk.

To British eyes it will seem that the heresy which
was latent in Tourville's instructions was a seed that
choked all the finer aspirations of the French navy.
In 1691 the plan of his cruise may possibly be defended
as sufficiently aggressive, since, seeing how unstable
was William's new throne, a resounding blow at
British trade, combined with an expected victory in
Ireland, might have been enough to upset it. But
afterwards the idea was stretched to occasions it would
not fit. It seems to have bred a belief that where
the object of the war plainly depended on winning
a real command of the sea, that object could yet
be attained by naval defensive operations. Many
times it is true a policy which had starved the navy
of France left no other course open to her seamen,
and had they in their inferiority attempted the offensive,
the end must have been swifter if not more certain.
In criticising the maritime history of France we must
be careful to distinguish policy from strategy. It was
not always the defensive strategy that was bad, but
the policy that condemned her admirals to negative

operations. Seeing that she was a continental Power
with continental aspirations, it was often a policy from
which her military exigencies permitted no escape.
Nevertheless the policy was twice accursed : it cursed
her when she was weak, and cursed her when she
was strong. The prolonged use of the defensive bred
a habit of mind which seems to have rendered her
incapable of striking hard when she had the strength.
In no other way at least can we account for the
behaviour of so high-spirited a nation when her
chance of revenge came in the War of American
Independence.

It is here in its moral reactions lies the danger of
the defensive, a danger so insidious in its working as to
tempt us never to utter the word. Yet with the voice
of Torrington, Kempenfelt, and Nelson in our ears, it
would be folly to ignore it for ourselves, and still more
to ignore the exhausting strain its use by our enemy
may impose upon us. It must be studied, if for
no other reasons than to learn how to break it
down. Nor will the study have danger, if only we
keep well in view the spirit of restless and vigilant
counter-attack which Kempenfelt and Nelson regarded
as its essence. True, some of the conditions which in
the days of sails made for opportunity have passed
away, but many still remain. Shifts of wind and
calms will no longer bring them, but weather thick
or violent can yet make seamanship, nimbleness, and
cohesion tell as it always did ; and there is no reason
to doubt that it is still possible for hard sea-training
to make "the activity and spirit of our officers and
seamen" give the results which Nelson so confidently
expected.

II

MINOR COUNTER-ATTACKS

For the weaker of two belligerents minor-attack has always exercised a certain fascination. Where a Power was so inferior in naval force that it could scarcely count even on disputing command by fleet operations, there remained a hope of reducing the relative inferiority by putting part of the enemy's force out of action. Such hopes were rarely realised. In 1587 Drake succeeded in stopping the Spanish invasion by such a counter-attack on the Cadiz division of the Armada while it was still unmobilised. In 1667 the Dutch achieved a similar success against our Chatham division when it was demobilised and undefended, and thereby probably secured rather more favourable terms of peace. But it cannot be said that the old wars present any case where the ultimate question of command was seriously affected by a minor counter-attack.

The advent of the torpedo, however, has given the idea a new importance that cannot be overlooked. The degree of that importance is at present beyond calculation. There is at least no evidence that it would be very high in normal conditions and between ordinarily efficient fleets. The comparative success of the opening Japanese attack on the Port Arthur squadron is the only case in point, and where only one case exists, it is necessary to use extreme caution in estimating its significance. Before we can deduce anything of permanent value we must consider very carefully both its conditions and results.

To begin with, it was a new experience of a new

class of weapon, and it by no means follows that the success of a new expedient will be repeated with anything like equal result. It will not be irrelevant again to recall the case of fireships. At the outset of the sailing era in 1588, this device prepared the way for a decisive success against a fleet in the open. In the succeeding wars the new weapon found a prominent place in the organisation of sea-going fleets, but its success was never repeated. Against ships in ill-defended harbours it did occasionally produce good results, and during the infancy of tactics its moral and even material effects in fleet actions were frequently demonstrated. But as naval science developed and the limitations of the weapon were more accurately measured, it was able to achieve less and less, till in the eighteenth century it was regarded as almost negligible. Even its moral effect was lost, and it ceased to be considered as a battle unit.

Now, if we examine closely the Port Arthur case, we shall find it pointing to the existence of certain inherent conditions not dissimilar from those which discredited fireships as a decisive factor in war. In spite of the apparently formidable nature of a surprise attack by torpedo the indications from the one case in point are that these conditions make for greater power in the defence than in the attack. The first condition relates to the difficulty of locating the objective accurately. It is obvious that for this kind of operation the most precise intelligence is essential, and of all intelligence the most difficult to obtain in war is the distribution of an enemy's fleet from day to day. The Japanese had fairly certain information that the bulk of the Port Arthur squadron was lying in the outer anchorage, but it had been constantly moving, and there was a report that three battleships had just been detached from it. The report was false, but the result was that of the five divisions of destroyers which the Japanese had available, two were diverted against Dalny, where no enemy was found. Such uncertainty must always exist, and in no circumstances is it likely to be less than where, as in the Japanese case, the attack is made before declaration, and while the ordinary channels of intelligence are still open.

Further, it is to be noted that in spite of the fact that relations for some weeks had been highly strained, and a surprise torpedo attack was regarded as probable, the Russians had taken no precautions to confuse their enemy. It is obvious that measures to prevent accurate locating can, and should, be taken in such cases. We may go further. From confusing the enemy by such means it is but a step to lead him to a wrong conclusion, and to lay for him a trap which may swallow up the bulk of his destroyer force in the first hours of the war. It is to be feared, however, that the risks of such an eventuality are so great in minor counter-attacks of this nature, that it will probably be very difficult to tempt an inferior enemy to expose his flotilla in this way.

This view receives emphasis from the second point which the Port Arthur case serves to demonstrate, and that is the great power of even the flimsiest defence against such attacks; in other words, the chances of success can scarcely ever be great enough to justify the risk. Everything was in favour of the Japanese. Orders had been issued in the Russian squadron for two or three nights previously to prepare for a torpedo attack, but so low had discipline fallen, that the orders were obeyed in a very perfunctory manner. Guns were not loaded, their crews were not at quarters, nor were the nets got out. The only real precaution taken was that two destroyers and no more had been sent out as guard patrol, but even they were forbidden to fire on anything they met until they had reported to the admiral or had themselves been fired on. Defence against a surprise attack could scarcely have been more feeble, and yet so high was the nervous tension in the attacking force, that it proved stronger than could reasonably have been expected. The mere existence of the patrol and the necessity of evading it threw the Japanese approach into a confusion from which it was unable to recover entirely, and the attack lost its essential momentum and cohesion. Again, defective as were the arrangements in the squadron itself, and lax as were its training and discipline, no torpedo hits were made, so far as we can judge, after the Russian guns and searchlights got into play.

Such development of strength in the defence seems inherent in the conditions of minor attack, and there appears to be no reason for expecting better results for such attacks in normal cases. But in deducing principles from the Port Arthur case, it must always be remembered that it was far from normal. It was a blow before declaration, when the menace of strained relations, though realised, had been almost entirely ignored by the Russians. In such exceptional and almost incredible circumstances a minor attack might always be counted on for a certain measure of success. To this we have to add the fact that the Russian squadron was not ordinarily efficient, but appears to have fallen into a lax condition such as could scarcely recur in the case of any other naval Power.

Finally, we must ask what, with every condition

abnormally in favour of the attack, was the actual material result? Did it have any real influence on the ultimate question of command? It is true that it so far swung the balance in favour of the Japanese that they were able to exercise the local control long enough to land their troops and isolate Port Arthur. But the Japanese plan for securing ultimate command rested on their power of taking Port Arthur by military operation and sustaining the siege from the sea. Yet in spite of every condition of success the physical effect of the blow was so small, that even without the help of an adequate dockyard the squadron recovered from it and became potent again before the siege could even be formed. The minor attacks which followed the first blow were all failures, and whether delivered at the port or upon the squadron in the open had no appreciable effect whatever.

At the same time it must be remembered that since that war the art of torpedo warfare has developed very rapidly. Its range and offensive power have increased in a higher ratio than the means of resisting it. Still those means have advanced, and it is probable that a squadron in a naval port or in a properly defended anchorage is not more easy to injure than it ever was; while a squadron at sea, so long as it constantly shifts its position, still remains very difficult to locate with sufficient precision for successful minor attack.

The unproved value of submarines only deepens the mist which overhangs the next naval war. From a strategical point of view we can say no more than that we have to count with a new factor, which gives a new possibility to minor counter-attack. It is a possibility which on the whole tells in favour of naval defence, a new card which, skilfully played in combination with defensive fleet operations, may lend fresh importance to the " Fleet in being." It may further be expected that whatever the effective possibilities of minor operations may ultimately prove to be in regard to securing command, the moral influence will be considerable, and at least at the beginning of a future war will tend to deflect and hamper the major operations and rob of their precision the lines which formerly led so frankly to the issue by battle.

In the absence of a sufficient volume of experience it would be idle to go further, particularly as torpedo attack, like fireship attack, depends for success more than any other on the spirit and skill of officers and men. With regard to the torpedo as the typical arm of mobile coastal defence, it is a different matter. What has been said applies only to its power towards securing command of the sea, and not to the exercise or to disputing the exercise of command. This is a question which is concerned with defence against invasion, and to that we must now turn.

CHAPTER IV

METHODS OF EXERCISING COMMAND

I

DEFENCE AGAINST INVASION

In methods of exercising command are included all operations not directly concerned with securing command or with preventing its being secured by the enemy. We engage in exercising command whenever we conduct operations which are directed not against the enemy's battle-fleet, but to using sea communications for our own purposes, or to interfering with the enemy's use of them. Such operations, though logically of secondary importance, have always occupied the larger part of naval warfare. Naval warfare does not begin and end with the destruction of the enemy's battle-fleet, nor even with breaking his cruiser power. Beyond all this there is the actual work of preventing his passing an army across the sea and of protecting the passage of our own military expeditions. There is also the obstruction of his trade and the protection of our own. In all such operations we are concerned with the exercise of command. We are using the sea, or interfering with its use by the enemy; we are not endeavouring to secure the use or to prevent the enemy from securing it. The two categories of operation differ radically in conception and purpose, and strategically they are on wholly different planes.

Logically, of course, operations for exercising command should follow those for securing command; that is to say, that since the attainment of command is the special object of naval warfare, and since that command can only be obtained permanently by the destruction of the enemy's armed forces afloat, it follows that in strictness no other objects should be allowed to interfere with our concentration of effort on the supreme end of securing command by destruction. War, however, is not conducted by logic, and the order of proceeding which logic prescribes cannot always be adhered to in practice. We have seen how, owing to the special conditions of naval warfare, extraneous necessities intrude themselves which make it inevitable that operations for exercising command should accompany as well as follow operations for securing command. War being, as it is, a complex sum of naval, military, political, financial, and moral factors, its actuality can seldom offer to a naval staff a clean slate on which strategical problems can be solved by well-turned syllogisms. The naval factor can never ignore the others. From the outset one or more of them will always call for some act of exercising command which will not wait for its turn in the logical progression. To a greater or less extent in all ordinary cases both categories of operation will have to be put in motion from the beginning.

Hence the importance of realising the distinction between the two generic forms of naval activity. In the hurry and stress of war confusion between them is easy. By keeping a firm grip upon the difference we can see at least what we are doing. We can judge how far any given operation that may be called for is a sacrifice of security to exercise, how far such a sacrifice may be justified, and how far the one end may be made to serve the other. By applying the distinction as a test much error may be avoided. The risk we take may be great, but we shall be able to weigh it accurately against the value of the end, and we shall take it with our eyes open and of set purpose. Above all, it will enable the Staff to settle clearly for each squadronal commander what is to be his primary objective, and what the object or purpose of the operations entrusted to him. It is above all in this last consideration, and particularly in the determination of the objective, that lies the main practical value of the distinction.

This will become clear the moment we begin to consider defence against invasion, which naturally takes the first place amongst operations for the exercise of control. Of all the current assumptions, not one is so confusing for the finer adjustments of strategy as that which affirms that the primary objective of our fleet is always the enemy's fleet. Of the battle-fleet and its attendant units it is of course true, so long at least as the enemy has a battle-fleet in being. It is true, that is, of all operations for securing control, but of operations for exercising control it is not true. In the case we have now to consider—defence against invasion—the objective of the special operations is, and always has been, the enemy's army. On this fundamental postulate our plans for resisting invasion have always been constructed from the year of the Armada to 1805.

In the old service tradition the point was perfectly well established. Admirals' instructions constantly insist on the fact that the transports are the " principal object." The whole disposition of the fleet during

Hawke's blockade in 1759 was based on keeping a firm hold on the transports in the Morbihan, and when he sought to extend his operations against the Rochefort squadron, he was sharply reminded by Anson that " the principal object of attention at this time " was, firstly, " the interception of the embarkations of the enemy at Morbihan," and secondly, " the keeping of the ships of war from coming out of Brest." Similarly Commodore Warren in 1796, when he had the permanent frigate guard before Brest, issued orders to his captains that in case of encountering enemy's transports under escort they were " to run them down or destroy them in the most expeditious manner possible previous to attacking the ships of war, but to preserve such a situation as to effect that purpose when directed by signal." Lord Keith's orders when watching Napoleon's flotilla were to the same effect. " Directing your chief attention," they run, " to the destruction of the ships, vessels, or boats having men, horses, or artillery on board (in preference to that of the vessels by which they are protected), and in the strict execution of this important duty losing sight entirely of the possibility of idle censure for avoiding contact with an armed force, because the prevention of debarkation is the object of primary importance to which every other consideration must give way." [1]

In tactics, then, the idea was the same as in strategy. The army was the primary objective round which all dispositions turned. In the French service the strength and soundness of the British practice was understood at least by the best men. When in 1805 Napoleon consulted Ganteaume as to the possibility

[1] *Admiralty Secretary's In-letters*, 537, 8th August 1803.

of the flotilla of transports effecting its passage by evasion, the admiral told him it was impossible, since no weather could avail to relax the British hold sufficiently. "In former wars," he said, "the English vigilance was miraculous."

To this rule there was no exception, not even when circumstances rendered it difficult to distinguish between the enemy's fleet and army as objectives. This situation could occur in two ways. Firstly, when the invading army was designed to sail with the battle-fleet, as in the case of Napoleon's invasion of Egypt; and secondly, when, although the design was that the two should operate on separate lines, our system of defence forced the fleet to come up to the army's line of passage in order to clear it, as happened in the case of the Armada and the French attempt of 1744.

In the latter case the invading army, whose objective was unknown, was at Dunkirk, and a French fleet was coming up the Channel to cover the passage. Sir John Norris, in command of the home fleet, was in the Downs. Though his name is now almost forgotten, he was one of the great founders of our naval tradition, and a strategist of the first order. In informing the Government of his plan of operations, he said he intended to proceed with his whole squadron off Dunkirk to prevent the transports sailing. "But," he says, "if they should unfortunately get out and pass us in the night and go northward, I intend to detach a superior force to endeavour to overtake and destroy them ; and with the remainder of my squadron either to fight the French fleet now in the Channel, or observe them and cover the country as our circumstances will admit of; or I shall pursue the embarkation with all my strength."

In this case there had been no time to organise a special squadron or flotilla, in the usual way, to bar the line of passage, and the battle-fleet had to be used for the purpose. This being so, Norris was not going to allow the presence of an enemy's battle-fleet to entice him away from his grip on the invading army, and so resolutely did he hold to the principle, that he meant if the transports put to sea to direct his offensive against them, while he merely contained the enemy's battle-fleet by defensive observation.

In the Egyptian case there was no distinction between the two objectives at all. Napoleon's expedition sailed in one mass. Yet in the handling of his fleet Nelson preserved the essential idea. He organised it into three "sub-squadrons," one of six sail and two of four each. "Two of these sub-squadrons," says Berry, his flag-captain, "were to attack the ships of war, while the third was to pursue the transports and to sink and destroy as many as it could"; that is, he intended, in order to make sure of Napoleon's army, to use no more than ten, and possibly only eight, of his own battle-ships against the eleven of the enemy.

Many other examples could be given of British insistence on making the enemy's army the primary objective and not his fleet in cases of invasion. No point in the old tradition was more firmly established. Its value was of course more strongly marked where the army and the fleet of the enemy endeavoured to act on separate lines of operation; that is, where the army took the real offensive line and the fleet the covering or preventive line, and where consequently for our own fleet there was no confusion between the two objectives. This was the normal case, and the reason it was so is simple enough. It may be stated at once, since it serves to enunciate the general principle upon which our traditional system of defence was based.

An invasion of Great Britain must always be an attempt over an uncommanded sea. It may be that our fleet predominates or it may be that it does not, but the command must always be in dispute. If we have gained complete command, no invasion can take place, nor will it be attempted. If we have lost it completely no invasion will be necessary, since, quite apart from the threat of invasion, we must make peace on the best terms we can get. Now, if the sea be uncommanded, there are obviously two ways in which an invasion may be attempted. Firstly, the enemy may endeavour to force it through our naval defence with transports and fleet in one mass. This was the primitive idea on which the Spanish invasion of Philip the Second was originally planned by his famous admiral, Santa-Cruz. Ripening military science, however, was able to convince him of its weakness. A mass of transports and warships is the most cumbrous and vulnerable engine of war ever known. The weaker the naval defence of the threatened country, the more devoutly will it pray the invader may use this device. Where contact with the enemy's fleet is certain, and particularly in narrow seas, as it was in this case, such a course will give the defender all the chances he could desire, and success for the invader is inconceivable, provided always we resolutely determine to make the army in its transports our main objective, and are not to be induced to break our head against its escort.

Where, however, contact is not certain, the invasion over an uncommanded sea may succeed by evasion of the defender's battle-fleet, as it did in the case of

Napoleon's invasion of Egypt. But that operation belongs to an entirely different category from that which we are now considering. None of the factors on which the traditional system of British defence is based were present. It was an operation over an open sea against a distant and undetermined objective that had no naval defence of its own, whereas in our own case the determining factors are permanent naval defence, an approximately determined objective, and a narrow sea where evasion by any force of invasion strength is impossible. Napoleon's exploit was in fact nothing more than the evasion of an open blockade which had no naval defence beyond it. The vital importance of these things will appear as we proceed and note the characteristics which marked every attempt to invade England. From such attempts we of course exclude the various descents upon Ireland, which, not being of invasion strength, fall into another class, to be dealt with hereafter.

Since the expedient of forcing an invasion by the strength of a powerful battleship escort has always been rejected as an inadmissible operation, the invader has had no choice but to adopt a separate line for his army, and operate with his fleet in such a way as may promise to prevent the enemy controlling that line. That, in short, is the problem of invasion over an uncommanded sea. In spite of an unbroken record of failure scored at times with naval disaster, continental strategists from Parma to Napoleon have clung obstinately to the belief that there is a solution short of a complete fleet decision. They have tried every conceivable expedient again and again. They have tried it by simple surprise evasion and by evasion through diversion or dispersal of our naval defence.

They have tried it by seeking local control through a local naval success prepared by surprise, or by attempting to entice our fleet away from home waters to a sufficient extent to give them temporarily local superiority. But the end has always been the same. Try as they would, they were faced ultimately by one of two alternatives—they must either defeat our covering battle-fleet in battle, or they must close their own battle-fleet on the transports, and so set up the very situation which it was their main design to avoid.

The truth is, that all attempts to invade England without command of the sea have moved in a vicious circle, from which no escape was ever found. No matter how ingenious or complex the enemy's design, a determined hold on their army as the primary naval objective has always set up a process of degradation which rendered the enterprise impracticable. Its stages are distinct and recurrent, and may be expressed as it were diagrammatically as follows:—

Two lines of operation having been decided on, the invading army is gathered at a point as close as possible to the coast to be invaded; that is, where the intervening sea is narrowest, and where the army's passage will be exposed to interference for the shortest time. The covering fleet will operate from a point as distant as convenient, so as to entice the enemy as far as possible from the army's line of passage. The defender replies by blockading the army's ports of departure with a flotilla of light vessels capable of dealing with transports, or by establishing a mobile defence of the threatened coasts which transports cannot break unaided, or more probably he will combine both expedients. The first fallacy of the invasion plan is then apparent. The narrower the sea, the easier it

is to watch.   Pure evasion becomes impossible, and it
is necessary to give the transports sufficient armed
strength by escort or otherwise to protect them against
flotilla attack.   The defender at once stiffens his flotilla
defence with cruisers and intermediate ships, and the
invader has to arrange for breaking the barrier with
a battle-squadron.   So weak and disturbing a position
is then set up that the whole scheme begins to give
way, if, that is, the defender has clung stubbornly
to the strategy we always used.   Our battle-fleet refused to seek out that of the invader.   It has always
held a position between the invader's fleet and the
blockaded invasion base, covering the blockade and
flotilla defence.   To enable a battle-squadron to break
our hold and to reinforce the army escort, the invader
must either force this covering position by battle, or
disturb it so effectively as to permit the reinforcing
squadron to evade it.   But since *ex hypothesi* he is
trying to invade without securing the command by
battle, he will first try to reinforce his transport escort
by evasion.   At once he is faced with new difficulty.
The reinforcement entails dividing his fleet, and this is
an expedient so vicious and disturbing to morale, that
no invader has ever been found to risk it.   And for
this reason.   To make evasion possible for the detached squadron, he must bring up the rest of his
force and engage the attention of the enemy's fleet,
and thus unless he is in very great superiority, and by
hypothesis is not—he runs the hazard of having his two
divisions beaten in detail.   This method has sometimes
been urged by Governments, but so loud have been the
protests both from the fleet and the army, that it has
always been dropped, and the invader finds himself at
the end of the vicious circle.   Unable to reinforce his

transport escort sufficiently without dividing his battle-fleet, he is forced to bring his whole force up to the army or abandon the attempt till command shall have been secured by battle.

Thus the traditional British system has never failed to bring about the deadlock, and it will be observed it is founded on making the invading army the primary objective. We keep a hold on it, firstly, by flotilla blockade and defence stiffened as circumstances may dictate by higher units, and secondly, by battle-fleet cover. It is on the flotilla hold that the whole system is built up. It is the local danger to that hold which determines the amount of stiffening the flotilla demands, and it is the security of that hold which determines the position and action of the battle-fleet.

A few typical examples will serve to show how the system worked in practice under all kinds of conditions. The first scientific attempt to work on two lines of operation, as distinguished from the crude mass methods of the Middle Ages, was the Spanish enterprise of 1588. Though internal support from Catholic malcontents was expected, it was designed as a true invasion, that is, a continuing operation for permanent conquest. Parma, the military commander-in-chief, laid it down that the Spanish fleet would have not only to protect his passage and support his landing, but also " to keep open his communications for the flow of provisions and munition."

In advising the dual line of operation, Parma's original intention was to get his army across by surprise. As always, however, it proved impossible to conceal the design, and long before he was ready he found himself securely blockaded by a Dutch flotilla supported by an English squadron. So firm indeed was the English hold on the army, that for a time it was overdone. The bulk of the English fleet was kept on the line of passage under Howard, while Drake alone was sent to the westward. It was only under the great sailor's importunity that the disposition, which was to become traditional, was perfected, and the whole fleet, with the exception of the squadron supporting the flotilla blockade, was massed in a covering position to the westward. The normal situation was then set up, and it could only have one result. Surprise was out of the question. Parma could not move till the blockade was broken, nor in face of the covering fleet could the Spanish fleet hope to break it by a sudden intrusion. The vague prospects the Spaniards had conceived of keeping the English fleet away from the line of passage by threatening a descent in the West Country or blockading it in a western port would no longer do. No such expedient would release Parma, and the Duke of Medina-Sidonia was ordered to proceed direct to Dunkirk if possible without fighting, there to break the blockade and secure the passage.

There was some idea in the King's mind that he would be able to do this without a battle, but Parma and every seasoned Spanish sailor knew that the English fleet would have to be totally defeated before the transports could venture out of port. Such a battle was indeed inevitable, and the English dispositions secured that the Spaniards would have to fight it under every disadvantage which was inherent in the plan of dual lines of operation. The English would secure certain contact at such a distance from the line of passage as would permit prolonged harassing attacks in waters unfamiliar to the enemy and close to their own sources of support and supply. No battle to the death would be necessary until the Spaniards were herded into the confined and narrow waters which the army's passage demanded, and where both sections of the British fleet would be massed for the final struggle. They must arrive there dispirited with indecisive actions and with the terrors of unknown and difficult seas at the highest point. All this was no matter of chance. It was inherent in the strategical and geographical conditions. The English dispositions had taken every advantage of them, and the result was that not only was the Spanish army unable even to move, but the English advantages in the final battle were so great, that it was only a lucky shift of wind that saved the Armada from being driven to total destruction upon the Dutch banks.

In this case, of course, there had been ample time to make the necessary dispositions. It will be well to follow it with an example in which surprise came as near to being complete as it is possible to conceive, and where the arrangements for defence had to be improvised on the spur of the moment.

A case in point was the French attempt of 1744. In that year everything was in favour of the invader. England was undermined with Jacobite sedition; Scotland was restless and threatening; the navy had sunk to what is universally regarded as its worst for spirit, organisation, and command; and the government was in the hands of the notorious "Drunken Administration." For three years we had been making unsuccessful war with Spain, and had been supporting Maria Theresa on the Continent against France, with the result that our home defence was reduced to its lowest ebb. The navy then numbered 183 sail—about equal to

that of France and Spain combined—but owing to the
strain of the war in the Mediterranean and Transatlantic
stations only forty-three, including eighteen of the
line, were available for home waters. Even counting
all cruising ships " within call," as the phrase then was,
the Government had barely one-fourth of the fleet at
hand to meet the crisis. With the land forces it was
little better. Considerably more than half the home
army was abroad with the King, who was assisting the Empress-Queen as Elector of Hanover.
Between France and England, however, there was no
war. In the summer the King won the battle of
Dettingen; a formal alliance with Maria Theresa
followed in the autumn; France responded with a
secret alliance with Spain; and to prevent further
British action on the Continent, she resolved to strike
a blow at London in combination with a Jacobite
insurrection. It was to be a " bolt from the blue "
before declaration and in mid-winter, when the best
ships of the home fleet were laid up. The operation
was planned on dual lines, the army to start from
Dunkirk, the covering fleet from Brest.

The surprise was admirably designed. The port of
Dunkirk had been destroyed under the Treaty of
Utrecht in 1713, and though the French had been re-
storing it secretly for some time, it was still unfit to
receive a fleet of transports. In spite of the warnings
of Sir John Norris, the senior admiral in the service,
the assembling of troops in its neighbourhood from the
French army in Flanders could only be taken for a
movement into winter quarters, and that no suspicion
might be aroused the necessary transports were secretly
taken up in other ports under false charter-parties, and
were only to assemble off Dunkirk at the last moment.

With equal skill the purpose of the naval mobilisation at Brest was concealed. By false information cleverly imparted to our spies and by parade of victualling for a long voyage, the British Government was led to believe that the main fleet was intended to join the Spaniards in the Mediterranean, while a detachment, which was designed to escort the transports, was ostensibly equipped for a raid in the West Indies.

So far as concealment was concerned the arrangement was perfect. Yet it contained within it the fatal ingredient. The army was to strike in the Thames at Tilbury; but complete as was the secrecy, Marshal Saxe, who was to command, could not face the passage without escort. There were too many privateers and armed merchantmen always in the river, besides cruisers moving to and fro on commerce-protection duty. The division, therefore, which we supposed to be for the West Indies was to be detached from the Brest fleet after it entered the Channel and was to proceed to join the transports off Dunkirk, while the Marquis de Roquefeuil with the main fleet held what British ships might be ready in Portsmouth either by battle or blockade.

Nothing could look simpler or more certain of success. The British Government seemed quite asleep. The blow was timed for the first week in January, and it was mid-December before they even began to watch Brest with cruisers regularly. On these cruisers' reports measures were taken to prepare an equal squadron for sea by the new year. By this time nearly twenty of the line were ready or nearly so at the Nore, Portsmouth, and Plymouth, and a press was ordered to man them. Owing to various causes the French had now to postpone their venture. Finally

it was not till February 6th that Roquefeuil was seen
to leave Brest with nineteen of the line. The news
reached London on the 12th, and next day Norris was
ordered to hoist his flag at Spithead. His instructions
were " to take the most effectual measures to prevent
the making of any descent upon the kingdoms." It
was nothing but news that the young Pretender had
left Rome for France that led to this precaution. The
Government had still no suspicion of what was brew-
ing at Dunkirk. It was not till the 20th that a Dover
smuggler brought over information which at last
opened their eyes.

A day or two later the French transports were seen
making for Dunkirk, and were mistaken for the Brest
fleet. Orders were consequently sent down to Norris
to follow them. In vain he protested at the interference. He knew the French were still to the westward of him, but his orders were repeated, and he had
to go. Tiding it up-Channel against easterly winds,
he reached the Downs and joined the Nore Division
there on the 28th. History usually speaks of this
false movement as the happy chance which saved the
country from invasion. But it was not so. Saxe had
determined not to face the Thames ships without
escort. They were ample to destroy him had he done
so. In truth the move which the Government forced
on Norris spoilt the campaign and prevented his
destroying the Brest fleet as well as stopping the
invasion.

Roquefeuil had just received his final orders off
the Start. He was instructed by all possible means
to bring the main British fleet to action, or at least to
prevent further concentration, while he was also to
detach the special division of four of the line under

Admiral Barraille to Dunkirk to escort the transports. It was in fact the inevitable order, caused by our hold on the army, to divide the fleet. Both officers as usual began to be upset, and as with Medina-Sidonia, they decided to keep company till they reached the Isle of Wight and remain there till they could get touch with Saxe and pilots for the Dover Strait. They were beset with the nervousness that seems inseparable from this form of operation. Roquefeuil explained to his Government that it was impossible to tell what ships the enemy had passed to the Downs, and that Barraille when he arrived off Dunkirk might well find himself in inferiority. He ended in the usual way by urging that the whole fleet must move in a body to the line of passage. On arriving off Portsmouth, however, a reconnaissance in thick weather led him to believe that the whole of Norris's fleet was still there, and he therefore detached Barraille, who reached Dunkirk in safety.

Not knowing that Norris was in the Downs, Saxe began immediately to embark his troops, but bad weather delayed the operation for three days, and so saved the expedition, exposed as it was in the open roads, from destruction by an attack which Norris was on the point of delivering with his flotilla of fireships and bomb vessels.

The Brest squadron had an equally narrow escape. Saxe and his staff having heard rumours of Norris's movement to the Downs had become seized with the sea-sickness which always seems to afflict an army as it waits to face the dangers of an uncommanded passage. They too wanted the whole fleet to escort them, and orders had been sent to Roquefeuille to do as he had suggested. All unconscious of Norris's presence in the Downs with a score of the line more powerful than his own, he came on with the fifteen he had still with his flag to close on Barraille. Norris was informed of his approach, and it was now he wrote his admirable appreciation, already quoted, for dealing with the situation.

"As I think it," he said, "of the greatest conse- quence to his Majesty's service to prevent the landing of these troops in any part of the country, I have . . . determined to anchor without the sands of Dunkirk, where we shall be in the fairest way for keeping them in." That is, he determined to keep hold of the army regardless of the enemy's fleet, and as Saxe's objective was not quite certain, he would do it by close blockade. "But if," he continued, "they should unfortunately get out and pass in the night and go northward [that is, for Scotland], I intend to detach a superior force to endeavour to overtake and destroy them, and with the remainder of my squadron either fight the French fleet now in the Channel, or observe them and cover the country as our circumstances will admit of; or I shall pursue the embarkation [that is, follow the transports] with all my strength." This meant he would treat the enemy's army offensively and their fleet defensively, and his plan was entirely approved by the King.

As to which of the two plans he would adopt, the inference is that his choice would depend on the strength of the enemy, for it was reported the Rochefort squadron had joined Roquefeuille. The doubt was quickly settled. On the morrow he heard that Roquefeuille was at Dungeness with only fifteen of the line. In a moment he seized all the advantage of the interior position which Roquefeuille's necessity to close on the army had given him. With admirable insight he saw there was time to fling his whole force at the enemy's fleet without losing his hold on the army's line of passage. The movement was made immediately. The moment the French were sighted "General chase" was signalled, and Roquefeuille was within an ace of being surprised at his anchorage when a calm stopped the attack. The calm was succeeded by another furious gale, in which the French escaped in a disastrous *sauve qui peut*, and the fleet of transports was destroyed. The outcome of it all was not only the failure of the invasion, but that we secured the command of home waters for the rest of the war.

The whole attempt, it will be seen, with everything in its favour, had exhibited the normal course of degradation. For all the nicely framed plan and the perfect deception, the inherent difficulties, when it came to the point of execution, had as usual forced a clumsy concentration of the enemy's battle-fleet with his transports, and we on our part were able to forestall it with every advantage in our favour by the simple expedient of a central mass on a revealed and certain line of passage.

In the next project, that of 1759, a new and very clever plan was devised for turning the difficulty. The first idea of Marshal Belleisle, like that of Napoleon, was to gather the army at Ambleteuse and Boulogne, and to avoid the assemblage of transports by passing it across the Strait by stealth in flat boats. But this idea was abandoned before it had gone very far for something much more subtle. The fallacious advantage of a short passage was dropped, and the army was to start from three widely separated points all in more open waters —a diversionary raid from Dunkirk and two more formidable forces from Havre and the Morbihan in

South Brittany. To secure sufficient control there was to be a concentration on the Brest fleet from the Mediterranean and the West Indies.

The new feature, it will be observed, was that our covering fleet—that is, the Western Squadron off Brest —would have two cruiser blockades to secure, one on either side of it. Difficult as the situation looked, it was solved on the old lines. The two divisions of the French army at Dunkirk and Morbihan were held by cruiser squadrons capable of following them over the open sea if by chance they escaped, while the third division at Havre, which had nothing but flat boats for transport, was held by a flotilla well supported. Its case was hopeless. It could not move without a squadron to release it, and no fortune of weather could possibly bring a squadron from Brest. Hawke, who had the main blockade, might be blown off, but he could scarcely fail to bring to action any squadron that attempted to enter the Channel. With the Morbihan force it was different. Any time that Hawke was blown off a squadron could reach it from Brest and break the cruiser blockade. The French Government actually ordered a portion of the fleet to make the attempt. Conflans however, who was in command, protested his force was too weak to divide, owing to the failure of the intended concentration. Boscawen had caught and beaten the Mediterranean squadron off Lagos, and though the West Indian squadron got in, it proved, as in Napoleon's great plan of concentration, unfit for further service. The old situation had arisen, forced by the old method of defence; and in the end there was nothing for it but for Conflans to take his whole fleet to the Morbihan transports. Hawke was upon him at once, and the disastrous day of Quiberon was the result. The Dunkirk division alone got free, but the smallness of its size, which permitted it to evade the watch, also prevented its doing any harm. Its escort, after landing its handful of troops in Ireland, was entirely destroyed; and so again the attempt of the French to invade over an uncommanded sea produced no effect but the loss of their fleet.

The project of 1779 marked these principles even more strongly, for it demonstrated them working even when our home fleet was greatly inferior to that of the enemy. In this case the invader's idea was to form two expeditionary forces at Cherbourg and Havre, and under cover of an overwhelming combination of the Spanish and French fleets, to unite them at sea and seize Portsmouth and the Isle of Wight. It was in the early summer we got wind of the scheme, and two cruiser squadrons and flotillas were at once formed at the Downs and Channel Islands to watch the French coasts and prevent the concentration of transports. Spain had not yet declared war, but she was suspected, and the main fleet, under the veteran Sir Charles Hardy, who had been Norris's second in command in 1744, was ordered to proceed off Brest and prevent any Spanish squadron that might appear from entering that port. The French, however, outmanœuvred us by putting to sea before Hardy could reach his station and forming a junction with the Spaniards off Finisterre. The combined fleet contained about fifty of the line, nearly double our own. The army of invasion, with Dumouriez for its Chief of the Staff, numbered some 50,000 men, a force we were in no condition to meet ashore. Everything, therefore, was in favour of success, and yet in the navy, at least, a feeling of confidence prevailed that no invasion could take place.

The brains of the naval defence were Lord Barham
(then Sir Charles Middleton) at the Admiralty and
Kempenfelt as Chief of the Staff in the fleet; and it is
to their correspondence at this time that we owe some
of the most valuable strategical appreciations we possess.
The idea of the French was to come into the Channel
in their overwhelming force, and while they destroyed
or held Hardy, to detach a sufficient squadron to break
the cruiser blockade and escort the troops across. Kempenfelt was confident that it could not be done. He
was sure that the unwieldy combined mass could be
rendered powerless by his comparatively homogeneous
and mobile fleet, inferior as it was, so long as he could
keep it at sea and to the westward. The appreciation
of the power of a nimble inferior fleet which he wrote
at this time has already been given.[1] When the worst
of the position was fully known, and the enemy was
reported off the mouth of the Channel, he wrote another
to Middleton. His only doubt was whether his fleet
had the necessary cohesion and mobility. " We don't
seem," he said, " to have considered sufficiently a
certain fact that the comparative force of two fleets
depends much upon their sailing. The fleet that sails
fastest has much the advantage, as they can engage or
not as they please, and so have always in their power
to choose the favourable opportunity to attack. I
think I may safely hazard an opinion that twenty-five
sail of the line coppered would be sufficient to harass
and tease this great unwieldy combined Armada so as
to prevent their effecting anything, hanging continually
upon them, ready to catch at any opportunity of a
separation from night, gale or fog, to dart upon the
separated, to cut off convoys of provisions coming to

[1] *Supra*, p. 223.

them, and if they attempted an invasion, to oblige their whole fleet to escort the transports, and even then it would be impossible to protect them entirely from so active and nimble a fleet."

Here we have from the pen of one of the greatest masters the real key of the solution—the power, that is, of forcing the mass of the enemy's fleet to escort the transports. Hardy, of course, knew it well from his experience of 1744, and acted accordingly. This case is the more striking, since defence against the threatened invasion was not the whole of the problem he had to solve. It was complicated by instructions that he must also prevent a possible descent on Ireland, and cover the arrival of the great convoys. In reply, on August 1st, he announced his intention of taking station ten to twenty leagues W.S.W. of Scilly, "which I am of opinion," he said, "is the most proper station for the security of the trade expected from the East and West Indies, and for the meeting of the fleets of the enemy *should they attempt to come into the Channel.*" He underlined the last words, indicating, apparently, his belief that they would not venture to do so so long as he could keep his fleet to the westward and undefeated. This at least he did, till a month later he found it necessary to come in for supplies. Then, still avoiding the enemy, he ran not to Plymouth, but right up to St. Helen's. The movement is always regarded as an unworthy retreat, and it caused much dissatisfaction in the fleet at the time. But it is to be observed that his conduct was strictly in accordance with the principle which makes the invading army the primary objective. If Hardy's fleet was no longer fit to keep the sea without replenishment, then the proper place to seek replenishment was on the invader's line of passage. So long as he was there, invasion could not take place till he was defeated. The allies, it was true, were now free to join their transports, but the prospect of such a movement gave the admiral no uneasiness, for it would bring him the chance of serving his enemy as the Spaniards were served in 1588. "I shall do my utmost," he said, "to drive them up the Channel." It is the old principle. If the worst comes to the worst, so long as you are able to force the covering fleet upon the transports, and especially in narrow waters, invasion becomes an operation beyond the endurable risks of war.

So it proved. On August 14th Count d'Orvilliers, the allied commander-in-chief, had made the Lizard, and for a fortnight had striven to bring Hardy to decisive action. Until he had done so he dared neither enter the Channel with his fleet nor detach a squadron to break the cruiser blockades at the invasion bases. His ineffectual efforts exhausted his fleet's endurance, which the distant concentration at Finisterre had already severely sapped, and he was forced to return impotent to Brest before anything had been accomplished. The allies were not able to take the sea again that campaign, but even had it been in their power to do so, Hardy and Kempenfelt could have played their defensive game indefinitely, and with ever-increasing chances, as the winter drew near, of dealing a paralysing blow.

There was never any real chance of success, though it is true Dumouriez thought otherwise. He believed the enterprise might have gone through if a diversion had been made by the bulk of the fleet against Ireland, and under cover of it a *coup de main* delivered upon the Isle of Wight, "for which," he said, "six or eight of the line would have been enough." But it is inconceivable that old hands like Hardy and Kempenfelt would have been so easily beguiled of their hold on the line of passage. Had such a division been detached up the Channel from the allied fleet they would surely, according to tradition, have followed it with either a superior force or their whole squadron.

The well-known projects of the Great War followed the same course. Under Napoleon's directions they ran the whole gamut of every scheme that ever raised delusive hope before. Beginning from the beginning with the idea of stealing his army across in flat-boats, he was met with the usual flotilla defence. Then came his only new idea, which was to arm his transport flotilla to the point of giving it power to force a passage for itself. We replied by strengthening our flotilla. Convinced by experiment that his scheme was now impracticable, he set his mind on breaking the blockade by the sudden intrusion of a flying squadron from a distance. To this end various plausible schemes were worked out, but plan after plan melted in his hand, till he was forced to face the inevitable necessity of bringing an overwhelming battle force up to his transports. The experience of two centuries had taught him nothing. By a more distant concentration than had ever been attempted before he believed he could break the fatal hold of his enemy. The only result was so severely to exhaust his fleet that it never could get within reach of the real difficulties of its task, a task which every admiral in his service knew to be beyond the strength of the Imperial Navy. Nor did Napoleon even approach a solution of the problem he had set himself—invasion over an uncommanded sea. With our impregnable flotilla hold covered by an automatic concentration of battle-squadrons off Ushant, his army could never even have put forth, unless he had inflicted upon our covering fleet such a defeat as would have given him command of the sea, and with absolute control of the sea the passage of an army presents no difficulties.

Of the working of these principles under modern conditions we have no example. The acquisition of free movement must necessarily modify their application, and since the advent of steam there have been only two invasions over uncommanded seas—that of the Crimea in 1854, and that of Manchuria in 1904—and neither of these cases is in point, for in neither was there any attempt at naval defence. Still there seems no reason to believe that such defence applied in the old manner would be less effective than formerly. The flotilla was its basis, and since the introduction of the torpedo the power of the flotilla has greatly increased. Its real and moral effect against transports must certainly be greater than ever, and the power of squadrons to break a flotilla blockade is more restricted. Mines, again, tell almost entirely in favour of defence, so much so indeed as to render a rapid *coup de main* against any important port almost an impossibility. In the absence of all experience it is to such theoretical considerations we must turn for light.

Theoretically stated, the success of our old system of defence depended on four relations. Firstly, there is the relation between the rapidity with which an invasion force could be mobilised and embarked, and the rapidity with which restlessness in foreign ports and *places d'armes* could be reported; that is to say, the chance of surprise and evasion are as the speed of preparation to the speed of intelligence.

Secondly, there is the relation of the speed of

convoys to the speed of cruisers and flotilla; that is
to say, our ability to get contact with a convoy after it
has put to sea and before the expedition can be dis-
embarked is as the speed of our cruisers and flotilla
to the speed of the convoy.

Thirdly, there is the relation between the destructive power of modern cruisers and flotillas against a
convoy unescorted or weakly escorted and the corresponding power in sailing days.

Fourthly, there is the relation between the speed
of convoys and the speed of battle-squadrons, which is
of importance where the enemy's transports are likely
to be strongly escorted. On this relation depends the
facility with which the battle-squadron covering our
mobile defence can secure an interior position from
which it may strike either the enemy's battle-squadron
if it moves or his convoy before it can complete its
passage and effect the landing.

All these relations appear to have been modified
by modern developments in favour of the defence. In
the first ratio, that of speed of mobilisation to speed
of intelligence, it is obviously so. Although military
mobilisation may be still relatively as rapid as the
mobilisation of fleets, yet intelligence has outstripped
both. This is true both for gaining and for conveying
intelligence. Preparations for oversea invasion were
never easy to conceal, owing to the disturbance of the
flow of shipping that they caused. Elaborate precautions were taken to prevent commercial leakage of
intelligence, but they never entirely succeeded. Yet
formerly, in the condition of comparative crudeness
with which international trade was then organised,
concealment was relatively easy, at least for a time.
But the ever - growing sensitiveness of world-wide

commerce, when market movements are reported from
hour to hour instead of from week to week, has
greatly increased the difficulty. And apart from the
rapidity with which information may be gathered
through this alert and intimate sympathy between
Exchanges, there is the still more important fact that
with wireless the speed of conveying naval intelligence
has increased in a far higher ratio than the speed of sea
transit.

As regards the ratio between cruiser and convoy
speeds, on which evasion so much depends, it is the
same. In frigate days the ratio appears to have been
not more than seven to five. Now in the case at any
rate of large convoys it would be nearly double.

Of the destructive power of the flotilla, growing as
it does from year to year, enough has been said already.
With the advent of the torpedo and submarine it has
probably increased tenfold. In a lesser degree the
same is true of cruisers. In former days the physical
power of a cruiser to injure a dispersing convoy was
comparatively low, owing to her relatively low excess
of speed and the restricted range and destructive
power of her guns. With higher speed and higher
energy and range in gun power the ability of cruisers to
cut up a convoy renders its practical annihilation almost
certain if once it be caught, and consequently affords a
moral deterrent against trusting to evasion beyond anything that was known before.

The increased ratio of battle-fleet speed to that of
large convoys is equally indisputable and no less important, for the facility of finding interior positions
which it implies goes to the root of the old system.
So long as our battle-fleet is in a position whence it can
cover our flotilla blockade or strike the enemy's convoy

in transit, it forces his battle-fleet in the last resort to close up on the convoy, and that, as Kempenfelt pointed out, is practically fatal to the success of invasion.

From whatever point of view, then, we regard the future chances of successful invasion over an uncommanded sea, it would seem that not only does the old system hold good, but that all modern developments which touch the question bid fair to intensify the results which our sea service at least used so confidently to expect, and which it never failed to secure.

II

ATTACK AND DEFENCE OF TRADE

The base idea of the attack and defence of trade may be summed up in the old adage, "Where the carcase is, there will the eagles be gathered together." The most fertile areas always attracted the strongest attack, and therefore required the strongest defence; and between the fertile and the infertile areas it was possible to draw a line which for strategical purposes was definite and constant. The fertile areas were the terminals of departure and destination where trade tends to be crowded, and in a secondary degree the focal points where, owing to the conformation of the land, trade tends to converge. The infertile areas were the great routes which passed through the focal points and connected the terminal areas. Consequently attack on commerce tends to take one of two forms. It may be terminal or it may be pelagic, terminal attack being the more profitable, but demanding the greater force and risk, and pelagic attack being the more uncertain, but involving less force and risk.

These considerations lead us directly to the paradox which underlies the unbroken failure of our enemies to exercise decisive pressure upon us by operations against our trade. It is that where attack is most to be feared, there defence is easiest. A plan of war which has the destruction of trade for its primary object implies in the party using it an inferiority at sea. Had he superiority, his object would be to convert that superiority to a working command by battle or blockade. Except, therefore, in the rare cases where the opposed forces are equal, we must assume that the belligerent who makes commerce destruction his primary object will have to deal with a superior fleet. Now, it is true that the difficulty of defending trade lies mainly in the extent of sea it covers. But, on the other hand, the areas in which it tends to congregate, and in which alone it is seriously vulnerable, are few and narrow, and can be easily occupied if we are in superior force. Beyond those areas effective occupation is impossible, but so also is effective attack. Hence the controlling fact of war on commerce, that facility of attack means facility of defence.

Beside this fundamental principle we must place another that is scarcely less important. Owing to the general common nature of sea communications, attack and defence of trade are so intimately connected that the one operation is almost indistinguishable from the other. Both ideas are satisfied by occupying the common communications. The strongest form of attack is the occupation of the enemy's terminals, and the establishment of a commercial blockade of the ports they contain. But as this operation usually requires the blockade of an adjacent naval port, it also constitutes, as a rule, a defensive disposition for our own trade, even when the enemy's terminal area does not overlap one of our own. In the occupation of focal areas the two ideas are even more inseparable, since most, if not all, such areas are on lines of communication that are common. It will suffice, therefore, to deal with the general aspect of the subject from the point of view of defence.

It was in conformity with the distinction between fertile and infertile areas that our old system of trade defence was developed. Broadly speaking, that system was to hold the terminals in strength, and in important cases the focal points as well. By means of a battle-squadron with a full complement of cruisers they were constituted defended areas, or "tracts" as the old term was, and the trade was regarded as safe when it entered them. The intervening trade-routes were left as a rule undefended. Thus our home terminals were held by two battle-squadrons, the Western Squadron at the mouth of the Channel, and the North Sea or Eastern Squadron with its head-quarters usually in the Downs. To these was added a cruiser squadron on the Irish station based at Cork, which was sometimes subordinate to the Western Squadron and sometimes an independent organisation. The area of the Western Squadron in the French wars extended, as we have seen, over the whole Bay of Biscay, with the double function, so far as commerce was concerned, of preventing the issue of raiding squadrons from the enemy's ports, and acting offensively against his Atlantic trade. That of the North Sea squadron extended to the mouth of the Baltic and the north-about passage. Its main function during the great naval coalitions against us was to check the operations of Dutch squadrons or to prevent the intrusion of French ones north-about against our Baltic trade. Like the Western Squadron, it threw out divisions usually located at Yarmouth and Leith for the protection of our coastwise trade from privateers and sporadic cruisers acting from ports within the defended area. Similarly, between the Downs and the Western Squadron was usually one or more smaller squadrons, mainly cruisers, and generally located about Havre and the Channel Islands, which served the same purpose for the Norman and North Breton ports. To complete the system there were flotilla patrols acting under the port admirals and doing their best to police the routes of the coastwise and local traffic, which then had an importance long since lost. The home system of course differed at different times, but it was always on these general lines. The naval defence was supplemented by defended ports of refuge, the principal ones being on the coast of Ireland to shelter the ocean trade, but others in great numbers were provided within the defended areas against the operations of privateers, and the ruins of batteries all round the British shores testify how complete was the organisation.

A similar system prevailed in the colonial areas, but there the naval defence consisted normally of cruiser squadrons stiffened with one or two ships-of-the-line mainly for the purpose of carrying the flag. They were only occupied by battle-squadrons when the enemy threatened operations with a similar force. The minor or interior defence against local privateers was to a large extent local; that is, the great part of the flotilla was furnished by sloops built or hired on the spot, as being best adapted for the service.

Focal points were not then so numerous as they have become since the development of the Far Eastern trade. The most important of them, the Straits of Gibraltar, was treated as a defended area. From the point of view of commerce-protection it was held by the Mediterranean squadron. By keeping watch on Toulon that squadron covered not only the Straits, but also the focal points within the sea. It too had its extended divisions, sometimes as many as four, one about the approaches to Leghorn, one in the Adriatic, a third at Malta, and the fourth at Gibraltar. In cases of war with Spain the latter was very strong, so as to secure the focal area against Cartagena and Cadiz. On one occasion indeed, in 1804–5, as we have seen, it was constituted for a short time an independent area with a special squadron. But in any case the Gibraltar area had its own internal flotilla guard under the direction of the port admiral as a defence against local privateers and pirates.

The general theory of these defended terminal and focal areas, it will be seen, was to hold in force those waters which converging trade made most fertile, and which therefore furnished an adequate field for the operations of raiding squadrons. In spite of the elaborate defensive system, such squadrons might, and sometimes did, intrude by surprise or stealth, and were then able to set at defiance both convoy escorts and the cruiser outposts. But, as experience proved, the system of terminal defence by battle-squadrons made it impossible for such raiding squadrons to remain long enough on the ground to cause any serious interruption or to do serious harm. It was only by a regular fleet of

superior strength that the system could be broken
down. In other words, the defence could only fall
when our means of local control was destroyed by
battle.

So much for the defended areas. With regard to
the great routes that connected them, it has been said
they were left undefended. By this is meant that the
security of ships passing along them was provided for,
not by patrols but by escort. The convoy system was
adopted, and the theory of that system is that while
vessels are on the great routes they are normally liable
only to sporadic attack, and they are consequently
collected into fleets and furnished with an escort sufficient to repel sporadic attack. In theory, cruiser escort
is sufficient, but in practice it was found convenient
and economical to assign the duty in part to ships-of-
the-line which were going out to join the distant
terminal squadron or returning from it for a refit or
some other reason; in other words, the system of
foreign reliefs was made to work in with the supple-
mentary escort system. Where no such ships were
available and the convoys were of great value, or
enemy's ships-of-the-line were known to be out, similar
units were specially detailed for convoy duty to go and
return, but this use of battle units was exceptional.

Such a method of dealing with the great routes is
the corollary of the idea of defended areas. As those
areas were fertile and likely to attract raiding squadrons,
so the great routes were infertile, and no enemy could
afford to spend squadrons upon them. It is obvious,
however, that the system had its weak side, for the
mere fact that a convoy was upon a great route tended
to attract a squadron, and the comparative immunity of
those routes was lost. The danger was provided for to

a great extent by the fact that the enemy's ports from which a squadron could issue were all within defended areas and watched by our own squadrons. Still, the guard could not be made impenetrable. There was always the chance of a squadron escaping, and if it escaped towards a critical trade-route, it must be followed. Hence there were times when the convoy system seriously disturbed our dispositions, as, for instance, in the crisis of the Trafalgar campaign, when for a short time our chain of defended areas was broken down by the escape of the Toulon squadron. That escape eventually forced a close concentration on the Western Squadron, but all other considerations apart, it was felt to be impossible to retain the mass for more than two days owing to the fact that the great East and West Indies convoys were approaching, and Villeneuve's return to Ferrol from Martinique exposed them to squadronal attack. It was, in fact, impossible to tell whether the mass had not been forced upon us with this special end in view.

In the liability to deflection of this kind lay the most serious strategical objection to the convoy system. It was sought to minimise it by giving the convoys a secret route when there was apprehension of squadronal interference. It was done in the case just cited, but the precaution seemed in no way to lessen the anxiety. It may have been because in those days of slow communication there could be no such certainty that the secret route had been received as there would be now.

Modern developments and changes in shipping and naval material have indeed so profoundly modified the whole conditions of commerce protection, that there is no part of strategy where historical deduction is more difficult or more liable to error. To avoid such error as far as possible, it is essential to keep those developments in mind at every step. The more important of them are three in number. Firstly, the abolition of privateering; secondly, the reduced range of action for all warships; and thirdly, the development of wireless telegraphy. There are others which must be dealt with in their place, but these three go to the root of the whole problem.

Difficult as it is to arrive at exact statistics of commerce destruction in the old wars, one thing seems certain—that the bulk of captures, which were reckoned in hundreds and sometimes even in thousands, were due to the action of privateers. Further, it seems certain that, reckoning at least by numbers, the greater part of the damage was done by small privateers operating close to their bases, either home or colonial, against coastwise and local traffic. The complaints of merchants, so far as they are known, relate mainly to this kind of work in the West Indies and home waters, while accounts of serious captures by large privateers on the high seas are comparatively rare. The actual damage done by the swarm of small vessels may not have been great, but its moral effects were very serious. It was impossible for the strongest Governments to ignore them, and the consequence was a chronic disturbance of the larger strategical dispositions. While these dispositions were adequate to check the operations of large privateers acting in the same way as regular cruisers, the smaller ones found very free play amidst the rib-work of the protective system, and they could only be dealt with by filling up the spaces with a swarm of small cruisers to the serious detriment of the larger arrangements. Even so, the proximity of the enemy's ports made escape so easy, that the work of repression was very ineffective. The state of the case was indeed almost identical with a people's war. The ordinary devices of strategy failed to deal with it, as completely as Napoleon's broadly planned methods failed to deal with the *guerilleros* in Spain, or as our own failed for so long in South Africa.

By the abolition of privateering, then, it would seem that the most disturbing part of the problem has been eliminated. It is, of course, uncertain how far the Declaration of Paris will hold good in practice. It is still open even to the parties to it to evade its restrictions to a greater or less extent by taking up and commissioning merchantmen as regular ships of war. But it is unlikely that such methods will extend beyond the larger privately owned vessels. Any attempt to revive in this way the old *picaresque* methods could only amount to a virtual repudiation of statutory international law, which would bring its own retribution. Moreover, for home waters at least, the conditions which favoured this *picaresque* warfare no longer exist. In the old wars the bulk of our trade came into the Thames, and thence the greater part of it was distributed in small coasting vessels. It was against this coastwise traffic that the small, short-range privateers found their opportunity and their richest harvest. But, now that so many other great centres of distribution have established themselves, and that the bulk of the distribution is done by internal lines of communication, the Channel is no longer the sole artery, and the old troublesome disturbance can be avoided without a vital dislocation of our commercial system.

The probability, then, is that in the future the whole problem will be found to be simplified, and

that the work of commerce protection will lie much
more within the scope of large strategical treatment
than it ever did before, with the result that the
change should be found to tell substantially in favour
of defence and against attack.

The reduction of range of action is scarcely less important. In the old days a cruising ship could be stored
for six months, and so long as she could occasionally
renew her fuel and water, she was free to range the sea
outside the defended areas for the whole of the period
with unimpaired vitality. For such pelagic operations
her movement was practically unrestricted. She could
run for two or three days from a superior enemy or
chase for as long without loss of energy, and she could
wait indefinitely at a likely spot, or change her ground,
as danger or hope of plunder dictated. So long as she
had men left to man her prizes, her power of mischief
was almost unlimited. All this is now changed. The
capacity of each cruise of a ship to-day is very small.
She is confined to short dashes within a strategically
defended area, or if she is bent on pelagic operations, is
compelled to proceed so far to find undefended waters
that her coal will scarcely permit of more than a few
days' actual cruising. A couple of chases at high speed
during that period may force her to return at once,
subject only to the precarious possibility of renewing
her coal from a prize. She has, further, to face the fact
that manning prizes must necessarily reduce her capacity for speed, which depends so much on a fully
manned engine-room. This will tend to jeopardise her
chances of return through or near defended areas. The
only escape from this difficulty is to sink the captured
ship. But this course has objections scarcely less
weighty than the other. No Power will incur the odium

of sinking a prize with all hands, and their removal to the captor's ship takes time, especially in bad weather, and the presence of such prisoners in a cruiser in any number soon becomes a serious check on her fighting power. In the case of large ships, moreover, the work of destruction is no easy matter. In the most favourable circumstances it takes a considerable time, and thus not only eats into the cruiser's endurance, but decreases her chances of evasion.

From these and similar considerations it is obvious that the possibilities of operations on the great trade-routes are much less extensive than they were formerly, while to speak of cruisers "infesting" those routes is sheer hyperbole. Under modern conditions it is scarcely more feasible than it would be to keep up a permanent blockade of the British Islands. It would require a flow of ships in such numbers as no country but our own can contemplate possessing, and such as could not be maintained without having first secured a very decided preponderance at sea. The loss of radius of action therefore, though it does not increase the power of defence, sensibly lessens that of attack by pelagic operations.

For the great increase in the powers of defence we must turn to the extraordinary development in the means of distant communication. Under former conditions it was possible for a cruising ship to remain for days upon a fertile spot and make a number of captures before her presence was known. But since most large merchantmen have been fitted with wireless installations, she cannot now attack a single one of them without fear of calling down upon her an adversary. Moreover, when she is once located, every ship within wireless reach can be warned of her presence and avoid her. She must widely and constantly shift her position, thereby still further reducing her staying power. On the whole, then, it would appear that in so far as modern developments affect the problem, they certainly render pelagic operations far more difficult and uncertain than they used to be. Upon the great routes the power of attack has been reduced and the means of evasion has increased to such an extent as to demand entire reconsideration of the defence of trade between terminal areas. The whole basis of the old system would seem to be involved. That basis was the convoy system, and it now becomes doubtful whether the additional security which convoys afforded is sufficient to outweigh their economical drawbacks and their liability to cause strategical disturbance.

Over and above the considerations already noticed, there are three others, all of which favour the security of our trade by permitting a much more extended choice of route. The first is, that steam vessels are not forced by prevailing winds to keep to particular courses. The second is, that the improvements in the art of navigation no longer render it so necessary to make well-known landfalls during transit. The third is, that the multiplication of our great ports of distribution have divided the old main flow of trade to the Channel into a number of minor streams that cover a much wider area and demand a greater distribution of force for effective attack. It will be obvious that the combined effect of these considerations is to increase still further the chances of individual vessels evading the enemy's cruisers and to lessen the risk of dispensing with escort.

Nor are the new practical difficulties of sporadic operations on the great routes the only arguments that

minimise the value of convoys. We have also to remember that while the number of vessels trading across
the ocean has enormously increased since 1815, it is
scarcely possible, even if the abolition of privateering
prove abortive, that the number of cruisers available
for pelagic attack could exceed, or even equal, the
number employed in sailing days. This consideration,
then, must also be thrown into the scale against convoys;
for it is certain that the amount of serious operative
damage which an enemy can do to our trade by pelagic
operation is mainly determined by the ratio which his
available cruiser strength bears to the volume of that
trade. This aspect of the question is, however, part of a
much wider one, which concerns the relation which the
volume of our trade bears to the difficulty of its defence,
and this must be considered later.

It remains, first, to deal with the final link in the old
system of defence. The statement that the great routes
were left undefended will seem to be in opposition to a
prevailing impression derived from the fact that frigates
are constantly mentioned as being "on a cruise." The
assumption is that they in effect patrolled the great
routes. But this was not so, nor did they rove the sea
at will. They constituted a definite and necessary part
of the system. Though that system was founded on a
distinction between defended terminals and undefended
routes, which was a real strategical distinction, it was
impossible to draw an actual line where the one sphere
began and the other ended. Outside the regularly
defended areas lay a region which, as the routes began
to converge, was comparatively fertile. In this region
enemies' cruisers and their larger privateers found the
mean between risk and profit. Here too convoys, as
they entered the zone, were in their greatest danger for

fear of their escorts being overpowered by raiding squadrons. Consequently it was the practice, when the approach of convoys was expected, to throw forward from the defended area groups of powerful cruisers, and even battleship divisions, to meet them and reinforce their escorts. Outward-bound convoys had their escorts similarly strengthened till they were clear of the danger zone. The system was in regular use both for home and colonial areas. In no sense did it constitute a patrol of the routes. It was in practice and conception a system of outposts, which at seasons of special risk amounted to an extension of the defended areas combining with a reinforcement of the convoy escorts. Focal points of lesser importance, such as Capes Finisterre and St. Vincent, were similarly held by one or two powerful cruisers, and if necessary by a squadron.

As has been already explained, owing to the peculiar conditions of the sea and the common nature of maritime communications, these dispositions were adopted as well for attack as defence, and the fertile areas, for the defence of which a frigate captain was sent "on a cruise," were always liable to bring him rich reward. His mission of defence carried with it the best opportunities for attack.

In the full development of the system patrol lines did exist, but not for the great routes. They were established to link up adjacent defended areas and as a more scientific organisation of the cruiser outposts. In 1805 the Gibraltar and the home areas were thus connected by a patrol line which stretched from Cape St. Vincent through the Finisterre focal area to Cape Clear, with a branch extending to the strategical centre off Ushant. The new system was introduced at a time when we had reason to expect

that the French and Spanish fleets were to be devoted
entirely to operations in small raiding squadrons
against our trade and colonies. Special provision
was therefore necessary to locate any such squadrons
that might elude the regular blockades, and to ensure
that they should be adequately pursued. The new
lines were in fact intelligence patrols primarily, though
they were also regarded as the only means of protecting efficiently the southern trade-route where it was
flanked by French and Spanish ports.[1]

The whole system, it will be observed, though not
conflicting with the main object of bringing the enemy's
fleets to action, did entail an expenditure of force
and deflecting preoccupations such as are unknown
in land warfare. Large numbers of cruisers had to
be employed otherwise than as the eyes of the battle-
squadrons, while the coming and going of convoys
produced periodical oscillations in the general distribution.

Embarrassing as was this commercial deflection in
the old wars, an impression appears to prevail that in
the future it must be much more serious. It is argued
plausibly enough not only that our trade is far larger
and richer than it was, but also that, owing to certain
well-known economic changes, it is far more a matter
of life and death to the nation than in the days when
food and raw material did not constitute the bulk of
our imports. In view of the new conditions it is held
that we are more vulnerable through our trade now

---

[1] It should be said that Cornwallis did not regard this system
as new, except for the extension from Finisterre to St. Vincent, which
Nelson advised. In acknowledging the order from Ushant he wrote,
" The instructions . . . are nearly the same as have generally been
given. I can therefore only guess why a copy of the order was sent
to me."—*Admiralty, In-letters*, 129, September 28, 1805.

than formerly, and that, consequently, we must devote
relatively more attention and force to its defence.

If this were true, it is obvious that war with a
strong naval combination would present difficulties
of the most formidable kind, greater indeed than
we have ever experienced; for since with modern
developments the demand for fleet cruisers is much
greater than formerly, the power of devoting cruisers
to trade defence is relatively much less.

It cannot be denied that at first sight the conclusion
looks irreproachable. But on analysis it will be found
to involve two assumptions, both of which are highly
questionable. The first is, that the vulnerability of a
sea Power through its maritime trade is as the volume
of that trade. The second is, that the difficulty of
defending sea-borne trade is also as its volume—that
is to say, the larger the amount of the trade, the larger
must be the force devoted to its protection. This idea
indeed is carried so far, that we are frequently invited
to fix the standard of our naval strength by comparing
it with the proportion which the naval strength of
other Powers bears to their sea-borne trade.

It is hoped that the foregoing sketch of our traditional system of trade defence will avail to raise a
doubt whether either assumption can be accepted
without very careful consideration. In the history of
that system there is no indication that it was affected
by the volume of the trade it was designed to protect.
Nor has any one succeeded in showing that the pressure
which an enemy could exert upon us through our
commerce increased in effect with the volume of our
sea-borne trade. The broad indications indeed are the
other way—that the greater the volume of our trade,
the less was the effective impression which an enemy

could make upon it, even when he devoted his whole naval energies to that end. It is not too much to say that in every case where he took this course his own trade dwindled to nothing, while ours continually increased.

It may be objected that this was because the only periods in which he devoted his main efforts to trade destruction were when we had dominated his navy, and being no longer able to dispute the command, he could do no more than interfere with its exercise. But this must always be so whether we have positively dominated his navy or not. If he tries to ignore our battle-fleets, and devotes himself to operations against trade, he cannot dispute the command. Whatever his strength, he must leave the command to us. He cannot do both systematically, and unless he attacks our trade systematically by sustained strategical operation, he cannot hope to make any real impression.

If, now, we take the two assumptions and test them by the application of elementary principles, both will appear theoretically unsound. Let us take first the relation of vulnerability to volume. Since the object of war is to force our will upon the enemy, the only way in which we can expect war on commerce to serve our end is to inflict so much damage upon it as will cause our enemy to prefer peace on our terms to a continuation of the struggle. The pressure on his trade must be insupportable, not merely annoying. It must seriously cripple his finance or seriously threaten to strangle his national life and activities. If his total trade be a hundred millions, and we succeed in destroying five, he will feel it no more than he does the ordinary fluctations to which he is accustomed in time of peace. If, however, we can destroy fifty millions, his trade equilibrium will be overthrown, and the issue of the war will be powerfully affected. In other words, to affect the issue the impression made on trade must be a percentage or relative impression. The measure of a nation's vulnerability through its trade is the percentage of destruction that an enemy can effect.

Now, it is true that the amount of damage which a belligerent can inflict with a given force on an enemy's commerce will vary to some extent with its volume; for the greater the volume of commerce, the more fertile will be the undefended cruising grounds. But no matter how fertile such areas might be, the destructive power of a cruiser was always limited, and it must be still more limited in the future. It was limited by the fact that it was physically impossible to deal with more than a certain number of prizes in a certain time, and, for the reasons already indicated, this limit has suffered a very marked restriction. When this limit of capacity in a given force is passed, the volume of commerce will not affect the issue; and seeing how low that capacity must be in the future and how enormous is the volume of our trade, the limit of destructive power, at least as against ourselves, provided we have a reasonably well-organised system of defence, must be relatively low. It must, in fact, be passed at a percentage figure well within what we have easily supported in the past. There is reason, therefore, to believe that so far from the assumption in question being true, the effective vulnerability of sea-borne trade is not in direct but in inverse proportion to its volume. In other words, the greater the volume, the more difficult it is to make an effective percentage impression.

Similarly, it will be observed that the strain of trade defence was proportioned not to the volume of that trade, but to the number and exposure of its terminals and focal points. Whatever the volume of the trade these remained the same in number, and the amount of force required for their defence varied only with the strength that could readily be brought to bear against them. It varied, that is, with the distribution of the enemy's bases and the amount of his naval force. Thus in the war of 1812 with the United States, the West Indian and North American areas were much more exposed than they had been when we were at war with France alone and when American ports were not open to her as bases. They became vulnerable not only to the United States fleet, but also in a much higher degree to that of France, and consequently the force we found necessary to devote to trade defence in the North Atlantic was out of all proportion to the naval strength of the new belligerent. Our protective force had to be increased enormously, while the volume of our trade remained precisely the same.

This relation of trade defence to terminal and focal areas is of great importance, for it is in the increase of such areas in the Far East that lies the only radical change in the problem. The East Indian seas were always of course to some extent treated as a defended area, but the problem was simplified by the partial survival in those regions of the old method of defence. Till about the end of the seventeenth century long-range trade was expected to defend itself, at least outside the home area, and the retention of their armament by East Indiamen was the last survival of the practice. Beyond the important focal area of St. Helena they relied mainly on their own power of resistance or to such escort as could be provided by the relief ships of the East Indian station. As a rule, their escort proper went no farther outward-bound than St. Helena, whence it returned with the homeward-bound vessels that gathered there from India, China, and the South Sea whaling grounds. The idea of the system was to provide escort for that part of the great route which was exposed to attack from French or Spanish colonial bases on the African coasts and in the adjacent islands.

For obvious reasons this system would have to be reconsidered in the future. The expansion of the great European Powers have changed the conditions for which it sufficed, and in a war with any one of them the system of defended terminal and focal areas would require a great extension eastward, absorbing an appreciable section of our force, and entailing a comparatively weak prolongation of our chain of concentrations. Here, then, we must mark a point where trade defence has increased in difficulty, and there is one other.

Although minor hostile bases within a defended area have lost most of their menace to trade, they have acquired as torpedo bases a power of disturbing the defence itself. So long as such bases exist with a potent flotilla within them, it is obvious that the actual provision for defence cannot be so simple a matter as it was formerly. Other and more complex arrangements may have to be made. Still, the principle of defended areas seems to remain unshaken, and if it is to work with its old effectiveness, the means and the disposition for securing those areas will have to be adapted to the new tactical possibilities. The old strategical conditions, so far as can be seen, are unaltered except in so far as the reactions of modern material make them tell in favour of defence rather than of attack.

If we desire to formulate the principles on which

this conclusion rests we shall find them in the two broad rules, firstly, that the vulnerability of trade is in inverse ratio to its volume, and secondly, that facility of attack means facility of defence. The latter, which was always true, receives special emphasis from modern developments. Facility of attack means the power of exercising control. For exercise of control we require not only numbers, but also speed and endurance, qualities which can only be obtained in two ways: it must be at the cost of armour and armament, or at the cost of increased size. By increasing size we at once lose numbers. If by sacrificing armament and armour we seek to maintain numbers and so facilitate attack, we at the same time facilitate defence. Vessels of low fighting power indeed cannot hope to operate in fertile areas without support to overpower the defence. Every powerful unit detached for such support sets free a unit on the other side, and when this process is once begun, there is no halting-place. Supporting units to be effective must multiply into squadrons, and sooner or later the inferior Power seeking to substitute commerce destruction for the clash of squadrons will have squadronal warfare thrust upon him, provided again the superior Power adopts a reasonably sound system of defence. It was always so, and, so far as it is possible to penetrate the mists which veil the future, it would seem that with higher mobility and better means of communication the squadronal stage must be reached long before any adequate percentage impression can have been made by the sporadic action of commerce destroyers. Ineffectual as such warfare has always been in the past, until a general command has been established, its prospects in the future, judged by the old established principles, are less promising than ever.

Finally, in approaching the problem of trade protection, and especially for the actual determination of the force and distribution it requires, there is a dominant limitation to be kept in mind. By no conceivable means is it possible to give trade absolute protection. We cannot make an omelette without breaking eggs. We cannot make war without losing ships. To aim at a standard of naval strength or a strategical distribution which would make our trade absolutely invulnerable is to march to economic ruin. It is to cripple our power of sustaining war to a successful issue, and to seek a position of maritime despotism which, even if it were attainable, would set every man's hand against us. All these evils would be upon us, and our goal would still be in the far distance. In 1870 the second naval Power in the world was at war with an enemy that could not be considered a naval Power at all, and yet she lost ships by capture. Never in the days of our most complete domination upon the seas was our trade invulnerable, and it never can be. To seek invulnerability is to fall into the strategical vice of trying to be superior everywhere, to forfeit the attainment of the essential for fear of risking the unessential, to base our plans on an assumption that war may be waged without loss, that it is, in short, something that it never has been and never can be. Such peace-bred dreams must be rigorously abjured. Our standard must be the mean of economic strength—the line which on the one hand will permit us to nourish our financial resources for the evil day, and on the other, when that day comes, will deny to the enemy the possibility of choking our financial vigour by sufficiently checking the flow of our trade.

III

ATTACK, DEFENCE, AND SUPPORT OF MILITARY EXPEDITIONS

The attack and defence of oversea expeditions are governed in a large measure by the principles of attack and defence of trade. In both cases it is a question of control of communications, and in a general way it may be said, if we control them for the one purpose, we control them for the other. But with combined expeditions freedom of passage is not the only consideration. The duties of the fleet do not end with the protection of the troops during transit, as in the case of convoys, unless indeed, as with convoys, the destination is a friendly country. In the normal case of a hostile destination, where resistance is to be expected from the commencement of the operations, the fleet is charged with further duties of a most exacting kind. They may be described generally as duties of support, and it is the intrusion of these duties which distinguish the naval arrangements for combined operations most sharply from those for the protection of trade. Except for this consideration there need be no difference in the method of defence. In each case the strength required would be measured by the dangers of interference in transit. But as it is, that standard will not serve for combined expeditions; for however small those risks, the protective arrangements must be sufficiently extensive to include arrangements for support.

Before dealing with this, the most complex aspect of the question, it will be well to dismiss attack. From the strategical point of view its principles differ

not at all from those already laid down for active
resistance of invasion. Whether the expedition that
threatens us be small or of invasion strength, the
cardinal rule has always been that the transports
and not the escort must be the primary objective of
the fleet. The escort, according to the old practice,
must be turned or contained, but never treated as a
primary objective unless both turning and containing
prove to be impracticable. It is needless to repeat
the words of the old masters in which this principle lies
embalmed. It is seldom that we find a rule of naval
strategy laid down in precise technical terms, but this
one is an exception. In the old squadronal instructions,
"The transports of the enemy are to be your principal
object," became something like a common form.

Nor did this rule apply only to cases where the
transports were protected by a mere escort. It held
good even in the exceptional cases where the military
force was accompanied or guarded by the whole
available battle strength of the enemy. We have
seen how in 1744 Norris was prepared to follow the
French transports if necessary with his whole force,
and how in 1798 Nelson organised his fleet in such
a way as to contain rather than destroy the enemy's
battle-squadron, so that he might provide for an
overwhelming attack upon the transports.

Exceptions to this as to all strategical rules may
be conceived. Conditions might exist in which, if
the enemy's battle-fleet accompanied his transports,
it would be worth our while, for ulterior objects of
our own, to risk the escape of the transports in order
to seize the opportunity of destroying the fleet. But
even in such a case the distinction would be little
more than academical; for our best chance of

securing a decisive tactical advantage against the enemy's fleet would usually be to compel it to conform to our movements by threatening an attack on the transports. It is well known that it is in the embarrassment arising from the presence of transports that lies the special weakness of a fleet in charge of them.

There is, however, one condition which radically differentiates comparatively small expeditions from great invasions and that is the power of evasion. Our experience has proved beyond dispute that the navy alone cannot guarantee defence against such expeditions. It cannot be sure of preventing their sailing or of attacking them in transit, and this is especially the case where an open sea gives them a free choice of route, as in the case of the French expeditions against Ireland. It is for this reason that, although an adequate navy has always proved sufficient to prevent an invasion, for defence against expeditions it must be supplemented by a home army. To perfect our defence, or, in other words, our power of attack, such an army must be adequate to ensure that all expeditions small enough to evade the fleet shall do no effective harm when they land. If in numbers, training, organisation, and distribution it is adequate for this purpose, an enemy cannot hope to affect the issue of the war except by raising his expeditions to invasion strength, and so finding himself involved in a problem that no one has ever yet solved for an uncommanded sea.

Still, even for expeditions below invasion strength the navy will only regard the army as a second line, and its strategy must provide in the event of evasion for co-operation with that line. By means of a just distribution of its coastal flotilla it will provide for getting contact with the expedition at the earliest

moment after its destination is declared. It will press
the principle of making the army its objective to the
utmost limit by the most powerful and energetic cruiser
pursuit, and with wireless and the increased ratio of
cruiser speed, such pursuit is far more formidable than
it ever was. No expedition nowadays, however successful its evasion, can be guaranteed against naval
interruption in the process of landing. Still less can it
be guaranteed against naval interference in its rear or
flanks while it is securing its front against the home
army. It may seek by using large transports to reduce
their number and secure higher speed, but while that
will raise its chance of evasion, it will prolong the
critical period of landing. If it seek by using smaller
transports to quicken disembarkation, that will decrease
its chances of evasion by lowering its speed and
widening the sea area it will occupy in transit. All
the modern developments in fact which make for
defence in case of invasion over an uncommanded sea
also go to facilitate timely contact with an expedition
seeking to operate by evasion. Nor must it be forgotten, since the problem is a combined one, that the
corresponding developments ashore tell with little less
force in favour of the defending army. Such appear to be
the broad principles which govern an enemy's attempts
to act with combined expeditions in our own waters,
where by hypothesis we are in sufficient naval strength
to deny him permanent local command. We may
now turn to the larger and more complex question of
the conduct of such expeditions where the naval conditions are reversed.

By the conduct, be it remembered, we mean not
only their defence but also their support, and for this
reason the starting-point of our inquiry is to be found,

as above indicated, in the contrast of combined expeditions with convoys. A convoy consists of two elements —a fleet of merchantmen and an escort. But a combined expedition does not consist simply of an army and a squadron. It is an organism at once more complex and more homogeneous. Its constitution is fourfold. There is, firstly, the army; secondly, the transports and landing flotilla—that is, the flotilla of flat-boats and steamboats for towing them, all of which may be carried in the transports or accompany them; thirdly, the "Squadron in charge of transports," as it came to be called, which includes the escort proper and the supporting flotilla of lighter craft for inshore work; and lastly, the "Covering squadron."

Such at least is a combined expedition in logical analysis. But so essentially is it a single organism, that in practice these various elements can seldom be kept sharply distinct. They may be interwoven in the most intricate manner. Indeed to a greater or less extent each will always have to discharge some of the functions of the others. Thus the covering squadron may not only be indistinguishable from the escort and support, but it will often provide the greater part of the landing flotilla and even a portion of the landing force. Similarly, the escort may also serve as transport, and provide in part not only the supporting force, but also the landing flotilla. The fourfold constitution is therefore in a great measure theoretical. Still its use is not merely that it serves to define the varied functions which the fleet will have to discharge. As we proceed it will be seen to have a practical strategical value.

From a naval point of view it is the covering squadron which calls first for consideration, because of the emphasis with which its necessity marks not only the distinction between the conduct of combined expeditions and the conduct of commercial convoys, but also the fact that such expeditions are actually a combined force, and not merely an army escorted by a fleet.

In our system of commerce protection the covering squadron had no place. The battle-fleet, as we have seen, was employed in holding definite terminal areas, and had no organic connection with the convoys. The convoys had no further protection than their own escort and the reinforcements that met them as they approached the terminal areas. But where a convoy of transports forming part of a combined expedition was destined for an enemy's country and would have to overcome resistance by true combined operations, a covering battle-squadron was always provided. In the case of distant objectives it might be that the covering squadron was not attached till the whole expedition assembled in the theatre of operations; during transit to that theatre the transports might have commerce protection escort only. But once the operations began from the point of concentration, a covering squadron was always in touch.

It was only where the destination of the troops was a friendly country, and the line of passage was well protected by our permanent blockades, that a covering squadron could be dispensed with altogether. Thus our various expeditions for the assistance of Portugal were treated exactly like commercial convoys, but in such cases as Wolfe's expedition to Quebec or Amherst's to Louisburg, or indeed any of those which were continually launched against the West Indies, a

battle-squadron was always provided as an integral part
in the theatre of operations. Our arrangements in the
Crimean War illustrate the point exactly. Our troops
were sent out at first to land at Gallipoli in a friendly
territory, and to act within that territory as an army of
observation. It was not a true combined expedition,
and the transports were given no covering squadron.
Their passage was sufficiently covered by our Channel
and Mediterranean fleets occupying the exits of the
Baltic and the Black Sea. But so soon as the original
war plan proved ineffective and combined offensive
operations against Sebastopol were decided on, the
Mediterranean fleet lost its independent character, and
thenceforth its paramount function was to furnish a
covering squadron in touch with the troops.

Seeing how important are the support duties of
such a force, the term "Covering squadron" may
seem ill-chosen to describe it. But it is adopted for
two reasons. In the first place, it was the one employed officially in our service on the last mentioned
occasion which was our last great combined expedition.
In preparing the descent on the Crimea, Sir Edmund
Lyons, who was acting as Chief of the Staff to Sir
James Dundas, and had charge of the combined operations, organised the fleet into a "Covering squadron"
and a "Squadron in charge of transports." In the
second place, the designation serves to emphasise
what is its main and primary function. For important
as it is to keep in mind its support duties, they must
not be permitted to overshadow the fact that its paramount function is to prevent interference with the
actual combined operations—that is, the landing,
support, and supply of the army. Thus in 1705, when
Shovel and Peterborough were operating against

Barcelona, Shovel was covering the amphibious siege
from the French squadron in Toulon.   Peterborough
required the assistance of the marines ashore to execute
a *coup de main*, and Shovel only consented to land
them on the express understanding that the moment
his cruisers passed the signal that the Toulon squadron
was putting to sea, they would have to be recalled to
the fleet no matter what the state of the land operations. And to this Peterborough agreed. The principle
involved, it will be seen, is precisely that which Lyons's
term " Covering squadron " embodies.

To quote anything that happened in the Crimean
War as a precedent without such traditional support
will scarcely appear convincing.   In our British way
we have fostered a legend that so far as organisation
and staff work were concerned that war was nothing
but a collection of deterrent examples.   But in truth
as a combined operation its opening movement both
in conception and organisation was perhaps the most
daring, brilliant, and successful thing of the kind we
ever did.   Designed as the expedition was to assist
an ally in his own country, it was suddenly called
upon without any previous preparation to undertake a
combined operation of the most difficult kind against
the territory of a well-warned enemy.   It involved a
landing late in the year on an open and stormy coast
within striking distance of a naval fortress which
contained an army of unknown strength, and a fleet
not much inferior in battle power and undefeated.
It was an operation comparable to the capture of
Louisburg and the landing of the Japanese in the
Liaotung Peninsula, but the conditions were far
more difficult.   Both those operations had been
rehearsed a few years previously, and they had been

long prepared on the fullest knowledge. In the Crimea everything was in the dark; even steam was an unproved element, and everything had to be improvised. The French had practically to demobilise their fleet to supply transport, and so hazardous did the enterprise appear, that they resisted its being undertaken with every military argument. We had in fact, besides all the other difficulties, to carry an unwilling ally upon our backs. Yet it was accomplished, and so far at least as the naval part was concerned, the methods which achieved success mark the culmination of all we had learnt in three centuries of rich experience.

The first of the lessons was that for operations in uncommanded or imperfectly commanded seas there was need of a covering squadron differentiated from the squadron in charge of transports. Its main function was to secure the necessary local command, whether for transit or for the actual operations. But as a rule transit was secured by our regular blockading squadrons, and generally the covering squadron only assembled in the theatre of operations. When therefore the theatre was within a defended terminal area, as in our descents upon the northern and Atlantic coasts of France, then the terminal defence squadron was usually also sufficient to protect the actual operations. It thus formed automatically the covering squadron, and either continued its blockade, or, as in the case of our attack on St. Malo in 1758, took up a position between the enemy's squadron and the expedition's line of operation. If, however, the theatre of operation was not within a terminal area, or lay within a distant one that was weakly held, the expedition was given its own covering squadron, in which the local squadron was more or less completely merged. Whatever, in fact, was necessary to secure the local control was done, though, as we have seen, and must presently consider more fully, this necessity was not always the standard by which the strength of the covering squadron was measured.

The strength of the covering squadron being determined, the next question is the position or "tract" which it should occupy. Like most other strategical problems, it is "an option of difficulties." In so far as the squadron is designed for support—that is, support from its men, boats, and guns—it will be desirable to station it as near as possible to the objective; but as a covering squadron, with the duty of preventing the intrusion of an enemy's force, it should be as far away as possible, so as to engage such a force at the earliest possible moment of its attempt to interfere. There is also the paramount necessity that its position must be such that favourable contact with the enemy is certain if he tries to interrupt. Usually such certainty is only to be found either in touch with the enemy's naval base or in touch with your own landing force. Where the objective is the local naval base of the enemy these two points, of course, tend to be identical strategically, and the position of the covering squadron becomes a tactical rather than a strategical question. But the vital principle of an independent existence holds good, and no matter how great the necessity of support, the covering squadron should never be so deeply engaged with the landing force as to be unable to disentangle itself for action as a purely naval unit in time to discharge its naval function. In other words, it must always be able to act in the same way as a free field army covering a siege.

Where the objective of the expedition is not the local naval base, the choice of a position for the covering squadron will turn mainly on the amount of support which the army is likely to require. If it cannot act by surprise, and serious military resistance is consequently to be expected, or where the coast defences are too strong for the transport squadron to overpower, then the scale will incline to a position close to the army, though the extent to which, under modern conditions, ships at sea can usefully perform the delicate operation of supporting an infantry attack with gun fire, except by enfilading the enemy's position, remains to be proved. A similar choice will be indicated where strong support of men and boats is required, as when a sufficiency of flat-boats and steam towage cannot be provided by the transports and their attendant squadron ; or again where the locality is such that amphibious operations beyond the actual landing are likely to be called for, and the assistance of a large number of boats and seamen acting with the army is necessary to give it the amphibious tactical mobility which it would otherwise lack. Such cases occurred at Quebec in 1759, where Saunders took his covering battle-squadron right up the St. Lawrence, although its covering functions could have been discharged even better by a position several hundreds of miles away from the objective; and again in 1800 at Alexandria, where Lord Keith ran the extremest hazard to his covering functions in order to undertake the supply of General Abercromby's army by inland waters and give him the mobility he required.

If, on the other hand, the transport squadron is able to furnish all the support necessary, the covering squadron will take station as close as possible to the enemy's naval base, and there it will operate according

to the ordinary laws of blockade. If nothing is desired
but to prevent interference, its guard will take the form
of a close blockade. But if there be a subsidiary purpose
of using the expedition as a means of forcing the enemy
to sea, the open form will be employed; as, for instance,
in Anson's case above cited, when he covered the St.
Malo expedition not by closely blockading Brest, but by
taking a position to the eastward at the Isle de Batz.

In the Japanese operations against Manchuria and
the Kuantung Peninsula these old principles displayed
themselves in undiminished vitality. In the surprise
descents against Seoul and at Takusan the work of
support was left entirely with the transport squadron,
while Admiral Togo took up a covering position far
away at Port Arthur. The two elements of the fleet
were kept separate all through. But in the operations
for the isolation and subsequent siege of Port Arthur
they were so closely united as to appear frequently indistinguishable. Still, so far as the closeness of the
landing place to the objective permitted, the two acted
independently. For the actual landing of the Second
Army the boats of the covering squadron were used,
but it remained a live naval unit all through, and was
never organically mingled with the transport squadron.
Its operations throughout were, so far as modern conditions permit, on the lines of a close blockade. To
prevent interference was its paramount function, undis-
turbed, so far as we are able to judge, by any subsidiary
purpose of bringing the enemy to decisive action.

All through the operations, however, there was a
new influence which tended to confuse the precision
of the old methods. Needless to say it was the torpedo and the mine. Their deflective pressure was curious and interesting. In our own operations against

Sebastopol, to which the Port Arthur case is most closely comparable, the old rules still held good. On the traditional principle, dating from Drake's attack on San Domingo in 1585, a landing place was chosen which gave the mean between facility for a *coup de main* and freedom from opposition; that is, it was chosen at the nearest practicable point to the objective which was undefended by batteries and out of reach of the enemy's main army.

In the handling of the covering squadron Admiral Dundas, the Commander-in-Chief, gave it its dual function. After explaining the constitution of the transport squadron he says, "The remainder of my force . . . will act as a covering squadron, and where practicable assist in the general disembarkation." With these two objects in mind he took a station near enough to the landing place to support the army with his guns if it were opposed, but still in sight of his cruisers before Sebastopol, and at such a distance that at the first sign of the Russians moving he would have time to get before the port and engage them before they could get well to sea; that is, he took a position as near to the army as was compatible with preventing interference, or, it may be said, his position was as near to the enemy's base as was compatible with supporting the landing. From either aspect in fact the position was the same, and its choice presented no complexity owing mainly to the fact that for the first time steam simplified the factors of time and distance.

In the Japanese case the application of these principles was not so easy. In selecting the nearest undefended point for a landing, it was not only batteries, or even the army in Port Arthur, or the troops dispersed in the Liaotung Peninsula that had to be considered, but rather, as must always be the case in the future, mines and mobile torpedo defence. The point they chose was the nearest practicable bay that was unmined. It was not strictly out of mobile defence range, but it so happened that it lay behind islands which lent themselves to the creation of fixed defences, and thus it fulfilled all the recognised conditions. But in so far as the defences could be turned by the Russian fleet a covering squadron was necessary, and the difficulty of choosing a position for it was complicated by the fact that the objective of the combined operations was not merely Port Arthur itself, but also the squadron it contained. It was necessary, therefore, not only to hold off that squadron, but to prevent its escape. This indicated a close blockade. But for close blockade a position out of night torpedo range is necessary, and the nearest point where such a position could be secured was behind the defences that covered the disembarkation. Consequently, in spite of what the strategical conditions dictated, the covering squadron was more or less continuously forced back upon the army and its supporting force, even when the support of the battle-squadron was no longer required.

In the conditions that existed nothing was lost. For the lines of the Japanese fixed defences were so near to the enemy's base, that by mining the entrance of the port Admiral Togo ensured that the enemy's exit would be slow enough for him to be certain of getting contact from his defended anchorage before the Russians could get far to sea. What would happen in a case when no such position could be secured is another matter. The landing place and supply base of the army must be secured against torpedo attack, and the principle of concentration of effort would suggest that the means of defence should not be attenuated by providing the covering squadron with a defended anchorage elsewhere. Thus it would appear that unless the geographical conditions permit the covering squadron to use one of its own national bases, the drift of recent developments will be to force it back on the army, and thus tend to confuse its duties with those of the transport squadron. Hence the increased importance of keeping clear the difference in function between the two squadrons.

To emphasise the principle of the covering squadron, these two cases may be contrasted with the Lissa episode at the end of the Austro-Italian War of 1866. In that case it was entirely neglected, with disastrous results. The Austrian admiral, Tegethoff, with an inferior fleet had by higher order been acting throughout on the defensive, and was still in Pola waiting for a chance of a counter-stroke. Persano with the superior Italian fleet was at Ancona, where he practically dominated the Adriatic. In July the Italians, owing to the failure of the army, were confronted with the prospect of being forced to make peace on unfavourable terms. To improve the position Persano was ordered to take possession of the Austrian island of Lissa. Wihout any attempt to organise his fleet on the orthodox British principle he proceeded to conduct the operation with his entire force. Practically the whole of it became involved in amphibious work, and as soon as Persano was thus committed, Tegethoff put to sea and surprised him. Persano was unable to disentangle a sufficient force in time to meet the attack, and having no compact squadron fit for independent naval action, he was decisively defeated by the inferior enemy. According to British practice, it was clearly a case where, if the operation were to be undertaken at all, an independent covering squadron should have been told off either to hold Tegethoff in Pola or to bring him to timely action, according to whether the island or the Austrian fleet was the primary objective. The reason it was not done may be that Persano was not given a proper landing force, and he seems to have considered that the whole strength of his fleet was needed for the successful seizure of the objective. If so, it is only one more proof of the rule that no matter what fleet support the landing operations may require, it should never be given in an imperfectly commanded sea to an extent which will deny the possibility of a covering squadron being left free for independent naval action.

The length to which the supporting functions of the fleet may be carried will always be a delicate question. The suggestion that its strength must be affected by the need of the army for the men of the fleet or its boats, which imply its men as well, will appear heretical. A battle-squadron, we say, is intended to deal with the enemy's battle-squadron and its men to fight the ships, and the mind revolts at the idea of the strength of a squadron being fixed by any other standard. Theoretically nothing can seem more true, but it is an idea of peace and the study. The atmosphere of war engendered a wider and more practical view. The men of the old wars knew that when a squadron is attached to a combined expedition it is something different from a purely naval unit. They knew, moreover, that an army acting oversea against hostile territory is an incomplete organism incapable of striking its blow in the most effective manner without the assistance of the men of the fleet.

It was the office, then, of the naval portion of the force not only to defend the striking part of the organism, but to complete its deficiencies and lend it the power to strike.   Alone and unaided the army cannot depend on getting itself ashore, it cannot supply itself, it cannot secure its retreat, nor can it avail itself of the highest advantages of an amphibious force, the sudden shift of base or line of operation.   These things the fleet must do for it, and it must do them with its men.[1]

The authority for this view is abundant.   In 1800, for instance, when General Maitland was charged with an expedition against Belleisle, he was invited to state what naval force he would require.   He found it difficult to fix with precision.   "Speaking loosely, however," he wrote, "three or four sail of the line and four or five active frigates appear to me to be properly adequate to the proposed service.   The frigates to blockade."   (Meaning, of course, to blockade the objective and prevent reinforcements reaching it from the mainland, always one of the supporting functions of the squadron attached to the transports.)   "The line-of-battle ships," he adds, "to furnish us with the number of men necessary for land operations."   In this case our permanent blockading squadrons supplied the cover, and what Maitland meant was that the battle-ships he asked for were to be added to the transport squadron not as being required for escort, but for support.   St. Vincent, who was then First Lord, not only endorsed his request, but gave him for disembarkation work one more ship-of-the-line than he had asked for.   At this time our general command of the sea had

---

[1] The Japanese in the late war attempted to do this work by means of a highly organised Army Disembarkation Staff, but except in perfect conditions of weather and locality it does not seem to have worked well, and in almost all cases the assistance of the Navy was called in.

been very fully secured, and we had plenty of naval force to spare for its exercise. It will be well to compare it with a case in which the circumstances were different.

When in 1795 the expedition under Admiral Christian and General Abercromby was being prepared for the West Indies, the admiral in concert with Jervis drew up a memorandum as to the naval force required.[1] The force he asked for was considerable. Both he and Jervis considered that the escort and local cover must be very strong, because it was impossible to count on closing either Brest or Toulon effectually by blockade. But this was not the only reason. The plan of operations involved three distinct landings, and each would require at least two of the line, and perhaps three, "not only as protection, but as the means by which flat-boats must be manned, cannon landed, and the other necessary services of fatigue executed." Christian also required the necessary frigates and three or four brigs "to cover [that is, support] the operations of the smaller vessels [that is, the landing flotillas doing inshore work]." The main attack would require at least four of the line and seven frigates, with brigs and schooners in proportion. In all he considered, the ships-of-the-line [the frigates being "otherwise employed"] would have to provide landing parties to the number of 2000 men "for the flat-boats, landing and moving guns, water, and provisions," and this would be their daily task. The military force these landing parties were to serve amounted to about 18,000 men.

[1] Sir Hugh Cloberry Christian was an officer of high distinction with a remarkable record of battle service. He had been serving as Howe's second captain just before his promotion to flag rank in 1795, and died as Commander-in-Chief at the Cape at the early age of fifty-one.

Lord Barham, it must be said, who as Sir Charles Middleton was then First Sea Lord, objected to the requirements as excessive, particularly in the demand for a strong escort, as he considered that the transit could be safeguarded by special vigilance on the part of the permanent blockading squadrons. The need for large shore parties he seems to have ignored. His opinion, however, is not quite convincing, for from the first he had taken up an antagonistic attitude to the whole idea of the expedition. He regarded the policy which dictated it as radically unsound, and was naturally anxious to restrict the force that was to be spent upon it. His opposition was based on the broad and far-sighted principles that were characteristic of his strategy. He believed that in view of the threatening attitude of Spain the right course was to husband the navy so as to bring it up to a two-Power standard for the coming struggle, and to keep it concentrated for decisive naval action the moment Spain showed her hand. In short, he stoutly condemned a policy which entailed a serious dissipation of naval force for a secondary object before a working command of the sea had been secured. It was, in fact, the arrangements for this expedition which forced him to resign before the preparations were complete. But it is to be observed that his objections to the plan were really due, not to the principle of its organisation, but to our having insufficient force to give it adequate naval support without prejudicing the higher consideration of our whole position at sea.[1]

It is obvious that the foregoing considerations,

[1] On analogous grounds almost every military critic has condemned the policy of this disastrous expedition as involving a dispersal of our slender military force at a time when everything called for its concentration in Europe.

beyond the strategical reactions already noted, will have another of the first importance, in that they must influence the choice of a landing place. The interest of the army will always be to fix it as near to the objective as is compatible with an unopposed landing. The ideal was one night's march, but this could rarely be attained except in the case of very small expeditions, which could be landed rapidly at the close of day and advance in the dark. In larger expeditions, the aim was to effect the landing far enough from the objective to prevent the garrison of the place or the enemy's local forces offering opposition before a footing was secured. The tendency of the navy will usually be in the opposite direction; for normally the further they can land the army away from the enemy's strength, the surer are they of being able to protect it against naval interference. Their ideal will be a place far enough away to be out of torpedo range, and to enable them to work the covering and the transport squadron in sound strategical independence.

To reduce these divergencies to a mean of efficiency some kind of joint Staff is necessary, and to ensure its smooth working it is no less desirable to ascertain, so far as possible, the principles and method on which it should proceed. In the best recent precedents the process has been for the Army Staff to present the limits of coast-line within which the landing must take place for the operation to have the desired effect, and to indicate the known practicable landing points in the order they would prefer them. It will then be for the Naval Staff to say how nearly in accordance with the views of the army they are prepared to act. Their decision will turn on the difficulties of protection and the essentials of a landing place from the point of view of weather, currents, beach and the like, and also in a secondary measure upon the extent to which the conformation of the coast will permit of tactical support by gun-fire and feints.   If the Naval Staff are unwilling to agree to the point or points their colleagues most desire, a question of balance of risk is set up, which the higher Joint Staff must adjust.   It will be the duty of the Naval Staff to set out frankly and clearly all the sea risks the proposal of the army entails, and if possible to suggest an alternative by which the risk of naval interference can be lessened without laying too heavy a burden on the army.   Balancing these risks against those stated by the army, the superior Staff must decide which line is to be taken, and each service then will do its best to minimise the difficulties it has to face.   Whether the superior Staff will incline to the naval or the military view will depend upon whether the greater danger likely to be incurred is from the sea or on land.

Where the naval conditions are fairly well known the line of operations can be fixed in this way with much precision.   But if, as usually happens, the probable action of the enemy at sea cannot be divined with sufficient approximation, then assuming there is serious possibility of naval interference, the final choice within the limited area must be left to the admiral. The practice has been to give him instructions which define in order of merit the points the army desire, and direct him to select the one which in the circumstances, as he finds them, he considers within reasonable risk of war.   Similarly, if the danger of naval interference be small and the local conditions ashore imperfectly known, the final choice will be with the general, subject only to the practicable possibilities of the landing place he would choose.

During the best period of our old wars there was seldom any difficulty in making things work smoothly on these lines. After the first inglorious failure at Rochefort in 1757 the practice was, where discretion of this kind had been allowed, for the two commanders-in-chief to make a joint coast-reconnaissance in the same boat and settle the matter amicably on the spot.

It was on these lines the conduct of our combined operations was always arranged thenceforth. Since the elder Pitt's time it has never been our practice to place combined expeditions under either a naval or a military commander-in-chief and allow him to decide between naval and military exigencies. The danger of possible friction between two commanders-in-chief came to be regarded as small compared with the danger of a single one making mistakes through unfamiliarity with the limitations of the service to which he does not belong.

The system has usually worked well even when questions arose which were essentially questions for a joint superior Staff. The exceptions indeed are very few. A fine example of how such difficulties can be settled, when the spirit is willing, occurred in the Crimea. The naval difficulties, as we have already seen, were as formidable as they could well be short of rendering the whole attempt madness. When it came to the point of execution a joint council of war was held, at which sat the allied Staffs of both services. So great were the differences of opinion between the French and British Generals, and so imperfectly was the terrain known, that they could not indicate a landing place with any precision. All the admirals knew was that it must be on an open coast, which they had not been able to reconnoitre, where the weather might at any time interrupt communications with the shore, and where they were liable to be attacked by a force which, until their own ships were cleared of troops, would not be inferior. All these objections they laid before the Council General. Lord Raglan then said the army now perfectly understood the risk, and was prepared to take it. Whereupon the allied admirals replied that they were ready to proceed and do their best to set the army ashore and support it at any point that should be chosen.

There remains a form of support which has not yet been considered, and that is diversionary movements or feints by the fleet to draw the enemy's attention away from the landing place. This will naturally be a function of the covering battle-squadron or its attendant cruisers and flotilla. The device appears in Drake's attack on San Domingo in 1585, an attack which may be regarded as our earliest precedent in modern times and as the pattern to which all subsequent operations of the kind conformed so far as circumstances allowed. In that case, while Drake landed the troops a night's march from the place, the bulk of the fleet moved before it, kept it in alarm all night, and at dawn made a demonstration with the boats of forcing a direct landing under cover of its guns. The result was the garrison moved out to meet the threat and were surprised in flank by the real landing force. Passing from this simple case to the most elaborate in our annals, we find Saunders doing the same thing at Quebec. In preparation for Wolfe's night landing he made a show of arrangements for a bombardment of Montcalm's lines below the city, and in the morning

with the boats of the fleet began a demonstration of
landing his marines.   By this device he held Montcalm
away from Wolfe's landing place till a secure footing
had been obtained.   Similar demonstrations had been
made above the city, and the combined result was that
Wolfe was able to penetrate the centre of the French
position unopposed.

Such work belongs of course to the region of
tactics rather than of strategy, but the device has been
used with equal effect strategically.   So great is the
secrecy as well as the mobility of an amphibious force,
that it is extremely difficult for an enemy to distinguish
a real attack from a feint.   Even at the last moment,
when a landing is actually in progress, it is impossible
for the defenders to tell that all the troops are being
landed at the one point if a demonstration is going
on elsewhere.   At Quebec it was not till Montcalm
was face to face with Wolfe that he knew he had to
deal with the whole British force.   Still less from a
strategical point of view can we be certain whether
a particular landing represents an advance guard or
is a diversionary operation to mask a larger landing
elsewhere.   This is a special difficulty when in the
case of large operations the landing army arrives in
echelon like the Second Japanese army.   In that
instance the naval feint was used strategically, and
apparently with conspicuous effect.   The Russians
were always apprehensive that the Japanese would
strike for Newchuang at the head of the Gulf of
Pe-chi-li, and for this reason General Stakelberg, who
had command of the troops in the peninsula, was not
permitted to concentrate for effective action in its
southern part, where the Japanese had fixed their
landing place.   Admiral Togo, in spite of the strain

on his fleet in effecting and securing.the disembarkation of the army, detached a cruiser squadron to
demonstrate in the Gulf. The precise effect of this
feint upon the Russian Staff cannot be measured with
certainty. All we know is that Stakelberg was held
back from his concentration so long that he was unable to strike the Japanese army before it was complete
for the field and able to deal him a staggering counter-
stroke.

This power of disturbing the enemy with feints
is of course inherent in the peculiar attributes of
combined expeditions, in the facility with which their
line of operation can be concealed or changed, and
there seems no reason why in the future it should be
less than in the past. Good railway connections in
the theatre of the descent will of course diminish the
effect of feints, but, on the other hand, the means
of making them have increased. In mine-sweeping
vessels, for instance, there is a new instrument which
in the Russo-Japanese War proved capable of creating
a very strong impression at small cost to the fleet.
Should a flotilla of such craft appear at any practicable
part of a threatened coast and make a show of clearing
it, it will be almost a moral impossibility to ignore the
demonstration.

On the whole then, assuming the old methods are
followed, it would seem that with a reasonable naval
preponderance the power of carrying out such operations
over an uncommanded sea is not less than it has proved
to be hitherto. The rapidity and precision of steam
propulsion perhaps places that power higher than
ever. It would at any rate be difficult to find in the
past a parallel to the brilliant movement on Seoul with
which the Japanese opened the war in 1904 It is

true the Russians at the last moment decided for political reasons to permit the occupation to take place without opposition, but this was unknown to the Japanese, and their arrangements were made on the assumption that their enemy would use the formidable means at his disposal to obstruct the operation. The risk was accepted, skilfully measured, and adequately provided for on principles identical with those of the British tradition. But, on the other hand, there has been nothing to show that where the enemy has a working command of the sea the hazard of such enterprises has been reduced. Against an enemy controlling the line of passage in force, the well-tried methods of covering and protecting an oversea expedition will no more work to-day than they did in the past. Until his hold is broken by purely naval action, combined work remains beyond all legitimate risk of war.

INDEX

THE END